ROALD DAHL

ROALD DAHL
Wales of the Unexpected

edited by

Damian Walford Davies

University of Wales Press
2016

www.uwp.co.uk

British Library CIP Data
A catalogue record for this book is available from the British Library.

ISBN 978-1-78316-940-5
eISBN 978-1-78316-941-2

Typeset by Marie Doherty
Printed by CPI Antony Rowe, Melksham

Contents

Acknowledgements

Excerpts from the published work and manuscripts of Roald Dahl are quoted by kind permission of the following: the Estate of Roald Dahl – © Roald Dahl Nominee Ltd; The Roald Dahl Museum and Story Centre, Great Missenden; the David Higham agency; Rily Publications (www.rily.co.uk); and as noted below in the case of individual titles:

Excerpts from *Charlie and the Chocolate Factory* by Roald Dahl, text copyright © 1964, renewed 1992 by Roald Dahl Nominee Limited. Used by permission of Alfred A. Knopf, an imprint of Random House Children's Books, a division of Penguin Random House LLC. All rights reserved.

Excerpts from *Charlie and the Great Glass Elevator* by Roald Dahl, text copyright © 1972, renewed 2000 by Roald Dahl Nominee Limited. Used by permission of Alfred A. Knopf, an imprint of Random House Children's Books, a division of Penguin Random House LLC. All rights reserved.

Excerpts from *James and the Giant Peach* by Roald Dahl, text copyright © 1961, renewed 1989 by Roald Dahl. Used by permission of Alfred A. Knopf, an imprint of Random House Children's Books, a division of Penguin Random House LLC. All rights reserved.

Excerpts from *Matilda*, copyright © 1988 by Roald Dahl. Used by permission of Viking Children's Books, an imprint of Penguin Young Readers Group, a division of Penguin Random House LLC.

Excerpts from *The Minpins*, copyright © 1991 by Felicity Dahl and the other Executors of the Estate of Roald Dahl. Used by permission of Viking Children's Books, an imprint of Penguin Young Readers Group, a division of Penguin Random House LLC.

Excerpts from *Boy: Tales of Childhood* © 1984 by Roald Dahl. Reprinted by permission of Farrar, Straus, and Giroux, LLC. All Rights Reserved.

Excerpts from *Going Solo* © 1986 by Roald Dahl. Reprinted by permission of Farrar, Straus, and Giroux, LLC. All Rights Reserved.

Excerpts from *The BFG* © 1982 by Roald Dahl. Reprinted by permission of Farrar, Straus, and Giroux, LLC. All Rights Reserved.

I am most grateful to the following for their advice, assistance and generosity: Sir Quentin Blake for the cover image; Catherine Butler; Georgia Glover at David Higham; Luke Kelly; Emma Schofield; Tom Solomon; Donald Sturrock; and Rachel White (collections manager and archivist at the Roald Dahl Museum and Story Centre, Great Missenden). I also thank those Dahl aficionados, Brychan Rhydderch Davies and Cristyn Rhydderch Davies.

List of Contributors

Ann Alston is Senior Lecturer in English at the University of the West of England, Bristol, where she specialises in children's literature. She is the author of *The History of the Family in English Children's Literature* (2008) and was co-editor of and contributor to the first collection of critical essays on Roald Dahl's children's books, *Roald Dahl* (New Casebooks; 2012).

Peter Finch is a poet, performer and psychogeographer. He was born in Cardiff, where he still lives. In his time he has been a sound-text manipulator, a literary entrepreneur, a magazine editor, publisher, bookseller and, more recently, CEO of Academi and its more recent incarnation, Literature Wales. His books include the *Real Cardiff* series, *Selected Later Poems* (2007), *Zen Cymru* (2010) and *Edging The Estuary* (2013). His most recent publication is *The Roots Of Rock: From Cardiff To Mississippi And Back* (2015). His web site is www.peterfinch.co.uk.

Kevin Mills is Professor of English Literature at the University of South Wales, where he teaches courses in Intertextuality, English Renaissance Literature, Nineteenth-century Literature, and Myth. Widely published on literary theory and Victorian literature, he is the author of *Justifying Language: Paul and Contemporary Theory* (1995); *Approaching Apocalypse: Unveiling Revelation in Victorian Writing* (2007); and *The Prodigal Sign: A Parable of Criticism* (2009). Three volumes of his poetry have been published by Cinnamon Press: *Fool* (2009), *Libra* (2012) and *Stations of the Boar* (2016).

Tomos Owen lectures in the School of English Literature at Bangor University, where he is Co-director of the MA in the Literatures of

Wales/Llenyddiaethau Cymru. His research focuses principally on modern and contemporary Welsh writing in English, and he is currently completing a monograph on Welsh writing in London at the turn of the twentieth century, to be published by University of Wales Press.

Richard Marggraf Turley is Professor of English Literature in the Department of English and Creative Writing at Aberystwyth University. In 2012, he was also appointed Professor of Engagement with the Public Imagination. He is author of several books on the Romantic poets, including *Keats's Boyish Imagination* (2004) and *Bright Stars: John Keats, Barry Cornwall and Romantic Literary Culture* (2009). He is the author of three poetry volumes, including *Wan-Hu's Flying Chair* (2009) and most recently a crime novel set in the Regency period, *The Cunning House* (2015).

Carrie Smith is Lecturer in English Literature in the School of English, Communication and Philosophy at Cardiff University. She is co-editor of *The Boundaries of the Literary Archive: Reclamation and Representation* (2013) and her published work on Ted Hughes focuses on questions of authenticity and voice in his poetry readings and recordings using original interviews and research undertaken in the BBC Written Archives. She has also published on Hughes's creative partnership with American artist Leonard Baskin. She is currently preparing a monograph on Hughes and the art of writing.

Siwan M. Rosser lectures in the School of Welsh at Cardiff University. She has published on subjects including childhood deaths in Welsh literature, children's fiction in translation, the construction of national identity in Edwardian children's literature and linguistic code-switching in contemporary young adult poetry. Her forthcoming monograph explores the evolving concept of childhood in nineteenth-century texts aimed at young readers. She is also co-founder of the annual Cardiff Children's Literature Festival and leads a European network on children's literature in minority languages.

Damian Walford Davies is Professor of English and Head of the School of English, Communication and Philosophy at Cardiff University. His recent publications include *Cartographies of Culture:*

New Geographies of Welsh Writing in English (2012), the poetry collections *Judas* (2015) and *Witch* (2012), and articles on the Romantic poets and cultures of trauma and illness. He is editor of *Counterfactual Romanticism* (forthcoming, 2017), *Romanticism, History, Historicism: Essays on an Orthodoxy* (2009), and, with Lynda Pratt, *Wales and the Romantic Imagination* (2007). He is currently editing *The Misfortunes of Elphin* for the Cambridge Edition of the novels of Thomas Love Peacock and is General Editor of the forthcoming *Oxford Literary History of Wales*.

Heather Worthington was Reader in English Literature at Cardiff University. Her research interests are nineteenth- and twentieth-century crime narrative, sensation fiction and children's literature. Her publications include *The Rise of the Detective in Early Nineteenth-century Popular Fiction* (2005), *Key Concepts in Crime Fiction* (2011) and contributions to *A Companion to Crime Fiction* (2010), *The Oxford History of the Novel in English: Vol II: The Nineteenth-Century Novel* (2012), and *Roald Dahl* (New Casebooks; 2012). She is on the Editorial Board of *Clues: A Journal of Detection*.

Introduction: Defamiliarising Dahl

Damian Walford Davies

1. Plural Dahl

Quentin Blake's cover illustration, drawn specially for this collection of essays, envisions an uncanny meeting. The young Roald Dahl – seven years old, perhaps, a new boy at the Cathedral School in well-heeled Llandaff, north-west of Cardiff – looks up with open-faced receptivity and inquisitiveness at his older self. The adult Dahl, not locked in garrulous conversation, it seems, but gazing intently down at himself, has a discernible stoop, the result of spinal trauma sustained when his Gloster Gladiator crashed in the Western Desert of Libya in September 1940. His features are in shadowed profile beneath his wide-brimmed hat. Boy (which is how the young Dahl would sign himself in two years' time in letters home from his English prep school in Weston-super-Mare) stands with his adult self, south-east of Llandaff Cathedral. The building's spire – damaged by a German parachute mine in the Cardiff Blitz in January 1941 – divides youth from age. The spire also seems to serve here as a sightline for the young Dahl's gaze, up to his six-foot-six, global-brand future. Quentin Blake has drawn the lofty figure resting on a tall stick that appears to offer a challenge to his younger self to measure up. Wearing his short-sleeved school shirt and maroon tie (still the school's colour), we encounter Boy fresh, perhaps, from perpetrating the fabled 'Great Mouse Plot' at Mrs Pratchett's local sweetshop.[1] The stick he holds in his right hand conjures the cane with which he will soon be thrashed by the headmaster – a beating that will prompt his outraged Norwegian mother, Sofie Magdalene, to remove her son to 'an *English* school' in 1925.[2]

The adult Dahl looks like an English countryman – a persona he inhabited (and ironised) from the late 1940s onwards as he established himself in a pastoral enclave around Great Missenden in Buckinghamshire. From here, this 'eccentric Arcadian', fêted in New York literary circles, regarded the 'inner citadel of literary London' (Donald Sturrock's formulations) with a mixture of scepticism, aversion and envy.[3] The persona of English maverick is unsettled and rendered uncanny in Blake's image by the Welsh location and by the fact that those long legs of Dahl's (which made the cockpits of fighter planes such tricky places) seem firmly rooted in Welsh soil. Further pluralising Dahl's cultural identity in the drawing is the fact that Blake's representation of the adult Dahl summons a pivotal figure in his early life: Joss Spivvis (his real name, Jones), the ex-Rhondda Valley miner who served as the Dahl family's gardener at their Llandaff villa, Cumberland Lodge – a stone's throw from the imagined location of the drawing.

But perhaps Boy and author *are* conversing, after all. Alternating between English and Norwegian, the adult Dahl might be relating a narrative about the '*boom bang woomph wham rat-tat-tat-tat-tat*' terror and thrill of aerial combat over Greece and Palestine, or telling his young self how the cathedral spire reminds him of the New York buildings that 'tapered off into a long sharp point – like an enormous needle sticking up into the sky' (in the words of *James and the Giant Peach*).[4] Perhaps they are discussing voyages out – Boy's imminent passage in a paddle steamer across the Bristol Channel from Cardiff docks to Weston, the journey of a later self to Dar es Salaam in Tanganyika to work for Shell, and Dahl's multiple crossings and flights to America – as well, of course, as the question of homecomings.

2. Dahl the Unhomely

The complex dynamics of Quentin Blake's image suggestively figure the paradoxes, hybrid identities, cultural and cartographic triangulations, multiple self-inscriptions and revisions that are excavated in *Roald Dahl: Wales of the Unexpected*, which is published to mark the centenary of Dahl's birth at Villa Marie in Fairwater Road, Llandaff, on 13 September 1916. Breaking new ground in its engagement with a writer now universally known as 'the world's number one storyteller', this collection of essays sets itself the task of defamiliarising Dahl and rendering him uncanny in both biographical and literary terms by exploring the place of Wales in his imagination and the complex registrations of his (Anglo-)Welsh alignments across the full range of his output. The eight essays published here reveal Wales to be a conditioning, paradigmatic presence – a crux – in Dahl's work, despite the fact that he was permanently resident in Wales only for the first nine years of his life.

Reading Dahl through a Welsh lens, and identifying the Welsh lenses through which Dahl himself sought a purchase on the world, are a means of contesting and correcting the received image of him as an 'English' writer. As Ann Alston and Heather Worthington emphasise in this volume, Dahl's anglocentrism was certainly reinforced by the cultural values of his Repton education and by those of his officer class during the war (and, in a different form, by his own subsequent performance of the countryman persona). However, these social and cultural allegiances are forever ironised in Dahl's work. Seeking to identify the Welsh genetics of his imagination, the essays in this volume are in tune with Dahl's own commitment, in his fiction for both adults and children, to the unexpected, to making strange. From the beginning of his writing career, Dahl was fascinated by in-between states and ex-centric perspectives. The early stories of *Over to You* (1946) can be read as psychologisations of difference, in particular those pieces in which Dahl inhabits the compound meta-perspectives and traumatised consciousness of the fighter pilot. Though the adult fiction of *Someone Like You* (1953), *Kiss, Kiss* (1960) and *Switch Bitch* (1974) was increasingly saturated in the grotesque and macabre, it retained a core element of the uncanny in the form of doublings, misrecognitions and hybrid and metamorphosed selves. The fantasy worlds of his fiction for children were fed by, and in turn fed into, the disordering conflation of realism, magic realism, fable and metafictional alienation effects that jolt the reader into new subject positions in the adult fiction. *Wales of the Unexpected* sets out to explore the link between Dahl's residual, interstitial Anglo-Welsh identity and the destabilising ironies, indeterminacies and hybridities of his work.

Dahl's latest biographer, Donald Sturrock, has valuably sought to excavate the plural cultural alignments and connected geographies of Dahl's work. Sturrock emphasises the importance of Dahl's formative relationship with America, to which he was posted as Assistant Air Attaché in 1942 and which he was to make his home in the early

1950s. He commuted restlessly between Buckinghamshire and New York in the late 1950s with his wife, Patricia Neal, and returned there frequently thereafter. As Sturrock emphasises, success was usually achieved in the US (not, however, without charges of vulgarity and tastelessness) before it was attained, with considerable effort, in Britain.[5] One might go further and speak legitimately of Dahl as an Anglo-American writer – or, in more nuanced terms (acknowledging his status as 'misfit' and 'outsider'), his negotiation of an Anglo-American persona.[6] Sturrock also lays great emphasis on what he sees as modalities of a 'gipsy' persona that Dahl self-consciously embraced as an expression of his free spirit and as a mode of resistance to cultural institutionalisation.[7] Dahl's Welsh birth, his boyhood in Radyr and Llandaff on the outskirts of Cardiff, and his father Harald's trajectory from Norway through Paris to the world's greatest coal-port have been duly noted – the facts are there in Dahl's *Boy: Tales of Childhood* (1984). However, there has hitherto been no sustained attempt to go beyond the descriptively factual to calibrate Dahl's Anglo-Welshness and explore the dynamics of his multidimensional identification with Wales across the *oeuvre*.

The essays in the present book argue for the existence of a complex (Anglo-)Welsh orientation in Dahl's work, which enhances our sense of the vital ex-centricity – the creative decentredness – identified by Sturrock. That hyphenated identity – necessarily bound up with Dahl's Norwegian heritage and with a vacillating Americaphilia – is a crucial element of a sensibility that was energised by cultural in-betweenness and which forever felt the need to relativise, and thus ironise, centres of authority and belonging. Considering 'the influence of northern European folk-tales' on the young Dahl, whose summer holidays were spent in Christiania (Oslo) and on the island of Tjøme, Norway (his Easter holidays were spent in Tenby), Jeremy Treglown in his 1994 biography remarks that 'Witches, and "hags" in general, took a particular hold. Not that in the 1920s you had to be Scandinavian, or a boy brought up in a matriarchy, to be scared of witches – particularly in druidical Wales.'[8] What *exactly* druids have to do with witches is unclear, and the cultural cliché at the end is not enlightening. However, Treglown rightly implies that in the Dahls' bilingual household in Wales, Norwegian cultural allegiances and those elements of the cultural and natural environments of Wales with which he came into contact complicated Dahl's fraught English/British identity.

They were factors of unbelonging. Recognising the ways in which his Anglo-Welshness was a productively troubling element of his cultural identity leads us to a more nuanced diagnosis of the reasons why he stood, to the end of his life, outside the pale of urbane English culture and in a tensely creative relation to American cultural hegemony.

In the title of the present volume (doubled uncannily from Kevin Mills's essay), 'Wales' puns with the unsaid 'tales', making the strangeness, the twists-in-the-tail, of that late-Dahl literary and TV brand, *Tales of the Unexpected*, the very matter of his Anglo-Welsh subjectivity. The essays in this book suggest that Dahl himself must, at some level, have been fascinated and exercised by the unexpectedness of Wales's presence in his work, its unexorcisable, necessary returns, and its role in sustaining both the dissenting energies of his imagination and those aspects of his worldview that were complicit with power. Hyphenisation is key. *Wales of the Unexpected* does not set out to identify some essentialist 'Welsh Dahl' (though that term is deployed – stringently – in the book). Rather, the contributors are concerned with more complex and plural cruxes of identity, with dynamics of acceptance *and* rejection, registration *and* elision, and with a sense of belonging that also grasps the reality of deracination. Further, the readings of Dahl offered in this volume identify multiple geographical locations in his life and work that suggestively triangulate with Wales and with his Anglo-Welsh affiliations. Bringing Dahl 'home' cannot result in a parochialisation, regionalisation or 'devolution' of Dahl since his very unhomeliness militates against such claustral emplacements.[9]

Academic engagements with Dahl's work began to appear in earnest in the 1990s, shortly after his death. It was 2012, however, before the first academic collection of essays – edited by Ann Alston and Catherine Butler – appeared from Palgrave. The ten essays in that volume range widely over his writings for children, representing second-generation Dahl criticism in their analysis of Dahl's linguistic inventiveness, his inflection of the fairy tale paradigm, his contribution to the feminist project, the place of the 'Criminal' in his work, his resistance to a conservative 'commodification of fantasy', filmic adaptations of his work and the interpretative power of Quentin Blake's illustrations. This pioneering volume was a much-needed intervention. At the same time, Catherine Butler acknowledged in her Introduction that Dahl scholars were engaged in remedial work: 'the field of Dahl studies is an underpopulated one, and a single volume of essays can

only begin the task of remedying that state of affairs.'[10] Further, recognised in the Palgrave collection is the absence of explorations of
the vital link between the children's books and the fiction for adults
– categories that remain unhelpfully (and unaccountably) compart-
mentalised in the critical literature, whose conceptual ambition this
volume seeks to enhance.[11]

On reading the manuscript of *James and the Giant Peach*, Dahl's agent,
Sheila St Lawrence, declared: 'I think you've done the undoable,
crossed the border between adult and juvenile.'[12] It was a border that
Dahl – a serial crosser of cultural borders – was to regard as necessarily permeable throughout his career. Extending holistic encounters
with Dahl's work into new territory, *Wales of the Unexpected* establishes
alignments of uncanny force between Dahl's adult fiction, the fiction
for children and for young adults, and his verse for young readers,
reading these bodies of work as mutually invigorating modalities of the
author's conflicted engagement with the world and with inherited literary traditions. Crossing the 'border' identified by St Lawrence has its
parallel in Dahl's penchant – analysed in this volume by Carrie Smith
– of 'passing material between fiction, essays and what one might
call "creative autobiography" or "autobiografiction"'.[13] Further, that
boundary crossing (or dialectic) can also be seen as a necessary aspect
of Dahl's negotiation of the hyphen between 'Anglo' and 'Welsh'. The
identification of Matilda as 'both child and grown-up all rolled into
one' in the second full draft of Dahl's novel of 1988 (held in the archive
of the Roald Dahl Museum and Story Centre at Great Missenden)
might be seen as Dahl himself, late in his career, serving notice of the
need to attend to the uncanny *hybridity* of his *oeuvre* in which a hyphenated identity is always in, and at, play.[14]

3. Frames and Registrations

As with their plural subject, so with the methods, approaches and
angles of entry of the essays in *Wales of the Unexpected*. Engaged in
creative interchange with one another, they encounter Dahl's work
through a variety of conceptual and theoretical lenses. Dahl's own
challenge to received paradigms is enacted in each contributor's will-
ingness to push Dahl studies into new territory in terms of both subject
and method, and Dahl emerges defamiliarised from each engagement.

The volume offers intertextual embeddings of Dahl's work in wider Welsh literary networks, traditions and structures of feeling alongside close readings of textual ghosts and 'betrayals' in Dahl's short stories. Historicist-deconstructionist contextualisations that amplify the lost biographical and cultural resonances of Dahl's texts interact with ground-breaking excavations of the Dahl archive and bold reinterpretations of core Dahlian motifs and figurations in the light of his Welsh experience, resourcefully recuperated. At the volume's close, an analysis of Dahl's movement across the borders of translation speaks to a 'creative-critical' performance of a physical journey across a number of local borders, with Dahl as the multiform quarry.

The variety of encounters with Dahl profiled above ensures that the danger of fixing a 'Welsh Dahl' is avoided. As a number of the contributors emphasise, Wales in Dahl's work is an elusive phenomenon, often legible only by inference or by creative triangulation with other, more explicitly summoned, locations. Certainly, *Wales of the Unexpected* is concerned with those moments in Dahl's work when Wales is directly (if always knottily) invoked. At the same time, the contributors emphasise that Wales and Welshness in Dahl's work are often inscribed as indeterminate, conflicted and paradoxical traces. Thus each is concerned to tackle different registrations of Wales in Dahl's work. Carrie Smith tracks Wales through the archive at Great Missenden and finds it inscribed, erased, redrafted, euphemistically refigured and elided again, but always undeniably present. Indeed, in her essay, Wales itself emerges as archival and palimpsestic – the very matter of revision (and of revisioning). Mapping *Charlie and the Chocolate Factory* – with a measure of Dahlian play – in relation to the Welsh industrial novel, Tomos Owen argues that Dahl's book of 1964 (not published in the UK until 1967) seems powerfully to summon certain categories of Welsh industrial fiction only to negate them, leaving them as conditioning absences. Kevin Mills reveals the ways in which Wales tantalisingly, hauntingly, 'rings for attention' in the echoing 'textual interstices' of Dahl's short stories. In his discussion of the significance of the aerial perspectives of the fighter pilot and acts of troubled 'homing' in Dahl's work, Richard Marggraf Turley establishes Dahl's war experience as constituting a trauma that evinces a 'compulsive desire for representation'. Wales itself emerges as a phenomenon that compulsively seeks representation in Dahl's work (the link between Wales, trauma and loss is multiply suggestive). In being fended off, Wales asserts itself. Relying

on the evidence afforded by the manuscripts of *Matilda*, my own essay
seeks to unpack a nodal point of personal and public trauma in the
novel that achieves a density of expression in and around a quotation
from Dylan Thomas in which Dahl's lost Welsh past and his fear of the
future are deeply embedded. Ann Alston's and Heather Worthington's
engagement with *The BFG* (1982) reveals the interpretative horizons
that open up when a classic Dahl text, with its paradoxical ethics of
resistance and control, are viewed anew through a Welsh lens in terms
of a cultural allegory of difference and assimilation. Here, Anglo-Welsh
identity is characterised by its very 'slipperiness' – in cultural-linguistic
as in textual terms. A Dahl who speaks in Welsh translation is Siwan
Rosser's subject. When read in the native tongue of his country of
birth, the global cultural brand is found to be 'not quite himself',
uncannily reoriented by the conditions of the target literary field, a
voice both 'foreign and familiar', resisted and naturalised. Conducting
– or rather being conducted by – a psychogeographical *dérive* that
extends the cartography of his previous explorations of Cardiff and
its hinterlands and which enhances the volume's acts of geographical
and cultural relocation, Peter Finch follows 'the Dahl scent' through
landscapes and a built environment that are themselves palimpsests.
He finds 'Welsh Dahl' to be a spectral presence, to be called into being
at one point only by means of a word game, his name and identity the
product, it seems, only of naming others.

4. 'Reading for Wales'

In his essay for this volume, Kevin Mills reveals the ways in which his
teasing Dahl text – the short story, 'The Landlady' (first published in
The New Yorker in 1959 before its appearance the following year in the
collection *Kiss, Kiss*) – 'seduces us into reading for Wales'. Carrie Smith
also speaks of the interpretative implications of 'Reading for a Welsh
Dahl'. Mills's 'reading for Wales' is appropriately wry and ambiguous,
signifying an interpretation that is hell-bent on finding textual traces of
Wales; an intervention made 'for the sake of Wales' (with the sense of
an underlying, coat-trailing cultural nationalist agenda); and a critical
act that amounts to a national sport. Mills acknowledges the critical peril of succumbing to the temptation creatively to infer traces of
Dahl's Welsh experience in the (merely) interstitial spaces of allusion,

alignment, analogy, resonance, echo and allegory. Such a reading runs the risk, he argues, 'of constriction and marginalisation'. At the same time, Mills emphasises that the ludic text seems actively to involve us in such Welsh play.[15] In 1983 Dahl published an anthology of ghost stories which he had in fact collected a quarter of a century earlier for a projected television series to be produced by Eddie Knopf, the half-brother of Dahl's American publisher, Alfred Knopf; Emlyn Williams was to be the 'introducer'. In his introduction to the collection, Dahl revealed the genesis of 'The Landlady':

> Good ghost stories, like good children's books, are damnably difficult to write. I am a short story writer myself, and although I have been doing it for forty-five years and have always longed to write just one decent ghost story, I have never succeeded in bringing it off. Heaven knows, I have tried. Once I thought I had done it. It was with a story that is now called *The Landlady*. But when it was finished and I examined it carefully, I knew it wasn't good enough . . . I simply hadn't got the secret. So finally I altered the ending and made it into a non-ghost story.[16]

As Mills reveals, the inflected 'non-ghost story' is itself a network of spectral signifiers of Wales. Once again Wales is the secret that insists on coming out; it is that which revision and retrospect yield.

Each of the contributors to *Wales of the Unexpected* is alive to the seductions of Dahl's texts, Dahl's life, and each is salutarily sceptical of gratuitously inferring suppressed or encoded negotiations with Wales in Dahl's work. And yet they all convincingly reveal how Dahl's Welshness achieves articulation – from explicit invocation to what Carrie Smith terms 'subscripts' to conditioning aporiae. Which, after all, is perhaps what the old Dahl and Boy are discussing in Quentin Blake's image on the cover.

Notes

1   See Roald Dahl, *Boy and Going Solo* (London: Puffin, 2008), pp. 35–7.
2   Dahl, *Boy and Going Solo*, p. 51.
3   See Donald Sturrock, *Storyteller: The Life of Roald Dahl* (London: HarperPress 2011), pp. 251, 491, 518.
4   Dahl, *Boy and Going Solo*, p. 339; Roald Dahl, *James and the Giant Peach* (London: Puffin, 2013 [1961]), p. 132.
5   See Sturrock, *Storyteller*, pp. 301, 309, 492.

6 Sturrock, *Storyteller*, pp. 301, 491.
7 See Sturrock, *Storyteller*, pp. 270–1.
8 Jeremy Treglown, *Roald Dahl: A Biography* (London: Faber and Faber 1994), p. 16.
9 I take the term 'claustral' in relation to Dahl from William Todd Schultz's analysis of spaces of trauma in Dahl's work; see 'Finding Fate's Father: Some Life History Influences on Roald Dahl's *Charlie and the Chocolate Factory*', *Biography*, 21/4 (Fall 1998), pp. 463–81.
10 Catherine Butler, 'Introduction', in *Roald Dahl* (New Casebooks), ed. Ann Alston and Catherine Butler (Basingstoke: Palgrave Macmillan, 2012), p. 12.
11 Butler, 'Introduction', p. 12. Laura Viñas Valle rightly claims that 'The general tendency in literary criticism has been to study Dahl's works in separate compartments as if he was a two-headed author writing distinctly for different audiences with no literary, thematic or stylistic links between the two,' but she proceeds to analyse the narrative voice in Dahl's children's books and the adult fiction in two separate sections, perpetuating the dualistic view; see 'The Narrative Voice in Roald Dahl's Children's and Adult Books', *Didáctica: Lengua y Literatura*, 20 (2008), p. 292.
12 Sturrock, *Storyteller*, p. 355.
13 See below, p. 13.
14 Roald Dahl Museum and Story Centre, RD/2/27/4, MS pages (no pagination), second full draft of *Matilda*.
15 See p. 59 below.
16 Roald Dahl (ed.), *Roald Dahl's Book of Ghost Stories* (London: Jonathan Cape, 1983), p. 18.

Works cited

Dahl, Roald, *Boy and Going Solo* (London: Puffin, 2008).
—, *James and the Giant Peach* (London: Puffin, 2013 [1961]).
— (ed.), *Roald Dahl's Book of Ghost Stories* (London: Jonathan Cape, 1983).

Butler, Catherine, 'Introduction', in *Roald Dahl* (New Casebooks), ed. Ann Alston and Catherine Butler (Basingstoke: Palgrave Macmillan, 2012), pp. 1–13.
Schultz, William Todd, 'Finding Fate's Father: Some Life History Influences on Roald Dahl's *Charlie and the Chocolate Factory*', *Biography*, 21/4 (Fall 1998), pp. 463–81.
Sturrock, Donald, *Storyteller: The Life of Roald Dahl* (London: HarperPress 2011).
Treglown, Jeremy, *Roald Dahl: A Biography* (London: Faber and Faber 1994).
Valle, Laura Viñas, 'The Narrative Voice in Roald Dahl's Children's and Adult Books', *Didáctica: Lengua y Literatura*, 20 (2008), pp. 291–308.

2

Inscription and Erasure:
Mining for Welsh Dahl in the Archive

Carrie Smith

1. Archival Identities

Roald Dahl's archive, held in the Roald Dahl Museum and Story Centre in Great Missenden, Buckinghamshire, occupies a physical space that embodies Jacques Derrida's desire in *Archive Fever* to shake up the 'limits, borders, and the distinctions' of the archive so that 'Order is no longer assured.'[1] Derrida's gleeful disorder is palpable in the reading room of the Dahl archive. Labelled 'The Chokey', in reference to the tall, narrow cupboard to which Miss Trunchbull consigns insubordinate pupils in *Matilda*, it overlooks the museum's courtyard where children run free, talk about their favourite Dahl books and eat 'Bruce Bogtrotter's chocolate cake'. As Antoinette Burton notes, 'the material spaces of archives exert tremendous and largely unspoken influences on their users, producing knowledges and insights which in turn impact the narratives they craft and the histories they write.'[2] The physical space of the Dahl archive, rather than being the seat of order and constraint, is infiltrated by the sound of one half of Dahl's audience – children. The Dahl archive is thus positioned between the joyful, riotous and anarchic energy of Dahl's readers and the ordered world of archival organisation and scholarly method symbolised by the numbered folders and drafts carefully preserved in meticulous order by Dahl himself.

The papers were preserved and ordered by Dahl to form a narrative for posterity. However, the sounds invading the archive serve as a salutary reminder that such spaces have the potential radically to rewrite inherited narratives. Little sustained scholarly attention has been devoted to Dahl's manuscripts. In this essay, I propose to excavate the archive with the aim of exploring published and draft material that illuminates the ways in which Dahl both inscribes and erases the formative Welsh contexts of his early experiences and their cultural and class markers. As Derrida notes, archives are often imagined as places in which origins can be discovered: the archive appears '*to efface itself*', he argues; 'it becomes transparent or unessential so as to let the *origin* present itself in person.'[3] Tracking the creative and biographical 'origins' of a Welsh Dahl in the archive draws into sharp relief an archive's potential both to reveal and to conceal. As already suggested, the location and space of an archive are necessarily part of this process. Were Dahl's archive to be located in Roald Dahl Plass in Cardiff, for example, a stone's throw from Y Senedd, the seat of the Welsh Government (and from the site of his father's shipbroking offices), would the Matter of Wales that is preserved in his papers speak more loudly?

Drawing together the references to Wales that recur throughout Dahl's archive involves taking on the seductive role of creative compositor – one who frames a cohesive narrative from disparate materials that Dahl's readers are unlikely ever to encounter first-hand. The researcher is engaged in an archaeological piecing together in which a 'montage of fragments . . . creates an illusion of totality and continuity.'[4] Burton describes such a method as involving 'complex processes of selection, interpretation, and even creative invention'.[5] Tracing, or rather chasing, a Welsh Dahl across reams of his distinctive yellow American legal paper and light Dixon Ticonderoga pencil strokes can certainly feel at times like 'creative invention'. Dahl's drafts often display evidence of whole pages of writing that have been rubbed out, leaving faint traces underneath the writing that remains. Thus when examining one of Dahl's 'first drafts', we are in fact looking at a second or even a third draft where the erased, ghostly first inscriptions lie in pressure marks beneath the visible writing. In bringing the archival process to the foreground and to the reader's sight, I argue that the only partially apprehended writing that lies tantalisingly out of reach is a serviceable metaphor for the presence of Wales itself within the papers in the archive. Reading for a Welsh Dahl involves attuning oneself to what one might term subscripts. These subscripts surface in explicit engagements with Wales but then disappear, only to reappear years later in inflected forms. This kind of creative reading requires the researcher to interpret significant absences alongside explicit presences. In the published work, Wales figures most explicitly in Dahl's 1984 fictionalised memoir *Boy*, yet his Welsh experience is also present anecdotally in the cookbook *Memories of Food at Gipsy House* (1991) and in another posthumous publication, *My Year* (1993), written just before his death, in which detailed observations of the world are interwoven with early memories. In the manuscript drafts of various pieces, registrations of the industrial experience of south Wales, and attendant questions of class and nationhood, are more prominent than in Dahl's published work. Paradoxically, a significant characteristic of Dahl's engagement with Wales is his gradual disengagement from it throughout the drafting process.

Dahl regularly blurred the line between fiction and autobiography, passing material between fiction, essays and what one might call 'creative autobiography' or 'autobiografiction'.[6] Archives allow us to explore these exchanges between fiction and autobiography and to calibrate what is elided or concealed during such processes. For example, the Dahl archive reveals that material relating to the author's childhood experiences in Wales, which ultimately found a place in *Boy: Tales of Childhood* (1984), was initially drafted for *The Witches* (1983).[7] Dahl's insistence that *Boy* was not an 'autobiography' but rather 'tales from childhood' allowed him a degree of creative freedom from the tyranny of fact, allowing him to (re)deploy material creatively within a flexible network of literary forms.

When asked about his upbringing on BBC Radio's iconic *Desert Island Discs* programme in 1979, Dahl replied that he was 'born and educated in England' and referred to himself as 'very English'.[8] The latter was a claim he made throughout his life. Yet at other times he was clearly aware of the distinctive Welshness of his early life. The fact that he physically aligned himself with Wales before sleep in his English prep school dormitory (an act of homing across dividing bodies of water explored by Richard Marggraf Turley in his essay in this volume) and his recollection of the sight of 'the coast of Wales lying pale and milky on the horizon' from the esplanade at Weston-super-Mare give some sense of Dahl's lasting conception of Wales as a separate imaginative entity and creative resource.[9] As Donald Sturrock notes, the Celtic cross that stands above the Welsh grave of his parents and his sister Astri 'suggest[s] perhaps a public commitment the Dahl family had made to the Welsh soil in which they had put down their roots'.[10] As embodied in Tŷ Mynydd, Radyr – the imposing house surrounded by farmland north of Cardiff, to which the family moved in 1918 – Wales was, as Sturrock emphasises, 'a kind of paradise, irretrievably taken from [him] at a very young age'.[11]

2. Insertions, Elisions, Traces: Drafts of 'Joss Spivvis' and 'The Wonderful Story of Henry Sugar'

In 1987, Dahl wrote an essay entitled 'Joss Spivvis' about his childhood friendship with the family's Welsh gardener at Cumberland Lodge, Llandaff. The piece was written for the 1987 anthology *When We Were Young: Memories of Childhood*, and has since been partially republished in *More About Boy* (2008), cementing its place in the canon of Dahl's writings about his boyhood.[12] Taking drafts of 'Joss Spivvis' as a case study, I evaluate the autobiografictional aspects of the essay to reveal how the archive gives us access to the ways in which a particular example of Dahl's Welsh experience is both elided and subtly registered in his published and unpublished work.

Dahl's 1975 novel, *Danny the Champion of the World*, has at its heart a moving father–son relationship. In an interview about the book that year with the *Western Mail*, Dahl recalled his own Welsh boyhood: 'It was a very happy childhood with haymaking, hay wagons and horses – that sort of thing. I have a strong feeling for Wales.'[13] Danny is nine years old in the novel, the same age as Dahl when he was sent away to St Peter's boarding school in Weston. I suggest that Dahl's sense of having lost, at a young age, the 'kind of paradise' that Wales represented is registered in a novel that both celebrates a close familial bond and acknowledges that this bond is intertwined with profound loss, figured by the death of Danny's mother. That loss gathers to itself the death of Harald Dahl five years before Roald's move from Wales. The central familial pairing in *Danny the Champion of the World*, however, is unusual in Dahl's *oeuvre*. It is more common in Dahl's books to encounter parent figures – grandparents, gardeners, teachers – rather than actual parents. As Ann Alston has argued, the 'biological family' is by no means valorised in Dahl's work (witness Miss Honey and Matilda, and James and the insects in the peach) and those familial relationships that are successful are often 'between one adult and one child'.[14] Echoed as it is in other fictional relationships throughout his work, Dahl's 1987 account of his relationship with the Welsh gardener named Jones – whom he called 'Joss Spivvis' – is crucial to our understanding of the dynamic between parent figures and their youthful charges in Dahl's *oeuvre*.

The letter inviting Dahl to contribute to *When We Were Young* explained that the compilers aimed to curate a book in which 'well known personalities from all walks of life write about a particularly memorable aspect of their childhood'; all proceeds were to go to the National Society for the Prevention of Cruelty to Children (NSPCC).[15] Dahl had considered offering a chapter from *Boy* for the editors to republish, but decided to write an original piece detailing his close friendship with the Dahls' gardener, the stories Joss Spivvis told the young Dahl of his boyhood in the Rhondda Valley, and the trips they took together to watch Cardiff City Football Club play at Ninian Park. The drafts of this piece show the evolution of Dahl's shaping of the Welsh context that lies at the heart of the essay – and of other fictional works that deal with similar themes. In a move that was to achieve fictional life in such characters as James in *James and the Giant Peach* (1961) and the boy in *The Witches* (1983), the young Dahl struck up the friendship with the gardener after a significant family loss – in Dahl's case, the deaths of his father and sister 'within a few weeks of one other'.[16] Dahl notes in *Boy* that his father was 'an expert gardener' – a fact that may have enhanced the strength of this new relationship at Cumberland Lodge, Llandaff.[17] Further, as we shall see, Jones and Harald Dahl were linked by the roles they played in the transformation of industrial south Wales in the late nineteenth and early twentieth centuries: the former as Rhondda Valley miner, working among the timber pit props that the Welsh called 'Norways' owing to their provenance, the latter as Norwegian shipbroker in Cardiff's 'coal metropolis'.[18]

Dahl had also fictionalised his relationship with the gardener a decade prior to the 'Joss Spivvis' essay in an early draft of the framing narrative for 'The Wonderful Story of Henry Sugar' that differs significantly from the piece that was published in 1977 in the volume of the same name. The archive reveals that rather than the rich, playboy adult of the published 'Henry Sugar', the protagonist of the framing narrative was initially a young boy from a wealthy family whose 'best friend was Arthur, the gardener'.[19] These early drafts of 'Henry

Sugar' begin to illustrate some of the inflections that the biographical material undergoes along cultural, national and class lines. Mirroring precisely the relationship between Jones and Dahl, Arthur and Henry eat lunch (provided by Arthur's wife) together in the 'harness-room': 'Two slices of white bread with a thick slab of cheese in between';[20] Jones and Dahl eat 'four Crawford's Crackers' each, 'lightly buttered and two large hunks of cheddar cheese' – a meal provided by 'Mrs Jones'.[21] (In the published 1987 essay, in the only comment on the difference in economic position between employer and employee, Dahl notes: 'Thinking back on it now, I am a bit surprised that my mother allowed that good woman to buy my lunch for me six days a week without recompense.'[22]) Dahl's decision to transform this real-life, pseudo-parental relationship into a variety of fictional forms across his work for children is testament to its significance. His letters from school consistently ask after Jones and conclude with 'Give my love to Alfhild, Else and Asta and Jones and the maids,' placing Jones next to his sisters in affection.[23] He also often asked after Jones's health and enquired as to the state of the garden, stating in one letter: 'It is very nice of Jones to keep a row of peas for me,' indicating the continuing exchange between young Dahl and Rhondda gardener through his letters to his mother.[24] However, Dahl's use of the gardener's surname, 'Jones', in his letters home (rather than the nickname he and his siblings gave him) suggests that this familial friendliness did not quite erase the etiquette of employer–employee relations in the context of letters to the matriarch, Sofie Magdalene.

In the first fictionalised version of this relationship, Arthur and Henry's friendship is terminated when the gardener slaughters a chicken, employing a method enjoined by the household cook by hanging it on a tree by its feet and 'inserting the point of the blade into the open beak of the chicken' in order to bleed the bird alive.[25] (The real-life Jones, in contrast to Arthur, tells the young Dahl how he saved his pit pony following the escape of flammable gas in the mine; though terrified, he 'wasn't going to leave [his] little pony behind to suffocate'.[26]) When Henry pleads with him to stop because the action is 'cruel', Arthur comments that he should not get 'worked up' because 'chickens are the stupidest things on this earth,' and asks Henry to look away.[27] In the drafts of Henry Sugar, the class and wealth of the Sugar family contrast starkly with the position of the gardener, whose duty this slaughter is. The bleeding of a chicken intended for Henry's dinner and the emphasis on looking away seem to register and euphemise the class gulf between boy and gardener – and, given the biographical context of the boy–gardener relationship, between Dahl and Joss Spivvis. The adult Dahl would certainly have had some sense of the level and social effects of unemployment in the Rhondda during the 1920s (it had risen from 2 per cent in 1921 to 20 per cent by 1929) – a social calamity that haunts the representation of Arthur the gardener in 'Henry Sugar' in the light of the 'Joss Spivvis' essay.[28]

The 'Henry Sugar' drafts elide the explicit Welsh context that would be supplied in the essay on Jones/Joss Spivvis. Similarly, the gardener's Welshness is far more prominent in the final, published 'Joss Spivvis' essay than it is in the first draft. Dahl's drafting allows access to his process of making visible certain cultural and socio-political markers of Joss Spivvis's Welsh identity – or rather, Dahl's own constructions of that identity. The first extant description of Jones is as follows: 'The gardener that my mother engaged to look after everything outdoors was a short, broad shouldered, middle-aged [*man*] <Welshman> with a pale brown moustache whose name was Jones.'[29] 'Welshman' is a left-hand marginal insert that appears to replace the erased 'man'. The addition points to a desire to give Jones cultural specificity (integral to the profile he goes on to offer) in the face of the possible assumption that the gardener was – as Dahl himself was understood to be – English. Similarly added – this time at the top of the page, with an arrow indicating its rightful place in the text – is the sentence in the published essay that identifies Jones as having 'the Welshman's love of speech and song', and which continues: 'when he was describing something to me his flowery sentences would hold me enthralled.'[30] Dahl draws on a recognisable national stereotype and, later in the piece, a broadly characterised class stereotype (as we shall see), which render Jones as a 'type' rather than an individual. Even as Dahl relates Jones's tales about his own life, together with specific memories of their relationship, Jones the gardener and former miner becomes, paradoxically, increasingly obscured.

The elements of Jones's stories and storytelling that Dahl so enjoys conform to the tropes associated in anglophone Welsh industrial fiction with the 'routine of a boy's first day down a colliery', which, as Stephen Knight has argued, often resonates with wider anxieties, serving as an 'objective correlative' for situations in which the individual feels powerless in the face of 'forces beyond personal control'.[31] Dahl records Jones's story as follows:

> 'Five o'clock every morning, six days a week we reported for work at the pithead,' he said, 'and me just a skinny little nipper wearing my grandad's worn-out old jacket as an overcoat, and I was always shivering shivering shivering. You don't half shiver at five in the morning when you're young and skinny. Then into the cage we all went and when they let go the winding-gear, we all dropped like a stone into the black black hole for miles and miles, and it fell so fast that your feet left the floor and your stomach came up to your throat, and every time I went down I thought the cable had broken and we were going to go right on falling until we came to the very centre of the earth where everything was white-hot boiling lava.'
>
> 'Did it ever crash Joss, that cage?'
>
> 'Lots of 'em crashed,' he said, 'But never with me in it or I wouldn't be here.'
>
> 'You mean the wire broke?'
>
> 'Not the wire,' he said, 'It was the brakes on the winding-gear that went wrong. And then the cage would go shooting downwards faster and faster for thousands of feet until it smashed into the bottom of the shaft and all the men inside would be turned into strawberry jam.'[32]

In its vivid, visceral and cartoonish evocation of violent disaster, the final line is characteristically Dahlian. Is this touch that of the mature Dahl, or is the author recalling the metaphorical energy of Jones the storyteller, whose capacity to 'enthral' made young Roald 'run all the way home' to spend half an hour with him after school and 'literally the whole of the day with him' during the holidays?[33] What is clear is that in communicating Jones's story, Dahl employs the figure of a young boy to highlight the 'isolation' and 'powerlessness' noted by Knight. The manuscript shows Dahl emphasising Jones's vulnerability before he goes on to detail Jones's response to the potential horror of firedamp as he sees the canary fall from his perch, calls the alarm and places himself in danger in order to safeguard the lives of the pit ponies for which he is responsible. The section of the essay that describes the descent of the pit cage has been worked over many times. As is characteristic of Dahl's method, a substantial draft has clearly been erased and written over. Traces of this erasure also indicate that this first rubbed-out version had significant sections of new text encircled and added in at a later point. This suggests that after initial drafting, the text was redrafted with insertions, then the original text and its insertions were erased and the text rewritten and further redrafted with new insertions including sections drafted on the verso and cued up with a 'PTO 1' on the front of the page. The following was added from a marginal bubble into the text: 'and I was always shivering, shivering, shivering. You don't half shiver at five in the morning when you're young and skinny'; in the previous sentence, 'worn-out' was added to the description of the hand-me-down jacket Jones was wearing as an overcoat. Significantly, these additions suggest Dahl's sensitivity to the conditions peculiar to Jones's hazardous occupation as part of the industrial capitalist machine in one of the seventy or so collieries operating in the Rhondda in the mid-1890s.

This presents a stark contrast to the Welsh matter of Dahl's own 'tales of childhood'. Rather than revolving around bicycles and sweet shops, Jones's tale centres on punishing work in the perilous darkness of a Rhondda mine. Dahl writes that he 'liked best of all when [Jones] told me about his own boyhood in the Rhondda Valley, when he was sent down the coalmines at the age of eleven'.[34] Dahl's autobiografiction – both 'Henry Sugar' and the 'Joss Spivvis' essay can be seen as modalities of such – begins to reveal some of the dissonances at the heart of the textual life of Dahl's inscriptions of Wales. Filtered through Dahl, Jones's reminiscences conform to the pattern of proletarian life writing collected in the Burnett Archive of Working Class Autobiographies.[35] As John Burnett notes, such autobiographers 'devote more space to their working experiences than to their family relationships, being particularly reticent about emotional and sexual matters'.[36] Claire Lynch explains that in such memoirs,

> work is shown to be the significant influence . . . from childhood onwards. From first jobs or apprenticeships, authors shape their narratives around work events including sporadic unemployment, gruesome building site accidents, and family traditions of working in the same trade.[37]

As such, an individual instance of life writing becomes 'indicative' of the lives of others 'of the same occupation or circumstance . . . a piece of evidence which contributes to an historical tableau'.[38] Dahl's Jones tells traditional stories of work and leisure time (such as going 'to see

the City play' at Ninian Park and eating jellied eels) that are stereotypical of Jones's social class. Dahl also notes Jones's mispronunciation of
the name of Cardiff City's Irish goalkeeper, Tom Farquharson (1900–
70), known as the 'Penalty King'; Dahl's mother explained that the
'correct' pronunciation is 'Farkerson', not 'Far-q-arson', as Jones had
it.[39] Through these types of details, Joss Spivvis becomes a representa-
tive of the proletariat who is 'alien enough to be marked as the stuff
of nostalgia'.[40] Jones, whose full name is not given and whose nickname replaces his name (which both erases his Welsh surname and
renders the individual untraceable), stands in for a whole class and
cultural experience. The drafts of the 'Joss Spivvis' essay show Dahl
erasing Jones's specificity as an individual with a particular life history in favour of stereotypical tropes of Welshness, the working class
and the Welsh industrial experience. The dialogue between various
inscriptions – manuscript and published – of Dahl's autobiografiction as it concerns the gardener figure demonstrates how the Welsh
context of this part of Dahl's life was also concealed in the drafts of
'Henry Sugar', thus removing a layer of complexity in the social and
cultural relationship between the young boy and the family employee.
Further, that social and cultural gulf is not explicitly explored owing to
the fact that Dahl's portrait of Jones oscillates problematically between
the representation of a Welsh surrogate father or father *manqué* (central
here is the link between Jones and Harald Dahl and their insertion in
the industrial economy of south Wales) and the depiction of Jones as
a powerless child at the mercy of circumstances beyond his control.
The latter is a figure at the centre of much of Dahl's fiction – a victim
whose subjection he often seeks to reverse.

3. Mining the Drafts of *Charlie and the Chocolate Factory*

An excavation of the archive reveals Jones and the Welsh proletarian
experience he represents to be an elided or euphemised – and thus
conditioning – presence in *Charlie and the Chocolate Factory* (1964), a
book in which a poor, malnourished young boy is born into an industrial landscape dominated by factories. I suggest that Jones's central
account of the descent of the pit cage into the Rhondda mine achieves
euphemised expression in the introduction into a late manuscript draft
of *Charlie* of Mr Wonka's elevator.

Although the earliest extant draft of *Charlie* does not include an elevator scene, it does, however, comprise elements that anticipate Dahl's later invocation of Jones's experience of going down the mine. The published book describes 'A great, craggy mountain made entirely of fudge, with Oompa-Loompas (all roped together for safety) hacking huge hunks of fudge out of its sides'.[41] In early drafts, this industrial space is allocated its own chapter, entitled 'The Vanilla Fudge Room', in which the expanse of fudge features as a '<u>colossal jagged mountain</u>' on which 'hundreds of men were working away' with 'picks and drills, hacking great hunks of fudge out of the mountain; and some of them, those that were high up in dangerous places, were roped together for safety.'[42] The blocks of fudge mined from the mountain are put into 'open waggons – into an endless moving line of waggons (rather like smallish railway waggons)' – or perhaps rather more like coal wagons or those drawn to illustrate his father's shipbroking business in *Boy*.[43]

The episode does not figure in the final version. However, reinforced by the memories that would eventually be creatively rendered in the 'Joss Spivvis' essay, the mining of the fudge establishes for the published book an industrial context that alters our understanding of those scenes involving ascents and descents in elevators that figure prominently in the novel as published (and in its sequel of 1972, *Charlie and the Great Glass Elevator*). The environment of extractive industry is slowly exorcised by Dahl from the drafts until it survives only in fleeting references, leaving in the published novel symbolic synecdoches – such as the elevator, which, as I shall show, takes on a punitive function in the novel – whose elided wholes can be reconstituted only through attention to the manuscript drafts. The elevator first makes its appearance in *Charlie* in the fourth draft of the novel. Mike Teavee complains that he is tired and wants to watch television; Mr Wonka suggests they should take the elevator. When they first enter the lift, the mining context that was present in 'The Vanilla Fudge Room' section of a previous draft is distilled in the form of the first elevator button label that Charlie Bucket reads: 'ROCK CANDY MINE – 10,000 FEET DEEP'.[44] Mike presses his chosen button. What follows is a description of the elevator's movement (unchanged from draft to published version) – 'suddenly, as though it had come to the top of the hill and gone over a precipice, it dropped like a stone and Charlie felt his tummy coming right up into his throat'[45] – that would be uncannily reprised in Dahl's recollection of Jones's account of the cage descending into the Rhondda mine: 'into the cage we all went and when they let go the winding-gear, we all dropped like a stone into the black black hole for miles and miles, and it fell so fast that your feet left the floor and your stomach came up to your throat.' Dahl's choice to deploy in the little-known 'Joss Spivvis' essay, over twenty years later, the same description he had used in one of his most famous books is telling. It should be noted that for Charlie, the elevator journey is exhilarating, not terrifying; for Mike Teavee, however, it is otherwise, given that the descent is meant by Wonka as a punishment for the boy's TV-generation indolence and barely suppressed violence. The re-engagement with Wales in the 1987 essay acknowledges the elision of Wales in the drafts of *Charlie and the Chocolate Factory*, just as it allows us to identify the Rhondda trace in the published *Charlie*. Just as Jones-Dahl remembers that 'every time I went down I thought the cable had broken and we were going to go right on falling until we came to the very centre of the earth where everything was white-hot boiling lava,' so Mrs Teavee, who feels vio-lently ill as a result of the journey to the 'Television-Chocolate Room', is terrified that 'the rope has broken.'[46] Dahl's appropriation and fictionalisation in *Charlie and the Chocolate Factory* of Jones's Rhondda mineshaft experience as punishment (in the case of Mike Teavee) and as a thrilling ride (for the Buckets) are suspect, even if a trace of Jones's terror is registered in the response of Mike's mother. Young Jones's fear is also inscribed in *Charlie and the Great Glass Elevator*, which begins with Charlie, his family and Mr Wonka aloft in the glass elevator. This sec-tion was an insertion written on the verso of the main draft but then crossed out. In Dahl's original drafting, rather than descending to hit the factory as in the published version, the elevator hits the ground. As this reality dawns on them, the passengers protest that they will be 'pulpified!', 'lixivated!', 'scrunched to a splodge!', 'Scrambled like eggs!', 'Splattered like splinters!', which anticipates Jones's comment in 'Joss Spivvis' – filtered, in 1987, through the discourse of *Charlie and the Chocolate Factory* – that if the cage 'smashed into the bottom of the shaft', 'all the men inside would be turned into strawberry jam.'[47] Such moments point to the fact that Dahl's Welsh experience survives in his published fiction as oblique registrations amplified by the frequencies of the archive. The archive reveals Dahl's distance from the material conditions of Welsh industrial capitalism at the turn of the twentieth century just as it brings to light the irresistible pressure of that world on his adult, middle-class, anglicised consciousness.

4. Origins in the Archive

The Great Missenden archive reveals the various forms in which Dahl
responded to Wales throughout his life, from the early school letters
back to Llandaff to a postcard from a hike up Snowdon in the 1930s
and material relating to family holidays in Tenby, to which Dahl also
brought his own children. However, in literary terms, as we have seen,
the archive allows us to track a process of elision as the matter of Wales,
and of a comfortably upper-middle-class Anglo-Welsh-Norwegian
childhood, are transformed into fiction. The evidence of the drafts
points to the dilution and erasure of complex national and socio-
economic contexts at moments of charged autobiografiction, alerting
us at the same time to the resonance of those absences and to the palimpsestic nature of Dahl's 'final' texts. To return to Derrida: Dahl's
archive is not a 'transparent' window that lets a Welsh origin 'present
itself'.[48] However, a carefully preserved archive such as Dahl's invites
critical acts of excavation that creatively undo 'the limits, borders, and
the distinctions' of the published canon.[49] The marginal and the elided
are conditioning forces that deconstruct the dominant tale of Dahl's
English self-fashioning.

Notes

[1] Jacques Derrida, *Archive Fever: A Freudian Impression*, trans. Eric Prenowitz
(Chicago: University of Chicago Press, 1996), p. 5. I would like to thank
Annie Price and Rachel White from the Roald Dahl Museum and Story
Centre for their generosity in support of my research for this chapter.

[2] Antoinette Burton, 'Introduction', in *Archive Stories: Facts, Fictions and the
Writing of History*, ed. Antoinette Burton (Durham, NC: Duke University
Press, 2005), p. 10.

[3] Derrida, *Archive Fever*, p. 93.

[4] See Michael Davidson, *Ghostlier Demarcations: Modern Poetry and the Material
World* (Berkeley and Los Angeles: University of California Press, 1997), p. 69;
and Achille Mbembe, 'The Power of the Archive and its Limits', in *Refiguring
the Archive*, ed. Carolyn Hamilton *et al.* (Dordecht: Kluwer Academic
Publishers, 2002), p. 21.

[5] Burton, 'Introduction', p. 8.

[6] This term was first coined in a 1906 essay by Stephen Reynolds in *The
Speaker* and has been naturalised in critical discourse; see for example Max
Saunders, *Self Impression: Life-writing, Autobiografiction, and the Forms of Modern
Literature* (Oxford: Oxford University Press, 2010).

7 The episodes 'A Visit to the Doctor' and 'Little Ellis and the Boil' were both included in early drafts of *The Witches*; the Roald Dahl Museum and Story Centre (hereafter RDMSC), RD/2/21/1.

8 BBC Radio 4, *Desert Island Discs* (27 October 1979), *http://www.bbc.co.uk/programmes/p009mwxx* (accessed 21 November 2015).

9 See Roald Dahl, *Boy: Tales of Childhood* (London: Puffin, 2013), pp. 85–6, 105.

10 Donald Sturrock, *Storyteller: The Life of Roald Dahl* (London: HarperPress, 2010), p. 39.

11 Sturrock, *Storyteller*, p. 45.

12 Roald Dahl, *More About Boy* (London: Penguin, 2008), pp. 19–23.

13 RDMSC, RD/1/4/6, Judy Hughes, 'Tale Feathers from a Retired Poacher', *Western Mail*, 30 October 1975.

14 Ann Alston, 'The Unlikely Family Romance in Roald Dahl's Children's Fiction', in *Roald Dahl* (New Casebooks), ed. Ann Alston and Catherine Butler (Basingstoke: Palgrave Macmillan, 2012), pp. 94, 96.

15 RDMSC, RD/6/2/26, drafts of 'Joss Spivvis'.

16 Roald Dahl, 'Joss Spivvis', in *When We Were Young: Memories of Childhood* (Newton Abbot: David & Charles Publishers, 1987), p. 13.

17 See Dahl, *Boy*, p. 12.

18 See Sturrock, *Storyteller*, pp. 27, 28 and Raymond Williams, *Who Speaks for Wales? Nation, Culture, Identity*, ed. Daniel Williams (Cardiff: University of Wales Press, 2003), p. 99.

19 RDMSC, RD/4/56/1/1, drafts of 'The Wonderful Story of Henry Sugar'.

20 RDMSC, RD/4/56/1/1, drafts of 'The Wonderful Story of Henry Sugar'.

21 Dahl, 'Joss Spivvis', p. 15.

22 Dahl, 'Joss Spivvis', p. 15.

23 RDMSC, RD/13/1/1/33, letter from Dahl to his mother, Sofie Magdalene, 21 February 1926.

24 RDMSC, RD/13/1/1/58, letter from Dahl to his mother, 25 July 1926.

25 RDMSC, RD/4/56/1/3, drafts of 'The Wonderful Story of Henry Sugar'. I am indebted to Annie Price for pointing out that this incident echoes the short story 'Pig' from *Kiss Kiss* (1960), in which a boy who is a vegetarian visits a slaughterhouse, sees a pig strung up and identifies emotionally with the animal.

26 Dahl, 'Joss Spivvis', p. 14.

27 RDMSC, RD/4/56/1/3, drafts of 'The Wonderful Story of Henry Sugar'.

28 Unemployment in the Rhondda would rise to 40 per cent by 1937; see Stephen Knight, *A Hundred Years of Fiction: From Colony to Independence* (Cardiff: University of Wales Press, 2004), p. 59 and John Davies, *A History of Wales* (London: Penguin, 1987), p. 471.

29 RDMSC, RD/6/2/26, drafts of 'Joss Spivvis'.

30 RDMSC, RD/6/2/26, drafts of 'Joss Spivvis'.

31 Knight, *A Hundred Years of Fiction*, p. 28.

32 Dahl, 'Joss Spivvis', pp. 13–14.
33 Dahl, 'Joss Spivvis', p. 13.
34 Dahl, 'Joss Spivvis', p. 13.
35 See *http://www.brunel.ac.uk/services/library/research/special-collections/collections/ burnett-archive-of-working-class-autobiographies*.
36 Quoted in Claire Lynch, '"Unlike Actors, Politicians or Eminent Military Men": The Meaning of Hard Work in Working Class Autobiography', *a/b: Auto/Biography Studies*, 25/2 (2010), p. 187.
37 Lynch, 'Unlike Actors', pp. 187–8.
38 Lynch, 'Unlike Actors', p. 189.
39 Dahl, 'Joss Spivvis', p. 16.
40 Lynch, 'Unlike Actors', p. 188.
41 Roald Dahl, *Charlie and the Chocolate Factory* (London: Puffin, 2010), p. 154.
42 RDMSC, RD/2/7/1/20 and 21, drafts of *Charlie and the Chocolate Factory*.
43 RDMSC, RD/2/7/1/21, drafts of *Charlie and the Chocolate Factory*.
44 Dahl, *Charlie and the Chocolate Factory*, p. 150.
45 Dahl, *Charlie and the Chocolate Factory*, p. 182.
46 Dahl, 'Joss Spivvis', pp. 13–14; Dahl, *Charlie and the Chocolate Factory*, p. 154.
47 RDMSC, RD/2/10/1/2, drafts of *Charlie and the Great Glass Elevator*; Dahl, 'Joss Spivvis', p. 14.
48 Derrida, *Archive Fever*, p. 93.
49 Derrida, *Archive Fever*, p. 5.

Works cited

Roald Dahl Museum and Story Centre, Great Missenden, RD/1/4/6, copy of Judy Hughes, 'Tale Feathers from a Retired Poacher', *Western Mail*, 30 October 1975.
—, RD/2/7/1/20 and 21, drafts of *Charlie and the Chocolate Factory*.
—, RD/2/10/1/2, drafts of *Charlie and the Great Glass Elevator*.
—, RD/2/21/1, early drafts of *The Witches*.
—, RD/4/56/1/1, drafts of 'The Wonderful Story of Henry Sugar'.
—, RD/4/56/1/3, drafts of 'The Wonderful Story of Henry Sugar'.
—, RD/6/2/26, drafts of 'Joss Spivvis'.
—, RD/13/1/1/33, letter from Dahl to his mother, Sofie Magdalene, 21 February 1926.
—, RD/13/1/1/58, letter from Dahl to his mother, 25 July 1926.

Dahl, Roald, *Boy: Tales of Childhood* (London: Puffin, 2013).
—, *Charlie and the Chocolate Factory* (London: Puffin, 2010).
—, 'Joss Spivvis', in *When We Were Young: Memories of Childhood* (Newton Abbot: David & Charles Publishers, 1987), pp. 13–16.
—, *More About Boy* (London: Penguin, 2008).

Carrie Smith

Alston, Ann, 'The Unlikely Family Romance in Roald Dahl's Children's Fiction', in *Roald Dahl* (New Casebooks), ed. Ann Alston and Catherine Butler (Basingstoke: Palgrave Macmillan, 2012), pp. 86–101.

Burton, Antoinette, 'Introduction', in *Archive Stories: Facts, Fictions and the Writing of History*, ed. Antoinette Burton (Durham, NC: Duke University Press, 2005), pp. 1–24.

Davidson, Michael, *Ghostlier Demarcations: Modern Poetry and the Material World* (Berkeley and Los Angeles: University of California Press, 1997).

Davies, John, *A History of Wales* (London: Penguin, 1987).

Derrida, Jacques, *Archive Fever: A Freudian Impression*, trans. Eric Prenowitz (Chicago: University of Chicago Press, 1996).

Knight, Stephen, *A Hundred Years of Fiction: From Colony to Independence* (Cardiff: University of Wales Press, 2004).

Lynch, Claire, '"Unlike Actors, Politicians or Eminent Military Men": The Meaning of Hard Work in Working Class Autobiography', *a/b: Auto/Biography Studies*, 25/2 (2010), pp. 186–202.

Mbembe, Achille, 'The Power of the Archive and its Limits', in *Refiguring the Archive*, ed. Carolyn Hamilton *et al.* (Dordrecht: Kluwer Academic Publishers, 2002), pp. 19–26.

Saunders, Max, *Self Impression: Life-writing, Autobiografiction, and the Forms of Modern Literature* (Oxford: Oxford University Press, 2010).

Sturrock, Donald, *Storyteller: The Life of Roald Dahl* (London: HarperPress, 2010).

Williams, Raymond, *Who Speaks for Wales? Nation, Culture, Identity*, ed. Daniel Williams (Cardiff: University of Wales Press, 2003).

3

How Sweet Was My Valley: Willy Wonka and the Welsh Industrial Novel

Tomos Owen

1. How Sweet

> They were looking down upon a lovely valley. There were green meadows on either side of the valley, and along the bottom of it there flowed a great brown river.
>
> ROALD DAHL, Charlie and the Chocolate Factory (1964)[1]

> My Valley, O my Valley, within me, I will live in you, eternally. Let Death or worse strike this mind and blindness eat these eyes if thought or sight forget you. Valley of the Shadow of Death, now, for some, but not for me, for part of me is the memory of you in your greens and browns, with everything of life happy in your deeps and shades, when you gave sweet scents to us, and sent forth spices for the pot, and flowers, and birds sang out for pleasure to be with you.
>
> RICHARD LLEWELLYN, How Green Was My Valley (1939)[2]

How sweet. Rich with greens and browns, vivid to the eye, fragrant to the nose, tantalising even to the tongue, the valleys described in these two novels have an evocative hold over their protagonists. The first quotation describes Charlie Bucket's arrival in the Chocolate Room of Willy Wonka's factory. Greeting the young boy is a hyper-real scene which, for all its pastoral beauty – down to its river and waterfall – is a confected landscape. The valley in Richard Llewellyn's novel is a symbolic and no less confected space. The verdure of the hillsides is threatened over the course of the novel by the growth of looming piles of slag, but the description above is not untypical of the rhapsodic and wistful tone of the protagonist-narrator, Huw Morgan. Both bucolic settings are framed by an industrial experience: Dahl's 'lovely valley' is housed within Willy Wonka's great factory, while the green Welsh valley of Llewellyn's novel is the setting for rapacious industrial expansion that unleashes forces that threaten to tear its social fabric apart.

But what, if anything, is to be gained from comparing Dahl's sugary landscape with Llewellyn's sugared apostrophe to a once green valley? This essay sets out to identify some of the unexpected and unlikely ways in which Dahl's most famous work of children's fiction speaks to a tradition of Welsh industrial fiction. If Welsh spaces left their imprint on Dahl's biography, then this essay contends that particular forms of Welsh writing leave traces in his work. Such an argument has consequences for our growing sense of the Welsh or Anglo-Welsh elements of Dahl's identity. What is at stake is not a kind of extraction of Wales or Welshness from the ore of Dahl's Wonka novels, much less his personal biography; Wales is not the golden ticket that grants final access to these texts. Nor is this essay an attempt to argue from absence, cheaply to re-insert Wales into those gaps in the text where the writing will not be drawn on nation or location. On the contrary, what is argued for is the possibility that thematic and formal literary structures with particular resonances in Welsh writing – namely those of industrial fiction – reverberate in the spaces of Dahl's text. A reading of *Charlie and the Chocolate Factory* as an industrial novel invokes structures of feeling from Welsh industrial fiction even as they are sugared and confected by the children's author.

Willy Wonka may be the candied capitalist and his author's most famous creation; for Dahl, however, Welsh coal and Welsh candy were there from the start. Though not the primary focus of this chapter, there are historical factors linking the Dahl family with Welsh industry. Biographers have identified the attraction of Welsh heavy industry for Dahl's father, Harald. Jeremy Treglown records that Harald settled in Cardiff in the 1880s, 'the boom years of the South Wales coalfields', when the town was one of the biggest cargo-shipping ports in the world.[3] More recently and in greater detail, Donald Sturrock has picked up the story by positioning Harald Dahl as part of a long history of correspondence and interaction between Norway and South Wales reaching back over a thousand years. 'By

1900', he notes, 'Cardiff was exporting 5 million tons of coal annually', and '[t]wo thirds of these exports left in Norwegian-owned vessels.'[4] Since 1868, Cardiff's docks had been home to a Norwegian church – a religious and social meeting-place for an exiled community. Sturrock relates the story of Harald Dahl's journey from Norway to Cardiff via Paris, where he made the acquaintance of his future business partner, Ludvig Aadnesen. The business of Aadnesen & Dahl grew from modest beginnings as a shipbroking venture managed from a single office on Cardiff's Bute Street to a thriving firm that traded in coal as well as providing ship supplies; these were successful times for the two Norwegian partners who found themselves at the heart of the great Welsh coal-shipping port that was in turn a gateway to global trade. In *Boy*, written in 1984 (the year of the British Miners' Strike), Dahl relates how Harald and Ludvig entered into the shipbroking business:

> All ships were steamships and these old steamers would take on hundreds and often thousands of tons of coal in one go. To the shipbrokers, coal was black gold.
>
> My father and his new-found friend, Mr Aadnesen, understood all this very well. It made sense, they told each other, to set up their shipbroking business in one of the great coaling ports of Europe. Which was it to be? The answer was simple. The greatest coaling port in the world at that time was Cardiff, in South Wales. So off to Cardiff they went . . .[5]

For Dahl's Boy, Welsh industry – lucrative, dynamic and international – is part of his own prehistory and formation. Coal constituted a (black) golden ticket by means of which Harald was able to achieve professional respect and handsome financial reward.[6] While Welsh industry was an attraction for Dahl *père*, Welsh industrial fiction emerges as an unexpected intertextual framework for Dahl *fils*. The industrial and industrialising society with which the Dahls were by now professionally connected found potent and varied expression through imaginative writing. The sweet seductiveness of heavy industry in the eyes of a young boy would be the focus of *Charlie and the Chocolate Factory* and its sequel, *Charlie and the Great Glass Elevator* (1972).

Bringing two seemingly discrete – even discordant – genres together, this essay explores how three elements common to Welsh industrial fiction are shared by Dahl's Wonka novels. First, *Charlie and the Chocolate*

Factory develops by describing the unfolding fascination of an innocent and naïve young boy in the face of a new industrial world that
is by turns cruel and incomprehensible, but always compelling and
strangely seductive. Structurally at least, there are several notable
Welsh industrial novels that operate by similar means, employing the
strategy of the child to achieve their characteristic effects. Second is
the seam of social and economic analysis that runs through a great
deal of Welsh industrial fiction. Fictional and literary responses to
Welsh industrial society took a range of different forms, from autobiographical writing (at varying degrees of displacement from their
authors' lives), to romance, to touristic 'regionalism', to more serious,
sustained and engaged critiques of the iniquities of industrial culture
and society. Dahl's Wonka novels are similarly fascinated by an industrial world that is ingenious to the point of alchemy, spectacular to the
point of terror. Third is how the depiction of racial difference can in
industrial fiction be difficult to swallow. The representation of Wonka's
factory workers, the Oompa-Loompas, in *Charlie and the Chocolate
Factory*, which generated significant controversy on first publication,
echoes other fraught and problematic textual representations of racial
otherness in Welsh industrial fiction. Taken together, these three
elements do not transform Dahl into a Welsh industrial writer in the
mould of Lewis Jones, Jack Jones and Gwyn Jones. Yet by 'industrialising' Dahl's Wonka novels from a Welsh perspective we might come to
think of them as being silently, invisibly formed by that which they do
not explicitly articulate. Wales does not stand 'behind' these texts, like
Wonka's factory behind its gates. But there are moments when *Charlie
and the Chocolate Factory* and *Charlie and the Great Glass Elevator* seem to
invoke – if only to deny – links with other kinds and traditions of writing. In the case of industrial fiction, this is a tradition of writing with
significant Welsh elements.

2. Boy

The title of his memoir would suggest that, for Dahl, the figure of the
boy is important and necessary. Charlie Bucket is the hero of Dahl's
novel and Wonka's eventual heir (though, as Jeremy Treglown notes,
this is 'more through inoffensiveness than for any positive merit').[7]
Though Charlie is indeed inoffensive, he retains a sense of wonder and

amazement at Wonka's factory as he and his grandfather are guided through it. It is a truism that children's literature is predicated on a concern with the experience and development of children; the child, and in particular the young boy, is also a significant figure and tool in the literature of industry. As a sensitive and delicate lad, entranced by both the spectacle and the functioning of industrial capitalism, Charlie Bucket (though he may not know it) has plenty of cousins on the pages of Welsh industrial fiction.

Raymond Williams and Stephen Knight have identified several structural problems confronting writers of industrial fiction in Wales. Knight notes that '[t]he form of the classic novel has frequently been described as inherently middle class, shaping an aesthetic that is deeply involved with the individual, with moralized choice and with many kinds of accepted hierarchy, social and discursive.'[8] The prob-lem, therefore, is how to make an individualist, middle-class form fit the communal, working-class experiences that defined industrial communities in Wales. In the Welsh context, Williams argues, the late arrival of industrial fiction – compared with the early arrival of industrialisation itself – is accounted for by the 'influence of the types of working-class community' still 'inaccessible' in English, the 'lack of motivated and competent middle-class observers' and the 'problems of the two languages and the relative unfamiliarity, in Welsh, of the appropriate realist form'.[9] These problems have literary and political implications. One available strategy, Williams suggests, is to 'accept one of the dominant forms [naturalism or classic realism] and to insert, to graft on to it, these other experiences, of work and struggle'.[10] Another alternative is to adapt existing forms and genres (life-writing and autobiography, for example). But '[t]he most accessible form, in this kind of novel, is the story of the family.'[11] By writing the story of a family, argues Williams, 'what is really being written, through it, is the story of a class; indeed effectively, given the local historical circum-stances, of a people.'[12] The development, conflict and depression of industrial society then come to bear on the family, first uniting it in struggle but also causing it to fragment. In such renderings of family experience, the figure of the young boy recurs frequently; time and again the experience of the boy – sensitive and often physically frail, and sometimes (to recall Treglown's description) inoffensive – is a tech-nical (and ideological) device that enables these novels to describe an industrial world both formative and alien.

'Family', notes Knight, 'is the centre of *Cwmardy*', Lewis Jones's 1937 left-wing fictional reworking of the working-class history of industrial south Wales from the late nineteenth century to the years following the end of the First World War.[13] Rolph Meyn has described the novel as an example of 'proletarian *Bildungsroman*' that stresses the protagonist's growth and class education.[14] The novel opens with Len, on whose growth to class consciousness there is a sustained focus, on the mountainside above the town of Cwmardy. His father, 'Big Jim, known to civil servants and army authorities as James Roberts', has 'stopped abruptly and let his eyes roam over the splendour of the mountain landscape'.[15] Jim is the archetypal hero-collier: in deed and physicality he is as massive as Mr Bucket is insipid. Looking plaintively down on the industrial town, Big Jim remembers 'the days long ago, when I did use to walk the fields of the North before I ever came down to work in the pits'; Len, 'puny' in his father's shadow, 'stood near by wondering what had caused this sudden halt' and 'surveyed the valley' covered with smoke 'like a blanket blotting out everything beneath'.[16] The son looking down at the industrial town with an initial sense of incomprehension and wonder – here in the literal shadow of his father – is another recurring motif in industrial novels: it positions the speaker outside of and at a distance from the industrial society that has been formative and influential. As Richard Marggraf Turley argues in this volume, aerial perspectives constitute a recurring motif in Dahl's work; by flying up and out of the factory at the conclusion of *Charlie and the Chocolate Factory*, Charlie, now in possession of the keys to the means of production, is afforded a panoramic view down over the town from which he has just emerged.[17]

Like Charlie Bucket, Dahl himself in *Boy* is at certain points a kid in a candy store. Recalling his time at Llandaff Cathedral School, Dahl writes:

> On the way to school and on the way back we always passed a sweet-shop. No we didn't, we never passed it. We always stopped. We lingered outside its rather small window gazing in at the big glass jars full of Bull's-eyes and Old Fashioned Humbugs and Strawberry Bonbons and Glacier Mints and Acid Drops and Pear Drops and Lemon Drops and all the rest of them. Each of us received sixpence a week for pocket-money, and whenever there was any money in our pockets, we would all troop in together to buy a pennyworth of this or that.[18]

Young Dahl's disposable income is invested, in this autobiographical account, back into confectionery. It is scarcely surprising to find that the sweetshop is figured as a seductive and alluring space in the young boy's memory. What is for Dahl's persona a fixture in the daily routine of a Welsh childhood is for Charlie Bucket a means of transportation from his meagre existence into what is almost a realm of fantasy, from delight at the taste of a morsel of chocolate to possession of the entire factory.

Even though their impelling drive is individualist, Dahl's Wonka novels also focus on family units and structures. Charlie lives in a small, dilapidated house on the edge of an industrial town with his parents and grandparents; his hapless father is made redundant from the toothpaste factory and both sets of grandparents spend their days sharing the same bed. Charlie is the only golden-ticket holder not to bring both his parents with him on the tour of Wonka's factory; Mr Bucket in fact declines the opportunity, and instead it is Grandpa Joe who accompanies him. Outside the gates early in the novel, the smell ('Oh, how he loved the smell!') heightens Charlie's desire to get inside.[19] Later, as 'the family begins to starve', Charlie again sniffs outside, 'taking deep swallowing breaths as though he were trying to *eat* the smell itself'.[20] Such is the ability of chocolate to conjure and summon desire, promising a kind of nourishment and satisfaction but ultimately vanishing into industrial air. Sam Leith has read *Charlie and the Chocolate Factory* as 'basically a fable about scarcity economics' and contends that the 'most blissful vision of perfection' offered by the novel 'is not access to Wonka's phantasmagoria: it's Charlie's husbanding of his birthday chocolate'.[21] This may be true, but at the miraculous moment when Charlie discovers the golden ticket he is driven by different impulses. On finding a fifty-pence piece on the street on his way home (notably, the purchase which yields the golden ticket is with money found, not earned or saved), Charlie resolves to 'buy one luscious bar of chocolate and eat it *all* up, every bit of it, right then and there'.[22] Inside the shop, Charlie devours his first bar and, instead of taking the change home to the family as he had initially resolved, he immediately purchases another bar; this is the one that contains the ticket. Self-motivated and greedy for the first time in the novel, Charlie's newly acquired capital is reinvested in the market economy; here, chocolate is the 'essence' of capitalism.[23] Having finally learned how to be a good capitalist, Charlie is duly rewarded for his individualism with the discovery of the golden ticket and the keys to the kingdom.

A discernible 'individualism and nostalgia' (in spite of a family story) have been identified by Knight in *How Green Was My Valley*, 'that thoroughgoing sentimentalisation of a national image'.[24] Here too, childhood confectionery is further sweetened in memory. In one of several wallowing descriptions of eating found in the novel (an ingredient in what Dai Smith has termed 'a veritable cornucopia of wholesome food, described again and again in the course of the book and kept perpetually before us'), Huw, like Dahl, recalls spending his Saturday penny to buy toffee from Mrs Rhys the Glasfryn:[25]

> She made the toffee in pans and then rolled it all up and threw it soft at a nail behind the door, where it stuck. Then she took a handful with both hands and pulled it towards her, then threw the slack back on the nail again. That went on for half an hour or more until she was satisfied it was hard enough, and then she let it lie to flatten out. Hours I have waited in her front room with my penny in my hand, and my mouth full of spit, thinking of the toffee, and sniffing the smell of sugar and cream and eggs. You could chew that toffee for hours, it seems to me now, and never lost [*sic*] the taste of it, and even after it had gone down, you could swallow and still find the taste hiding behind your tongue.[26]

Again, how sweet. Ian Bell has drawn attention to the novel's peculiar kind of ancestor-worship, its suspicion of all forms of modernity and its glorification of the past simply because it is the past.[27] The toffee here is both material and numinous. It has to be pulled and slackened, thrown on nails, stretched and hardened; but it also stays on the tongue, evanescent yet lingering, satisfying yet also always conjuring more desire.

Alun Lewis's short story 'The Housekeeper' (1942) leaves a different taste. Here too, the boy, Jackie, features prominently in the story of an industrial family; like *Charlie*, his father Penry is made redundant from the industrial workforce (Mr Bucket clears snow to make ends meet, while Penry must scour the tips and slag heaps in search of pieces of coal for the fires in the house). This is no sugar-coated industrial childhood. In a powerful passage, Myfanwy, the 'Welsh Mam' of the story, allows her son to visit the sweetshop of Granny Geake, a place she had herself frequented as a child:

She remembered buying at Granny Geake's herself. The smelly little parlour with its oilcloth counter ranged with great paradisical glass
bottles, smooth and round and filled with coloured sweets; and the thrilling moment when Granny took the thick glass lid off and plunged her
hands into the bottle, sifting the sweets like diamonds; and then at the
last moment changing your mind and deciding instead to buy a bag of
sherbet or a barley stick or a Turkish Delight . . . She had a big white wen
on her neck that fascinated the children, and behind her silver-rimmed
spectacles her eyes hid in her pouched and wrinkled flesh. She had been
like that when Myfanwy went there to spend; nothing was changed in
Granny Geake's, neither the delight of the sweets nor the fascination of
the wen; when she thought of the children Myfanwy thought of her own
childhood; nothing had changed. She hoped Jackie would not forget to
offer Granny a loshin . . .[28]

Granny Geake, toothless and cystic, is figured as a strange and grotesque figure, almost a witch; she certainly finds her correlatives in
Dahl's depictions of women (Mrs Pratchett, the harridan-proprietor
of the Llandaff sweetshop described in the early chapters of *Boy* fits
this mould). The sweets, glistening like diamonds, establish a connection between confectionery and material, economic value. Here, as in
Wonka's factory, the allure of sweetness can also be tinged with cruelty,
the cure and the poison equally sweet. For Myfanwy, whose thoughts
structure the narrative, Jackie's visits to Granny Geake's shop provide
continuity and a generational link of shared experience between mother
and son. Yet while Llewellyn has Huw Morgan in *How Green Was My
Valley* rhapsodising as the taste of the toffee lingers long and undimmed
on the tongue, Alun Lewis moves to a minor key: Myfanwy muses that
'she was glad she had the children, although she knew it would be better for them if they hadn't been born.'[29] For Lewis at least, no amount
of sugar can sweeten the bitterness of family life in this industrial valley.

3. Industry

There is a hole in Charlie Bucket. Throughout *Charlie and the Chocolate
Factory*, he is associated with want and incompleteness: the 'small
wooden house on the edge of a great town' lacks space; Mr Bucket 'was
never able to make enough to buy one half of the things that so large

a family needed'; the meals consist of boiled potatoes and cabbage; and even though they do not starve, every member of the family 'and especially little Charlie himself . . . went about from morning till night with a horrible empty feeling in their tummies'.[30] For all its richness and wonder, the wafting odour outside Wonka's factory gates lacks any actual nutritional value. And as the novel shows, there is a teasing quality to both chocolate and capital: a taste of either will always leave you wanting more. If in *Boy* it is Welsh coal that is described as black gold, in the Wonka novels chocolate is the ambrosial stuff. However delicious the experience, consumers of Wonka-brand chocolate invariably go back for another bite; however scrumptious the writing, generations of readers have similarly returned to the novel again and again.[31] In the Dahl universe, chocolate exists in what the philosopher Slavoj Žižek describes as 'curved space – the nearer you get to it, the more it eludes your grasp (or the more you possess it, the greater the lack)'.[32]

Across his body of work, Žižek has written repeatedly on the correspondences between the Marxian notion of 'surplus value' and the Lacanian concept of 'surplus-enjoyment'. There could scarcely be a more appropriate setting than a chocolate factory – where the motives of profit and the cravings of the sweet tooth are equally insatiable – for demonstrating what Žižek describes as 'the link between the capitalist dynamics of surplus-value and the libidinal dynamics of surplus-enjoyment'.[33] Mark I. West reads Willy Wonka as a 'symbol', arguing that '[i]n many ways he represents the child's libidinal drives, the desires to indulge in sensuous pleasures and act out aggressive fantasies'.[34] Wonka's language and behaviour certainly spill over to excess and violence in the spaces of Dahl's writing – and this overspill has captivating and dangerous consequences. As David Harvey has noted, 'Capitalism, in short, is a social system internalizing rules that ensure it will remain a permanently revolutionary and disruptive force in its own world history'.[35] Having invented a new kind of chewing gum that replicates the experience of eating a three-course meal (and brings about the downfall of Violet Beauregarde), Wonka excitedly declares: '[I]t will change *everything*! It will be the end of all kitchens and all cooking! . . . No more buying meat and groceries!'[36] Comprehensive change and continuous revolution identify Wonka as the paradigmatic and matchless industrialist he is. Žižek further suggests that this permanent self-revolutionising is part of capitalism's 'immanent want of balance . . . incessant development is the only way for it to resolve again and again . . . its own fundamental, constitutive, imbalance.'[37] A similar structure, Žižek argues, is in operation in the notion of surplus-enjoyment:

> it is not a surplus which simply attaches itself to some 'normal', fundamental enjoyment, because *enjoyment as such emerges only in this surplus*, because it is constitutively an 'excess'. If we subtract the surplus we lose enjoyment itself, just as capitalism, which can survive only by incessantly revolutionizing its own material conditions, ceases to exist if it 'stays the same', if it achieves an internal balance.[38]

In the world of Willy Wonka's factory, enough is never as good as a feast. In this reading, Augustus Gloop (who, according to Mark West, 'symbolizes gluttony'), emerges as an ethically consistent hero of the novel: greedy and keen to consume all he sees in the edible valley of the Chocolate Room, he obeys to the fullest extent the command on which the landscapes of the novel insist.[39] For all the Oompa-Loompas' reprimands ('*Augustus Gloop! Augustus Gloop! / The great big greedy nincompoop!*'), Gloop's demise reveals a gluttony that is in no simple way a personal or moral failure, but which rather informs the very ecology of Wonka's chocolate utopia.[40]

The Welsh industrial novel, meanwhile, emerges from hell. Taking his cue from George Borrow's description of the approach to Merthyr Tydfil in *Wild Wales* (1862), Raymond Williams argues that '[S]o conscious a view of a sketch for Hell is one of the ways of seeing which led to the industrial novel.'[41] For middle-class observers like Borrow, standing at a distance and looking in (and usually down) on the industrial town, the inhabitants of this inferno are viewed only as 'figures attendant on a landscape', their culture, labour and way of life a mystery.[42] What emerges later is writing from the inside, a sense of 'what it is like to live in hell, and slowly, as the disorder becomes an habitual order, what it is like to get used to it, to grow up in it, to see it as home'.[43] This way of seeing offers a new lens on Dahl's novel. *Charlie and the Chocolate Factory* affords two principal representations of industrial capitalism. The first, which governs Charlie's life and that of his family, is Mr Bucket's experience as a cap-screwer at the toothpaste factory.[44] The second, within sight of the Buckets' family home, is Wonka's chocolate factory. According to Charlie's grandparents, the latter is 'about *fifty* times as big as any other!'[45] It is a 'tremendous, marvellous place' with 'huge iron gates leading into it, and a high wall surrounding it, and smoke belching from its chimneys, and strange whizzing sounds coming from deep inside it'.[46] Exuding the aroma of chocolate for half a mile in all directions, Wonka's factory is enticing and compelling, attractive and enthralling.

Speculating as to the source of the labour on which Wonka's factory depends, Charlie muses to Grandpa Joe, 'there *must* be people working there', to which his grandfather replies, 'Not *people*, Charlie. Not *ordinary* people, anyway.'[47] Short, shadowy figures are seen, backlit, in the factory windows late at night. Wonka closes the factory amid fears of corporate espionage, and the labour that sustains and drives the factory after it reopens is figured as a mystery in the text: 'nobody knows' whom Mr Wonka is employing in the factory. The workers in this dark (chocolate) satanic mill are the Oompa-Loompas. Glimpsed *ab extra*, the staff are merely staffage within the industrial landscape. Charlie's eventual tour of the factory in *Charlie and the Chocolate Factory*, and his trip in the lift in *Charlie and the Great Glass Elevator*, are journeys into the very workings of Wonka's chocolate empire, trajectories that can be read as a descent similar to those encountered in Welsh industrial fiction:

> The place was like a gigantic rabbit warren, with passages leading this way and that in every direction . . .
>
> 'Notice how all these passages are sloping downwards!' called out Mr Wonka, 'We are now going underground! *All* the most important rooms in my factory are deep down below the surface!'[48]

The depiction of the first trip underground is a recurrent trope in the Welsh industrial novel. It often figures as an instance of the sensitive lad's first encounter with the world of adult work that has hitherto been the domain of the father. Down goes Huw in *How Green Was My Valley*:

> And the ground fell from underfoot, and we dropped, with a scream from the wind, into darkness, so dark that you thought you saw lights and your knees were loose and bent.
>
> Hundreds of times I went down, but I never got over the drop of the cage.[49]

The endless fall of the injured pilot into morphia's layered darknesses in Dahl's story 'A Piece of Cake' (1946) comes to mind: 'Then it became darker because the sun and the day were in the fields far away at the top of the cliff . . . I kept my eyes open and watched the darkness turn from grey-black to black, from black to jet black and from jet black to pure liquid blackness.'[50] In Lewis Jones's *Cwmardy*, descent and submersion prefigure otherworldly, underworld ontologies:

> The descent now became even steeper. Len compared it to the sheer mountain drop near the quarry, and the thought made him long for the first time that morning to be back again in the sun. He had never dreamed of this interminable tram in the darkness of the pit. Thinking of the world above prompted him to ask: 'How far be we down, dad?'[51]

This is a Stygian descent, away from the familiar warmth and light of the morning into the darkness of chthonic toil below. On his first descent into the underworld of Wonka's factory in the glass elevator, Charlie glimpses the button for 'ROCK CANDY MINE – 10,000 FEET DEEP'.[52] Later, among the sights is 'A great, craggy mountain made entirely of fudge, with Oompa-Loompas (all roped together for safety) hacking huge hunks of fudge out of its sides'.[53] On his trip in *Charlie and the Great Glass Elevator*, Charlie 'caught a glimpse of what seemed like an enormous quarry with a steep craggy-brown rock-face, and all over the rock-face there were hundreds of Oompa-Loompas working with picks and pneumatic drills'.[54] They work the richest rock-candy deposit in the world, at the heart of Wonka's extractive economy. Despite his own lowly origins, Charlie's way of seeing has more in common with the middle-class view identified by Raymond Williams: he sees 'A village of Oompa-Loompas, with tiny houses and streets and hundreds of Oompa-Loompa children no more than four inches high playing in the streets'.[55] *Charlie and the Great Glass Elevator* plunges even deeper underground; West notes that the journey into Minusland (to which we shall return) has an absurd, almost surreal, quality.[56] If the surreal involves an exploration of the unconscious mind, the trope of descent – in industrial fiction and the Wonka novels – is never merely physical and is often figured in psychological terms. Charlie is overwhelmed as the elevator descends and 'hundreds, literally hundreds of astonishing sights kept flashing by outside': streets of Oompa-Loompa dwellings (terrace-like, perhaps); a gusher of oily liquid chocolate; a rock-candy mountain quarried by Oompa-Loompas.[57] Things are different below the surface.

Alongside Dahl's own historic and familial connections with Welsh industry, the presence of these tropes drawn from Welsh industrial fiction in the Wonka novels should not be misread as coded references to Wales – or even Welsh industrial fiction – to be critically mined from the texts. Nonetheless, as Raymond Williams makes clear, ways of seeing are crucial in industrial writing. In turn, Welsh industrial fiction can offer new – and sometimes uncomfortable – ways of looking at *Charlie and the Chocolate Factory* and its sequel.

4. The Oompa-Loompenproletariat

In the Wonka novels, the workforce sings in its enslavement. While the Marxian concept of the Lumpenproletariat refers to those individuals submerged beneath or excluded from the industrial process, Dahl's Oompa-Loompenproletariat is totally co-opted by it. The Oompa-Loompas are among Dahl's most distinctive creations; their arrival on the pages of Dahl's novel – as with their arrival at Wonka's factory – was the source of animated debate. Introducing the Oompa-Loompas to the touring guests, Willy Wonka enumerates a string of characteristics that reads as a check-list of stereotypical representations of the Welsh industrial proletariat: 'They are wonderful workers. They all speak English now. They love dancing and music. They are always making up songs. I expect you will hear a good deal of singing today from time to time.'[58] Obedient, anglicised, songful, they ensure the efficient functioning of Wonka's industrial machine. Occasionally, as the novel shows, they are sacrificed to that machine. This Oompa-Loompenproletariat generated public controversy in ways that also resonate unexpectedly, I suggest, with the politics of Welsh industrial fiction.

Charlie's first glimpse of Wonka's workforce is part of his view across the chocolate valley:

> The tiny men – they were no larger than medium-sized dolls – had stopped what they were doing, and now they were staring back across the river at the visitors . . .
>
> 'But they can't be *real* people,' Charlie said.
>
> 'Of course they're real people,' Mr Wonka answered. 'They're Oompa-Loompas.'[59]

Inside the factory, Wonka completes his colonial master-narrative of the arrival of the Oompa-Loompas – a myth of origin on which Grandpa Joe had speculated outside the factory gates. The thousands of hands made redundant by Wonka when he closed the factory were replaced by Oompa-Loompas, 'Imported direct from Loompaland'.[60] They are literally a captive labour force: in the course of the tour, Wonka reveals that the high temperature in the factory is maintained because the Oompa-Loompas could not survive the climate outside ('They'd perish if they went outdoors in this weather! They'd freeze to death!', he exclaims).[61] They are fed on, and paid in, cacao beans, to which they are practically addicted ('You had only to *mention* the word "cacao" to an Oompa-Loompa and he would start dribbling at the mouth').[62] Wonka's qualities as a chocolatier are matched by his skill and opportunism as a colonialist; he remarks that he liaised with the leader of the tribe in his tree-top dwelling to bring the Oompa-Loompas – harried by predators in their native land – to the chocolate factory to work. Wonka imports a workforce who will literally work for beans.

In their biographies of Dahl, Jeremy Treglown and Donald Sturrock both outline the response to the novel's representation of the Oompa-Loompas. Sturrock notes that the story went through six different rewrites, and that '[a]t the beginning, there were no Oompa-Loompa factory workers and no Grandpa Joe to look after Charlie.'[63] First drafts of the story have Charlie as a 'small NEGRO boy', but it was the published novel's racial representation of the Oompa-Loompas that caused controversy.[64] In 1969, the National Association for the Advancement of Colored People (NAACP) wrote to David L. Wolper, the producer of the film adaptation of *Charlie and the Chocolate Factory*, to express its disapproval of the project on the basis of perceived racism in the book. In the first edition of the novel, published by Knopf in America in 1964, the Oompa-Loompas are portrayed as African pygmies 'from the very deepest and darkest part of the jungle where no white man had ever been before'. As Sturrock relates, '[f]or the NAACP, the Oompa-Loompas seemed clearly to reinforce a stereotype of slavery that American blacks were trying to overcome.'[65]

Mark West notes that Dahl 'was a bit taken aback'; Sturrock remarks that 'this conclusion came as a complete shock.'[66] Dahl seems to have been unaware of the possibility that his Oompa-Loompas could be read in this way. Lucy Mangan's conclusion is that changes in

cultural and social attitudes around the politics of race connected with
the Civil Rights movement had 'outpaced Roald Dahl, and indeed
his agents and editors'; Sturrock quotes Dahl's letter to the publisher
Bob Bernstein angrily describing the response of the NAACP as 'real
Nazi stuff'.[67] Dahl ultimately rewrote the passages relating to the
Oompa-Loompas, changing their appearance in the revised 1973 edition of the novel, in which they hail not from darkest Africa but rather
from the Loompaland jungle (though they are still portrayed as primi-
tives, living in trees and tribal communities). They appear in the 1971
film with green hair and orange skin.

Following the NAACP controversy, Dahl received a letter from a
group of librarians from Madison, Wisconsin, expressing dismay at the
passages 'with racist implications' in the novel.[68] Further, Lois Kalb
Bouchard identifies the infantilisation of the Oompa-Loompas in the
first edition of the novel and their exploitation in Wonka's factory.[69]
Bouchard includes in her critique the fact that the Oompa-Loompas
are experimented on in the development of Wonka's fantastic con-
fections. This is certainly the case across both of the Willy Wonka
novels. In *Charlie and the Chocolate Factory*, a huge black beard grows
thickly from the chin of an Oompa-Loompa who is testing Wonka's
everlasting gobstopper; it is revealed that twenty Oompa-Loompas
have been experimented on and that each – like Violet Beauregarde
– has inflated into a giant blueberry; and an old Oompa-Loompa has
floated away, having drunk from a test batch of fizzy lifting drinks,
never to be seen again. In *Charlie and the Great Glass Elevator*, Wonka
develops Wonka-Vite, an elixir that reverses the ageing process, by
experimenting on Oompa-Loompas, and in the process consigns some
unfortunates to Minusland, a kind of underworld for those who have
had their ages subtracted into a negative value.[70] It is clear that Wonka
considers the lives of individual members of his workforce to be
expendable even if they are collectively essential for the effective functioning of the factory. Neither novel pauses or lingers on the demise of
any single Oompa-Loompa; rather, Wonka's momentum carries the
narrative, and the tour of the factory, onwards in cavalier spirit.

Greater attention is given to the misadventures of the other child
ticket-holders who, through their own individual failings, are lured
to ruin within the factory. It is at these points in the narrative, after
the downfall of each of the silly children, that the Oompa-Loompas
emerge and in song bemoan the victims' moral and personal failings:

"'There they go again!" said Mr Wonka. "I'm afraid you can't stop them singing.'"[71]

Treglown and West have noted that the Oompa-Loompas function as a kind of Greek chorus, moralising in the aftermath of the children's demise.[72] If the Oompa-Loompenproletariat is not expending its labour, it is being pulled into the cogs of the machine; or, it is singing. These three elements – labour, disaster and song – are recurrent, though greatly varying, structural and thematic concerns in a significant body of Welsh industrial fiction. Indeed, they crystallise into a stereotype. Again, it is to Llewellyn's *How Green Was My Valley* (or its film adaptation by John Ford) that we must turn if, as Knight puts it, 'facile stereotype and personalized sentiment are what you want'.[73] Ian Bell claims that 'Whatever you think of it, the novel is the most pervasive and influential fabrication of Wales and the Welsh ever invented.'[74] Following Huw's convalescence after a long illness, the Morgan house is visited by '[h]undreds of people':

> The choir came up in a crowd and I could hear them singing as they walked up the Hill, beautiful indeed . . .
> Everywhere was singing, all over the house was singing, and outside the house was alive with singing, and the very air was song.[75]

So harmonious is this view of community that the people and their song merge into the landscape itself. This mellifluousness belongs not only to the song but also, by extension, to the entire community and its way of life; it is fondly remembered by Huw as characteristic of the integrated, coherent culture of his youth. It is also the kind of saccharine detail that led Raymond Williams to describe the text as the 'export version of the Welsh industrial experience'.[76] In a particularly waspish reading of the novel, Stephen Knight goes as far as to claim that the book 'basically created a stereotype that could be said to have done significant harm to Wales over the years as a land of Black and White Taffy minstrels'.[77] Knight's reference to minstrelsy in his analysis of the novel's contribution to representations of Wales identifies the imbrication of song and race as a defining aspect of the Welsh industrial novel.[78]

As with the Wonka novels, however, the initial impression of sweetness can leave a bitter taste. Llewellyn's valley can sing to a much more unsettling tune. In the novel's most sinister passage, a small girl is 'savaged' on the mountainside and Mr Gruffydd, the minister, assembles a vigilante group to apprehend the culprit:

> [S]triking up a hymn as he went, down toward the village Mr Gruffydd led us. The boots of the men beat time upon the ground, and their voices flung the anthem before them, and the blaze of the torches lit their bearded faces and struck sparks from their eyes.[79]

As Ian Bell notes, the minister effectively 'conducts a kind of pogrom of its immigrants', namely the dehumanised, mongrel Irish, Scottish, English and 'inter-breed Welsh' who constitute what Huw describes as 'a living disgust'.[80] Ultimately – and with no intervention from officers of the law or the state – the father and brothers of the dead girl are allowed by the community to carry off and lynch the culprit on the mountainside. Led by fundamentalist zeal, and singing together with frightful exhilaration, the chorus here metes out a brutal justice.

The Oompa-Loompas in the revised edition of *Charlie and the Chocolate Factory* are an industrial proletariat-cum-Greek chorus. Their status and song are also informed by a tradition of minstrelsy (or an exaggerated or caricatured performance of racial origin) that survives from the novel's early drafts and, indeed, from the first published version. The songs they are so prone to making up are performed at those moments when justice – or at least some sort of comeuppance – has been dealt out to the ill-fated child contestants. In its choric function and its minstrelsy the Oompa-Loompenproletariat reinforces the values of the factory and the industry that have co-opted it; it is a workforce conscripted by the ideology of industrial capitalism – and which sings in its conscription.

5. Conclusion: Welsh Minusland

Mark West argues that the 'contemporary industrial area' inhabited by the central characters in *Charlie and the Chocolate Factory* 'has a sense of universality to it' owing to Dahl's refusal to situate it within an identifiable geographic location; the great town on whose outskirts the Bucket family lives 'could be practically any large city in England or America'.[81] He is of course correct to state that the town is anonymous and undecidable as the text refuses to yield a precise location.

However, it is possible to suggest that a point of triangulation here is Wales. What West reads as universality may be reread as specificity: the anonymous and universal may yet be silently conditioned by the local and particular. Žižek elucidates his idea of the 'Non-All' with a joke derived from Ernst Lubitsch's film *Ninotchka* (1939). The hero of the film visits a coffee-shop and orders coffee without cream, only to be informed that the establishment has run out of cream, and must instead serve coffee without milk. Žižek notes:

> In both cases the customer gets coffee alone, but this One-coffee is each time accompanied by a different negation, first coffee-with-no-cream, then coffee-with-no-milk . . . What we encounter here is the logic of dif-ferentiality, where the lack itself functions as a positive feature.[82]

Such logic, whereby that which is absent or negated nonetheless conditions that which remains, structures the category of Welsh Industrial Dahl. *Charlie and the Chocolate Factory* invokes, if only to negate, Welsh industrial fiction. As this essay has argued, there are moments in Dahl's novels when thematic and generic structures that are paradigmatic in industrial and Welsh industrial writing are summoned: race, industry, song, disaster, the figure of the boy. That said, neither the novel nor its sequel makes any direct reference to Wales or Welsh writing, nor is there any *direct* invocation of specific Welsh industrial texts. Yet, as Wonka shows in his journey into Minusland in *Charlie and the Great Glass Elevator*, negation still counts.

As with the surplus-enjoyment that is the taste of chocolate itself, Welsh Dahl exists in curved space. Elusive and always decentred, Welsh Dahl evades us, however much we try to grasp it. Wales and traditions of Welsh industrial writing constitute the invisible and unfixed elements that can never definitively be apprehended but which nonetheless whizz in and around the Wonka novels. Thus if Welsh Dahl or Welsh Industrial Dahl signifies as a critical category, it is in those evanescent moments that fizz tantalizingly on the tongue but then seem to vanish almost, but not quite, without a trace. How sweet.

Notes

[1] Roald Dahl, *Charlie and the Chocolate Factory* (London: Puffin, 2013 [1964; rev. edn 1973]), p. 77.

2   Richard Llewellyn, *How Green Was My Valley* (Harmondsworth: Penguin, 1991 [1939]), p. 215.

3   Jeremy Treglown, *Roald Dahl: A Biography* (London: Faber and Faber, 1995), p. 10.

4   Donald Sturrock, *Storyteller: The Life of Roald Dahl* (London: HarperPress, 2011), p. 28.

5   Dahl, *Boy: Tales of Childhood* (1984), in *Boy and Going Solo* (London: Puffin, 2013), pp. 13–14.

6   Sturrock describes how the wealth acquired from the shipbroking business enabled the Dahls to live comfortably in large houses in Llandaff and Radyr. See Chapter Two of *Storyteller*, 'Shutting Out the Sun', pp. 28–39.

7   Treglown, *Roald Dahl*, p. 139.

8   Stephen Knight, '"A New Enormous Music": Industrial Fiction in Wales', in *Welsh Writing in English*, ed. M. Wynn Thomas (Cardiff: University of Wales Press, 2003), p. 49.

9   Raymond Williams, 'The Welsh Industrial Novel', in *Who Speaks for Wales? Nation, Culture, Identity*, ed. Daniel Williams (Cardiff: University of Wales Press, 2003), pp. 99–100. Williams's essay was first published in 1979.

10 Williams, 'The Welsh Industrial Novel', p. 101.

11 Williams, 'The Welsh Industrial Novel', p. 105.

12 Williams, 'The Welsh Industrial Novel', p. 105.

13 Knight, 'A New Enormous Music', p. 69.

14 Rolph Meyn, 'Lewis Jones's *Cwmardy* and *We Live*: Two Welsh Proletarian Novels in Transatlantic Perspective', in *British Industrial Fictions*, ed. Stephen Knight and H. Gustav Klaus (Cardiff: University of Wales Press, 2000), p. 128.

15 Lewis Jones, *Cwmardy and We Live* (Cardigan: Parthian/Library of Wales, 2006), p. 3.

16 Jones, *Cwmardy and We Live*, pp. 4, 3, 6.

17 See Dahl, *Charlie and the Chocolate Factory*, p. 168.

18 Dahl, *Boy and Going Solo*, pp. 31–2.

19 Dahl, *Charlie and the Chocolate Factory*, p. 8.

20 Dahl, *Charlie and the Chocolate Factory*, p. 48.

21 Sam Leith, 'Willy Wonka Economics', *Prospect* (July 2015), p. 82.

22 Dahl, *Charlie and the Chocolate Factory*, p. 51.

23 This phrase is borrowed from Humphrey McQueen's history of capitalism and Coca-Cola, *The Essence of Capitalism: The Origins of Our Future* (London: Profile, 2001).

24 Knight, 'A New Enormous Music', p. 72.

25 David (Dai) Smith, 'Myth and Meaning in the Literature of the South Wales Coalfield – The 1930s', *The Anglo-Welsh Review*, 25/56 (1976), p. 32.

26 Llewellyn, *How Green Was My Valley*, p. 12.

27 See Ian A. Bell, 'How Green *Was* My Valley?', *Planet*, 73 (February/March 1989), pp. 3–9.

28 Alun Lewis, 'The Housekeeper', *Collected Stories*, ed. Cary Archard (Bridgend: Seren, 1995), p. 100. 'Loshin' = a sweet.

29 Alun Lewis, 'The Housekeeper', p. 100.

30 Dahl, *Charlie and the Chocolate Factory*, pp. 5, 6.

31 Too much chocolate, as we all know, is not good for our health. Sturrock quotes from an essay by the Canadian children's author Eleanor Cameron which argues that the book's pleasures are like candy: the novel is 'delectable and soothing . . . but leaves us poorly nourished with our taste dulled for better fare'. Quoted in Sturrock, *Storyteller*, p. 496.

32 Slavoj Žižek, *The Fragile Absolute, or, Why is the Christian Legacy Worth Fighting For?* (London and New York: Verso, 2008), p. 21.

33 Žižek, *The Fragile Absolute*, p. 19.

34 Mark I. West, *Roald Dahl* (New York: Twayne, 1992), p. 69.

35 David Harvey, *The Condition of Postmodernity: An Enquiry into the Origins of Cultural Change* (Oxford: Blackwell, 1990), p. 107.

36 Dahl, *Charlie and the Chocolate Factory*, p. 111.

37 Žižek, *The Sublime Object of Ideology* (London and New York: Verso, 2008), p. 53.

38 Žižek, *The Sublime Object of Ideology*, p. 54.

39 West, *Roald Dahl*, p. 68.

40 Dahl, *Charlie and the Chocolate Factory*, p. 93.

41 Williams, 'The Welsh Industrial Novel', pp. 95–6.

42 Williams, 'The Welsh Industrial Novel', p. 96.

43 Williams, 'The Welsh Industrial Novel', p. 96.

44 Sam Leith notes that the chocolate produced at Wonka's factory is what renders necessary the toothpaste produced at the toothpaste factory; Leith, 'Willy Wonka Economics', 82.

45 Dahl, *Charlie and the Chocolate Factory*, p. 10.

46 Dahl, *Charlie and the Chocolate Factory*, pp. 7–8.

47 Dahl, *Charlie and the Chocolate Factory*, p. 17.

48 Dahl, *Charlie and the Chocolate Factory*, p. 75.

49 Llewellyn, *How Green Was My Valley*, p. 337.

50 Roald Dahl, *The Collected Short Stories of Roald Dahl* (London: Penguin, 1992), p. 231.

51 Jones, *Cwmardy and We Live*, p. 145.

52 Dahl, *Charlie and the Chocolate Factory*, p. 140.

53 Dahl, *Charlie and the Chocolate Factory*, p. 144.

54 Dahl, *Charlie and the Great Glass Elevator* (London: Puffin, 2013 [1972]), p. 140.

55 Dahl, *Charlie and the Chocolate Factory*, p. 144.

56 West, *Roald Dahl*, p. 76.

57 Dahl, *Charlie and the Great Glass Elevator*, pp. 140–2.

58 Dahl, *Charlie and the Chocolate Factory*, p. 86.

59 Dahl, *Charlie and the Chocolate Factory*, p. 82.

60 Dahl, *Charlie and the Chocolate Factory*, p. 83.

61   Dahl, *Charlie and the Chocolate Factory*, p. 73.

62   Dahl, *Charlie and the Chocolate Factory*, p. 84.

63   Sturrock, *Storyteller*, pp. 396, 397.

64   Sturrock, *Storyteller*, p. 397.

65   Sturrock, *Storyteller*, p. 493.

66   West, *Roald Dahl*, p. 71; Sturrock, *Storyteller*, p. 493.

67   Lucy Mangan, *Inside Charlie's Chocolate Factory: The Complete Story of Willy Wonka, The Golden Ticket, and Roald Dahl's Most Famous Creation* (New York: Puffin, 2014), p. 32; Sturrock, *Storyteller*, p. 493.

68   Sturrock, *Storyteller*, p. 495.

69   Lois Kalb Bouchard, '*Charlie and the Chocolate Factory*: A New Look at an Old Favourite', in *Racism and Sexism in Children's Books*, ed. Judith Stinton (London: Writers and Readers, 1979), pp. 41–4.

70   See Dahl, *Charlie and the Chocolate Factory*, p. 124 and *Charlie and the Great Glass Elevator*, p. 143.

71   Dahl, *Charlie and the Chocolate Factory*, p. 161.

72   See West, *Roald Dahl*, p. 68. Treglown describes the Oompa-Loompas as 'a kind of comic Greek chorus' in the revised drafts of the novel; see Treglown, *Roald Dahl*, p. 142.

73   Knight, 'A New Enormous Music', p. 73.

74   Bell, 'How Green *Was* My Valley?', pp. 3–4.

75   Llewellyn, *How Green Was My Valley*, p. 79.

76   Williams, 'The Welsh Industrial Novel', p. 108.

77   Knight, 'A New Enormous Music', p. 74.

78   Daniel Williams has recently explored the politics of race, including minstrelsy, in the literature of the Welsh coalfield, contending that 'a striking characteristic of the Welsh industrial novel is that social changes are often linked to changes in the racial composition of society', with Llewellyn's *How Green Was My Valley* standing as a paradigmatic example. See Daniel G. Williams, *Black Skin, Blue Books: African Americans and Wales, 1845–1945* (Cardiff: University of Wales Press, 2012), p. 193. See also the section '"Ain't We All Black Down That Pit?" Race and the Welsh Industrial Novel', pp. 184–205.

79   Llewellyn, *How Green Was My Valley*, p. 188.

80   Llewellyn, *How Green Was My Valley*, pp. 189, 190.

81   West, *Roald Dahl*, p. 67.

82   Audun Mortensen (ed.), *Žižek's Jokes (Did You Hear the One about Hegel and Negation?)* (Cambridge, MA: MIT Press, 2014), p. 47.

Works cited

Dahl, Roald, *Boy: Tales of Childhood* (1984), in *Boy and Going Solo* (London: Puffin, 2013).

—, *Charlie and the Chocolate Factory* (London: Puffin, 2013 [1964; rev. edn 1973]).

—, *The Collected Short Stories of Roald Dahl* (London: Penguin, 1992).

Bell, Ian A., 'How Green *Was* My Valley?', *Planet*, 73 (February/March 1989), pp. 3–9.

Bouchard, Lois Kalb, '*Charlie and the Chocolate Factory*: A New Look at an Old Favourite', in *Racism and Sexism in Children's Books*, ed. Judith Stinton (London: Writers and Readers, 1979), pp. 41–4.

Harvey, David, *The Condition of Postmodernity: An Enquiry into the Origins of Cultural Change* (Oxford: Blackwell, 1990).

Jones, Lewis, *Cwmardy and We Live* (Cardigan: Parthian/Library of Wales, 2006).

Knight, Stephen, '"A New Enormous Music": Industrial Fiction in Wales', in *Welsh Writing in English*, ed. M. Wynn Thomas (Cardiff: University of Wales Press, 2003), pp. 47–90.

Leith, Sam, 'Willy Wonka Economics', *Prospect* (July 2015), p. 82.

Lewis, Alun, 'The Housekeeper', *Collected Stories*, ed. Cary Archard (Bridgend: Seren, 1995), pp. 94–105.

Llewellyn, Richard, *How Green Was My Valley* (Harmondsworth: Penguin, 1991 [1939]).

McQueen, Humphrey, *The Essence of Capitalism: The Origins of Our Future* (London: Profile, 2001).

Mangan, Lucy, *Inside Charlie's Chocolate Factory: The Complete Story of Willy Wonka, The Golden Ticket, and Roald Dahl's Most Famous Creation* (New York: Puffin, 2014).

Meyn, Rolph, 'Lewis Jones's *Cwmardy* and *We Live*: Two Welsh Proletarian Novels in Transatlantic Perspective', in *British Industrial Fictions*, ed. Stephen Knight and H. Gustav Klaus (Cardiff: University of Wales Press, 2000), pp. 124–36.

Mortensen, Audun (ed.), *Žižek's Jokes (Did You Hear the One about Hegel and Negation?)* (Cambridge, MA: MIT Press, 2014).

Smith, David, 'Myth and Meaning in the Literature of the South Wales Coalfield – The 1930s', *The Anglo-Welsh Review*, 25/56 (1976), pp. 21–42.

Sturrock, Donald, *Storyteller: The Life of Roald Dahl* (London: HarperPress, 2011).

Treglown, Jeremy, *Roald Dahl: A Biography* (London: Faber and Faber, 1995).

West, Mark I., *Roald Dahl* (New York: Twayne, 1992).

Williams, Daniel G., *Black Skin, Blue Books: African Americans and Wales, 1845–1945* (Cardiff: University of Wales Press, 2012).

Williams, Raymond, 'The Welsh Industrial Novel', in *Who Speaks for Wales? Nation, Culture, Identity*, ed. Daniel Williams (Cardiff: University of Wales Press, 2003), pp. 95–111.

Žižek, Slavoj, *The Fragile Absolute, or, Why is the Christian Legacy Worth Fighting For?* (London and New York: Verso, 2008).

—, *The Sublime Object of Ideology* (London and New York: Verso, 2008).

4

Wales of the Unexpected:
Kiss, Kiss

Kevin Mills

One distant bell-note, faintly reverberating

DYLAN THOMAS, *Under Milk Wood*

Kiss, kiss: both greeting and parting. One kiss may suggest immediate contact; adding the second leaves room for various species of doubt. One might imagine a faux intimacy or gestural bonhomie that fulfils a social function in the absence of true fondness or regard. When the phrase is vocalised or written (rather than performed in simulated osculation), the sense of distance-in-proximity is even more pronounced, as if even a token bodily representation would be too close for comfort, or too far from the truth.

Then again, we might imagine a message ending with two letters – xx: a short run of barbs marking, protecting, a boundary. Maybe, as such, they serve as a last line of defence against loss of intimacy, connectedness, while signifying that very possibility. Or the second cross might be read as negating what precedes it, indicating error without erasing it, making of the text a record of its own failure. The double cross (xx) might be a betrayal, or it might deny one betrayal with another: betray by denying the betrayal.

The phrase 'kiss, kiss' removes itself from the body, denies the need for a physical act. It betrays itself as discourse by means of a conventional doubling. We kiss; we do not kiss, kiss; the repetition is not of action but of articulation: joining and separation. Twice over.

In cultures where the Christian myth has currency, we know not to trust even the single kiss where lips actually touch the flesh of another. Does doubling the kiss add to or cross out the greeting/parting/treachery?

Kiss, Kiss is the title of Dahl's third collection of adult short stories.[1] Bearing in mind the manifold possibilities, worries and complexities already outlined, I want to read that title (in the light of some aspects of the stories) as a self-troubling, unstable gesture towards Wales in which Dahl affectionately betrays and lovingly dismisses the land of his birth. Published in 1960, first in the USA and, later the same year, in the UK, the collection was the product of divided geographical loyalties. As Donald Sturrock notes, 'For a period of five years – 1955–60 – Roald and Pat commuted between Great Missenden and New York, with occasional sojourns in Los Angeles if Pat was working there.'[2] The notional locations of the stories in *Kiss, Kiss* reflect that transatlantic lifestyle: some are set in New York, some in England. None is set in Wales. Wales is (very nearly) absent.

But if, under the sign of the double kiss (or the double cross), presence and absence disrupt and betray one another, distance and proximity intermingle, then it is possible that Wales is not far from view. That is not to suggest, in a perverse way, that the very non-appearance of Wales is enough to make it significant to the collection's imaginative universe; rather, it is to argue that the text betrays, with the narrative equivalent of a peck on the cheek, that Dahl's native country is a shaping absence. It is as if a lost land, submerged by some Atlantic catastrophe, determined the form of the current coastline, carving out the bay around which the country curves. Legends have arisen intimating that, on certain occasions, one might hear the bells of the inundated kingdom peal beneath the waves.[3]

Before we can allow ourselves to hear the bells, it would be as well to acknowledge the 'kiss' by means of which the text seduces us into reading for Wales. It occurs in 'The Landlady' – the story that opens *Kiss, Kiss* – as an entry in the guest-book of a small bed-and-breakfast in Bath:

> He found the guest-book lying open on the piano, so he took out his pen and wrote down his name and address. There were only two other entries above his on the page, and, as one always does with guest-books, he started to read them. One was a Christopher Mulholland from Cardiff. The other was Gregory W. Temple from Bristol.[4]

The protagonist, Billy Weaver, has travelled west from London by train, arriving at about nine o'clock in the evening. Cold weather and the lateness of the hour prompt him to seek accommodation for the night, and a station porter directs him to The Bell and Dragon hotel. En route he notices a small, homely-looking guest house and (fatefully) elects to stay there. Just as he disembarks from the westbound train in Bath before it reaches Wales, so he ends his walk short of The Bell and Dragon. It may, or may not, be significant that *Kiss, Kiss* was originally due to be published in the USA in 1959: the year in which Wales adopted *Y Ddraig Goch* – The Red Dragon – as its national flag.[5] One component of the name of the unreached hotel obviously evokes the Welsh emblem; the relevance of the other term needs teasing out. But I shall have to detain you a little longer before responding to the bell, since the name 'The Bell and Dragon' may have nothing at all to do with our interest in Wales.

Google 'The Bell and Dragon' and you'll find links to a number of inns and hotels in southern England. They all belong, in fact, to a chain called 'Bel and the Dragon', which would seem to have taken its curious name from either of two ancient tales: one an apocryphal addition to the biblical Book of Daniel; the other (older) version a Babylonian creation myth.[6] It seems unlikely that this modern hospitality business or its putative source texts have any bearing on our story. We should turn, perhaps, towards another possibility: that 'The Bell and Dragon' renames 'The George and Dragon', the name of a pub in Bath since the late nineteenth century.[7] The dragon survives; the patron saint of England is banished, to be replaced by a bell. This may signify little or nothing were it not for another apparently unimportant detail in Dahl's text. On reading the entry in the guest-book – 'Christopher Mulholland, 231 Cathedral Road, Cardiff' – Billy Weaver is given pause for thought: 'That's funny, he thought suddenly. Christopher Mulholland. It rings a bell.'[8] The bell rings for a memory of, or associated with, Wales: the only mention of the country, or any part of it, in the entire collection. Coming across the bell rung by a Cardiffian, the reader with Wales in mind cannot but be reminded of the dragon.

Mulholland – the tintinnabulating name – encodes a variety of geopolitical possibilities. Dahl, who had been resident in the USA, a visitor to Hollywood and a hobnobber with movie stars, would have known LA's famous Mulholland Drive, but historically the surname is associated closely with Ireland: 'Mulholland is the name of three distinct septs which arose independently in various parts of Ireland, the most notable being the Mulhollands of Loughinsholin, County Derry, who were Keepers of *the Bell of St. Patrick*.'[9] So the peal in Billy's head might be that of St Patrick's bell, which expands the hermeneutical as well as the geopolitical terrain by adding to the list of potentially operative contexts. It is a multiaccentual sign suggestive of more than one location, a range of possible memories, none of which either Billy or the reader can recover. Adhering to the classic constraints of the short story, giving the reader no details of the protagonist's history or his wider social milieu, Dahl refuses us further guidance in the matter of where we might be taken by the involuntary mental resonance. The sound of the bell neither guides us home nor suggests any definite direction; it merely offers a range of options to consider. As he sits with the landlady sipping tea that tastes of bitter almonds, and looking at her stuffed animals, Billy's fate becomes clear to the reader: he will be the woman's next taxidermic project. On the brink of recalling something (possibly something about Cardiff), he is poisoned by his deceptively benign English landlady and preserved here between locales. He might well have been spared this end had he been able to respond with greater clarity to the chime.

If Billy's narrative seizure holds him fast on the cusp of Wales, both geographically and psychologically, unable even to summon to consciousness its significance to his predicament, his is only the first case of enforced stasis or close containment the reader of *Kiss, Kiss* encounters. In 'William and Mary', William dies and his brain is preserved alive and conscious in a 'white enamel bowl about the size of a wash basin'; 'The Way Up to Heaven' traps Mr Foster in a lift where he is left to die; the protagonist of 'Georgy Porgy' ends up incarcerated in a padded cell; 'Pig' tells the story of the naïve country-bred Lexington who, shortly after discovering the exciting diversity of New York, finds himself slung upside down and 'wriggling like a fish' at the end of a chain in a meat processing plant.[10] The material constraints imposed on these characters resonate with, and might be read as taking the reader back to, the case of Billy, captured and frozen near the border. But they echo too Dahl's own self-sequestration:

> His writing hut represented part of an effort not only to recreate his own early childhood but to improve on it. As a boy in the 1920s, Roald used

to hide up a tree in order to write his diary; at Repton, there had been the photography darkroom. His garden shed was a more substantial place in which to work, where he could commemorate, and fantasize about his past ... Here he transported himself back to his earliest infancy. Even beyond. 'It's a lovely place to work,' he told an interviewer. 'It's small and tight and dark and the curtains are always drawn and it's a kind of womb.'[11]

As it takes the writer back to the womb and to infancy, the gestating cell is also, of course, a representation of early life in Llandaff and Radyr, recalled from somewhere beyond the tightly drawn borders of Wales. The traveller, flyer, migrant and nomad depicted by both of Dahl's biographers, Treglown and Sturrock, gathered himself, his mementoes, trophies and souvenirs into that small physical and psychic space, reminiscent in certain respects of the fighter planes into which he had folded his tall frame during the war. Sturrock makes the connection: 'his claustrophobic, dark writing hut itself became a surrogate cockpit.'[12] Freedom in restraint – the open spaces experienced only from within a snugly proportioned capsule – is refigured in the formal restriction of Dahl's first literary métier: the short story. The stories take the form of, emerge from, and recreate various kinds of physically and/or psychologically enclosed spaces. But unlike the 'lovely' womb, their confines are typically destructive, carceral, contorting, immobilising, deathly. Such ambivalence would seem to reflect, *inter alia*, what Wales had become for Dahl's imagination.

While Billy Weaver's journey ends in immobility, in permanent entrapment on the English side of the border, the name Mulholland impels the reader further west from Bath towards Wales, Ireland, America. Following Billy's dangerous lead, we might truncate our occidental journey and go no further than Wales. But we should do so in the knowledge that reading for Wales runs the risk of constriction and marginalisation, of having to squeeze ourselves into textual interstices that might be womb-like, but which equally may prove entombing.

For reasons already indicated, going no further than Wales in this context means responding to the sound of the bell. Like the kiss, the bell's ring has no fixed or reliable meaning. Bells can summon, wake, remind, warn, proclaim, mourn, locate and, as Ivan Pavlov famously demonstrated, condition. As I read, and write, I am conditioning myself to see the dragon and to think of Wales with each peal, knell, toll, chime, bong, dong or tinkle. And *Kiss, Kiss* (like Dylan Thomas's *Under Milk*

Kevin Mills

Wood and Idris Davies's lyric from *Gwalia Deserta* known as 'The Bells of Rhymney') is a textual carillon: some kind of bell sounds in most of the stories – doorbells, telephones, jangling bracelets and alarm clocks.

Non-linguistic texts, bells have no addressee. Wales has to be listened for in these sounds by whoever will; inferred from the slightest, all-but-invisible hint; sought out at edges and margins as if we were telepathic or clairvoyant recipients of messages never intended for us. But Wales's presence/absence, its distance-in-proximity, is not only *evoked* by the sounding of bells; the bells *figure* it too. That is to say, the peals both recall the unrepresented country by marking its absence, and ventriloquise the call of a distant sender. Here, Wales might be thought of as an unseen force telecommunicating with the reader through the text of *Kiss, Kiss*, as if the country were a spirit ringing bells at a séance. In a text littered with corpses, it would not be unreasonable to expect them to communicate – if only as signifiers of silence – the lost, buried or drowned.

As in 'The Landlady', bells and corpses play significant roles in another story from *Kiss, Kiss*, 'The Way Up to Heaven'. Mrs Foster, tortured by a fear of being late and by a husband who does all he can to exacerbate her anxieties with procrastination and delay, finds herself presented, unexpectedly, with a means of taking revenge. She catches a flight from her home city of New York to visit family in Paris, knowing (or at least strongly suspecting) that her dilly-dallying spouse is trapped in the lift of their six-storey house. A crucial detail hints at the implications of her abandoning him: 'It was a gloomy place, and few people came to visit them.'[13] She must suspect, or even hope, that she is leaving him to die. A bell tolls towards the end of the tale when, six weeks later, she returns home:

> The taxi drew up before the house on Sixty-second Street, and Mrs Foster persuaded the driver to carry her two large cases to the top of the steps. Then she paid him off and rang the bell. She waited, but there was no answer. Just to make sure, she rang again, and she could hear it tinkling shrilly far away in the pantry, at the back of the house. But still no-one came.
>
> So she took out her own key and opened the door herself.[14]

Ringing the bell and waiting, rather than letting herself in straight away, is Mrs Foster's way of testing the results of her actions: someone

56

might have found and released her husband. The reference to the pantry suggests that she is not sure that one of the four servants referred to earlier in the story hasn't returned early from their six-week vacation. The unanswered bell is confirmation: Mr Foster is still in the lift.

I would like, of course, for there to be some way in which the lack of an answer to the doorbell might be shown to evoke Wales or Welshness, but here it is the text that fails to respond. Reading it in, from, or for Wales, fosters a silence that might be deadly for this essay, leaving me with no more than a faint echo of the distant shrill tinkle in Billy Weaver's (now dead) head. But then it is precisely this kind of failure that I need to exploit as the bells continue to ring. Like Mrs Foster, I have to take out my own (hermeneutic) key and open the door myself.

In common with most bells, the doorbell is a form of tele-communication – communication at a distance. Simultaneously, its ring signifies a blind contiguity: a distance-in-proximity whereby appellant and respondent are relatively close but remain separated. Almost the inverse of the phrase 'kiss, kiss', which fends off greater intimacy, it invites, expresses a hope for, a closer, unimpeded encounter. Such might be the semiotics of doorbells in everyday usage. But in Dahl's story, the doorbell, normally functioning according to a simple binary code (sound/no-sound), becomes an expression of something less easily categorised. Mrs Foster is neither hoping for nor expecting a face-to-face encounter; she rings the bell in the hope that it will *not* be answered. Its chime becomes a signal akin to the echo-locating call of a bat: it has no specific addressee; it feeds back information without the intervention of a respondent. In the multiple possibilities encoded by the sound of the bell – its play of presence and absence, proximity and distance, response and non-response, life and death – the stories invite speculation about a set of relations between what is there to be read and what might have to be inferred from silence.

Little of what actually happens to Mr Foster is explicit in the text. That is the peculiar art of the short story: it leaves, by design, room for the reader to make their own substantive inferences. The bell in 'The Way Up to Heaven' figures such a reading process inasmuch as to read can be compared to making soundings and interpreting the resonances. I hear in Mrs Foster's use of the bell an echo of Billy Weaver's mental ring that furnishes him with no answer; the corpse of Mr Foster shut up in the broken elevator reprises Billy's fate in the aftermath of an unanswered call. It is almost as if Mrs Foster has read, or is reading,

'The Landlady' by Roald Dahl; the story of Billy Weaver chimes with her need to know who is dead and it teaches her the importance of interpreting the bell's elusive and unstable signifiers.

What Billy fails to understand from the ringing is the Welsh connection, and every time the text rings a bell, the failure recurs. But in that failure it is possible to read a kind of shaping submergence: what *can't* be recovered at the sound of the bell is Wales. Since the information Mrs Foster gleans from her unanswered call is precisely what Billy needed to hear (that is, news of a death), Wales, perhaps, *is* the corpse: the index of an absent presence at the core of the text. It is figured in the lifeless but undecomposed body of Christopher Mulholland from Cardiff, Billy's bell-ringing predecessor: 'But my dear boy', the landlady chillingly confides, 'he never left. He's still here.' [15]

But corpses do not necessarily mark the end of a life in *Kiss, Kiss*. The story 'William and Mary' seems to have been based on accounts of an experiment conducted in Russia in 1940 to keep the head of a dog alive after the death of its body. The fictional doctor, John Landy, refers explicitly to this experiment in his pitch to a terminally ill human guinea pig (the William of the story's title) for permission to do the same to him when the time comes.[16] Shortly before his death, William writes at length to his wife Mary explaining that he has agreed to allow Landy to keep his brain alive, with one eye attached to it, in a basin. By the time Mary receives and reads the letter, the deed has already been done. Like Mrs Foster, she sees the opportunity to settle the score with a husband who had bullied her throughout their married life; she will take him home and make him witness in silence her joyous transgression of all his rules, proscriptions and impositions.

There is an obvious similarity between the key details of 'William and Mary' and those of 'The Landlady'. Both stories hinge on the will to preserve something of the individual after death. For the landlady it is the body; for the doctor, the brain. The scene in which the former comments on the youth and beauty of her victims to the dying Billy (he has already ingested some of the poisoned tea) is paralleled by one in which Landy imagines the 'great thoughts', 'solutions' and 'ideas' that might occur to the mind of a Doctor of Philosophy such as William, undistracted by the inconvenient needs and pleasures of the flesh. Billy is hollowed out and immobilised by taxidermy while, inversely, William is stripped of external flesh and reduced to permanent stasis in his basin. So it is perhaps no accident that the name

Landy is a contraction of 'landlady'; tellingly, the difference is a lost 'lad', perhaps a (cryptic) allusion to the missing seventeen-year-old Christopher Mulholland.[17] If 'William and Mary' represents a complement to 'The Landlady' – is the brain, one might say, to the other's body – then the physical fate of one victim suspended just outside of Wales is contrasted with the mental fate of the other, trapped in the heart of England (the story is set in Oxford). But since William's plight also mirrors that of Billy and Christopher, the heart of England might be a place in which to reflect on, remember, or preserve Wales. We may well be reminded of Dahl recreating his infancy in a womb-like writing shed in Buckinghamshire.

In his disembodied afterlife, William becomes a figure of distance-in-proximity, there but not completely there – a shaping but infinitely vulnerable presence/absence around which Mary's new life will unfold on her terms rather than his. Suggesting both his complete subjection and his total immersion in the life of the mind stripped of almost all physical sensation, the diminished remnant of his flesh is literally submerged, like an inundated land under the waves And if no warning bell sounded a cautionary note in his head before it was too late, the text at least allows the faintest of echoes to reverberate from the liquid world he comes to inhabit: William's brain lies 'in the basin, submerged in *Ringer's* Solution'.[18]

At times it seems almost as if the text of *Kiss, Kiss* invites the reader to look for, but not find, Wales; it rings bells that elicit no response. When, just a few paragraphs into 'Pig', the soon-to-be-dead father of baby Lexington uses his own doorbell, he and his wife are left unattended: 'So he rang the bell. They waited. Nothing happened.'[19] If the bell has prompted us to think of Wales, the lack of an answer should prepare us to be disappointed: the story mentions (in the first two pages) a Scottish nurse and 'three cops of Irish extraction', yet there is no Welsh presence.[20] Set mainly in New York, not even the widely reported death of Dylan Thomas in that city in 1953 – the year in which work on *Kiss, Kiss* commenced – provoked Dahl to place any Welsh people there.[21]

Perhaps the strangest, and most suggestive, non-appearance of Wales occurs when the orphaned ten-year-old Lexington, now living in Virginia with his octogenarian Aunt Glosspan, discovers a talent for cooking. He experiments with ingredients and flavours, so that 'hardly a day went by without some new delectable creation being set upon the table.'[22] A list of exemplary dishes follows that includes 'Dutch rarebit'. The *OED* describes the etymology of 'rarebit' as an 'alteration of *rabbit* in Welsh Rabbit', the association with Wales being definitive. In *A Dictionary of Toponyms*, Nigel Viney is even clearer about the specificity of the connection between the dish and the country: '*Welsh rarebit* was originally *Welsh rabbit,* an eighteenth-century mockingly derisive name for toasted cheese. It was altered, perhaps by Welshmen, to *Welsh rarebit,* the latter word only being used anywhere in this way.'[23] While 'Dutch Rarebit' features in some cookbooks, it would appear to be a version of the Welsh delicacy made with either Edam or Gouda.[24] The dish's close association with Wales makes the presence of the Dutch derivative in the imaginative work of a Welsh-born author seem almost perverse, as if it were there both to evoke and to conceal its own origins.

Lexington's interest in food leads directly to his demise. Raised to be a vegetarian in a remote house in the Blue Ridge Mountains, he moves to New York on the death of his guardian. Encountering meat for the first time in a city diner, and being astonished at its delectable taste, he sets out to investigate its source. At an abattoir in the Bronx, to which he has been directed by the diner's cook, he and his fellow visitors are fed into the butchery process. Eating seems to be dangerous in *Kiss, Kiss,* both physically and psychologically, because it testifies to the implication of humans in the predatory instincts and habits of carnivores and engenders a concomitant fear of predation. A troubled and troubling relationship with food is a material factor in three other stories: in 'Royal Jelly', consumption of that potent apian substance leads to the transmogrification of a human baby into a queen bee; 'The Champion of the World' involves the feeding to pheasants of raisins stuffed with sleeping pills; and the narrator of 'Georgy Porgy' recounts a childhood memory of witnessing a mother rabbit swallowing its newborn kit.

'Georgy Porgy' is a comic but nonetheless disturbing psychological tale centring on zoophagy, or the fear of it, narrated by a man who turns out to be insane. Free-thinking and capable, his mother had tried to educate him in the ways of the world until she was killed in an accident when the narrator was ten years old. The event has had devastating consequences for the narrator – a grown man and a curate when the story opens – which unfold as the tale progresses. Recounting the circumstances of his mother's death, he tells of his childhood sex education, which involved being taken down to the garage by his mother in the middle of the night to witness a pet rabbit giving birth. Pointing out the maternal instincts of the doe, the parental pedagogy was fatefully anthropomorphic:

> 'See how she's fondling it and kissing it all over! There! She's *really* kissing it now, isn't she! Exactly like me and you.'
> I peer closer. It seems a pretty queer way of kissing to me.
> 'Look!' I scream. 'She's eating it!'
> And sure enough, the head of the baby rabbit is now disappearing swiftly into the mother's mouth.[25]

Turning round, the traumatised boy found his mother looking down at him and, panicked by the suddenly shocking comparison, ran off into the night, terrified of sharing the kit's fate. Giving chase, his mother was hit by a car and killed. As he ran, the boy heard her in close pursuit: 'I can hear the jingle of bracelets coming up behind me in the dark, getting louder and louder as she keeps gaining on me.'[26] The sonorous bracelets are an integral aspect of the memory of his mother:

> She was a wonderful woman, my mother. She used to wear huge bracelets on her wrists, five or six of them at a time, with all sorts of things hanging from them and tinkling against each other as she moved. It didn't matter where she was, you could always find her by listening for the noise of those bracelets. It was better than a cowbell.[27]

Her death is marked by a sudden cessation of the ringing: 'then there is silence, and I notice that the bracelets aren't jingling behind me any more.'[28]

The narrator of 'Georgy Porgy' is terrified of physical contact with women. Single and surrounded by nubile female parishioners, he perceives himself to be engaged in a constant battle to fend them off. Most terrifying of all is the prospect of being kissed. Unwittingly given alcohol at a party, he finds himself attracted (tipsily) to a female guest who tries to kiss him in the 'Georgian' summer house; his sanity completely breaks down and he believes himself to have been swallowed alive by her. The story's title, 'Georgy Porgy', then, is an ironic allusion to the figure in the nursery rhyme who 'kissed the girls and made them cry'. Its evocation of kissing and its turning of the kiss into a threatening and fearful gesture powerfully contribute to the significance of the collection's title. The narrator actively seeks to enjoy the company of women, but wants to forestall any physical contact. When the kiss becomes a matter of bodily contact rather than of discursive exchange, he falls into a psychotic state from which he never recovers. He ends the story in a padded cell believing it to be the digestive tract of his attacker.

By virtue of etymology, if for no other reason, the *rarebit* in 'Pig' recalls the baby-swallowing *rabbit* in 'Georgy Porgy'. The resonance is not unimportant since Lexington and the protagonist of 'Georgy Porgy' both end up as food – the former physically, the latter psychologically. Perhaps by denying rarebit its Welsh origin, the text disguises a fear of being swallowed alive by the (Welsh) motherland. 'Georgy', and the 'Georgian' attribution of the summer house in which the crisis occurs, mark the return of the patron saint of England (displaced in the name of The Bell and Dragon). In this recrudescence, the text might be read as reasserting its Englishness and, inversely, to encode a fear of *not* being English. Or not English enough. What initially threatens to swallow 'Georgy' in his 'Georgian' retreat is the mother whose seemingly predatory pursuit, like the name Christopher Mullholland, *rings bells*.

Judging by what his biographers write, Dahl's relationship with England and Englishness was even less straightforward than his disposition towards Wales. Sturrock sees him as an 'outsider' but one who often yearned for England when away from it: 'During the Second World War, when he was in Africa and the Middle East as a pilot and in Washington as a diplomat, it was not Norway he craved for, nor the valleys of Wales he had loved as a child, but the fields of rural England.' Despite that craving, he remained an uneasy Englishman: 'In truth Dahl was always an outsider, the child of Norwegian immigrants, whose native land would become for their son an imaginative refuge.'[29] Nor do the national complications end with divergent desires; identity itself is unsettled:

> As with many children of emigrants, Roald would take on the manners and identity of his adopted home with the zeal of a convert ... Ironically, however, the one British ancestor he did publicly acknowledge was the Scots patriot William Wallace.[30]

The transatlantic Dahl who wrote the stories making up *Kiss, Kiss* was no less riven, as is evident from the collection's geographical ambilocation and its out-of-kilter depiction of England. Treglown draws attention to Malcolm Bradbury's review of the volume in *The New York Times Review of Books*: 'Dahl's England was, [Bradbury] rightly said, a curious place, "rather like the England in British Travel Association ads in *The New Yorker*. Deliberately, he makes it a bit more rural, a bit more quaint, a bit more lively than it really is, a foreigner's England, perhaps."'[31] David Rudd makes a similar point about Dahl's oblique orientation, from a linguistic perspective:

> Dahl had a particular animosity towards what he saw as the Great Grammatizator, which can be seen to represent the language of the establishment, of a Great Britain that, reluctantly, he found himself a part of. He learned its ways, certainly, but kept himself on its margins, both geographically and mentally.[32]

Irreconcilable differences multiply. Treglown again: 'Although in various ways, his apparent contradictions were of a piece, there are points at which he simply can't be reconciled with himself. More than most people, he was divided between the things he was and those he wanted to be'.[33] The self-marginalising outsider, whose imagination flees to Norway for refuge yet who longs for the heart of England, who restlessly crosses and recrosses the Atlantic, is pursued with love and menace through the pages of *Kiss, Kiss* by mother Wales, her bracelets now jingling, now falling silent.

The title *Kiss, Kiss* fends off real physical contact with the mouth of another, just as the narrator of 'Georgy Porgy' tries to keep the hungry mouths of women at bay, fearing that the kiss might be a prelude to ingestion. His peculiar psychopathology engenders a terror of being returned alive to the interior of the maternal body. Metonymically, the story encodes a fear, afflicting the whole volume, of being pulled back into Wales by a kind of textual/cultural peristalsis. But if *Kiss, Kiss* keeps Wales at a safe distance (or at a distance that it imagines to be safe), the text also acknowledges that the kiss and what comes after might have generative consequences. Having been 'swallowed', the narrator of 'Georgy Porgy' ends up in a comfortably confined space: 'this isn't such a bad place, and I have made myself as comfortable as I possibly can. It is a small chamber.' 'A lovely place to work . . .

small and tight . . . a kind of womb', maybe. In this sanctum he writes his story, becoming the fictive author of 'Georgy Porgy': 'I find that writing is a most salutary occupation at a time like this, and I spend many hours each day playing with sentences.'[34] Similarly confined to the small, tight spaces of the text, Wales writes itself, plays out its (custodial) sentence, and rings for attention.

Notes

1. KISS is also an acronym, standing for 'Keep it simple, stupid'. Coined in the mid-twentieth century by American aircraft engineer Kelly Johnson, it is associated with what became known as the 'Kiss Principle', a development of Occam's razor. *Technopedia* defines it as 'a design rule that states that systems perform best when they have simple designs rather than complex ones': *http://www.techopedia.com/definition/20262/* (accessed 15 September 2015). It bears an obvious relation to definitions of the short story such as that offered by the *Encyclopædia Britannica*: 'The form encourages economy of setting, concise narrative, and the omission of a complex plot.'

2. Donald Sturrock, *Storyteller: The Life of Roald Dahl* (London: HarperPress, 2010), p. 348.

3. In some versions of the legend of *Cantre'r Gwaelod* (the Drowned Hundred under Cardigan Bay), bells of the submerged kingdom can occasionally be heard ringing.

4. Roald Dahl, 'The Landlady', *The Collected Short Stories of Roald Dahl* (London: Penguin, 1992), p. 7.

5. According to Donald Sturrock, Alfred Knopf dropped *Kiss, Kiss* from his 1959 autumn publication list. This appears to have been a result of his personal dislike for the stories (*Storyteller*, p. 352).

6. See E. A. Wallis Budge, *The Babylonian Legends of the Creation and the Fight Between Bel and the Dragon* (London: Harrison and Sons, 1921). One might also note that in the Irish tale 'The Dream of Aengus', the protagonist meets Caer Ibormeith at Lough Bel Dracon.

7. See *http://georgeanddragonbath.co.uk/* (accessed 21 September 2015).

8. Dahl, *The Collected Short Stories*, p. 7.

9. *http://www.surnamedb.com/Surname/Mulholland* (accessed 21 September 2015). Emphasis mine.

10. Dahl, *The Collected Short Stories*, pp. 31, 171.

11. Jeremy Treglown, *Roald Dahl: A Biography* (San Diego: Harcourt Brace and Company, 1994), p. 126.

12. Sturrock, *Storyteller*, p. 154.

13. Dahl, 'The Way Up to Heaven', *The Collected Short Stories*, p. 38.

14. Dahl, *The Collected Short Stories*, p. 47.

15 Dahl, *The Collected Short Stories*, p. 9.

16 The 'medical film' Landy refers to as the source of his ideas is available on YouTube: *https://www.youtube.com/watch?v=K_T8OuYIfhM*.

17 Dahl's fondness for wordplay is explored by David Rudd, '"Don't Gobblefunk Around with Words": Roald Dahl and Language', in *Roald Dahl* (New Casebooks), ed. Ann Alston and Catherine Butler (Basingstoke: Palgrave Macmillan, 2012), pp. 51–69.

18 Dahl, *The Collected Short Stories*, p. 23; emphasis mine. 'Ringer's Solution: a physiological saline solution that typically contains, in addition to sodium chloride, salts of potassium and calcium. Named after Sydney Ringer (1834–1910), English physician' (*OED*).

19 Dahl, *The Collected Short Stories*, p. 154.

20 Dahl, *The Collected Short Stories*, pp. 154–5.

21 Had Dahl travelled west into upstate New York, he might have found an unexpected, eerie reminder of Wales. The shape of Erie County (NY), on the shores of the great lake, bears an uncanny resemblance to the contours of Wales, with the landmass of Grand Island occupying the position of the isle of Anglesey. A town called Wales lies to the southeast. Sturrock reveals that in 1945 Dahl was stationed at 'Camp X' which lay directly north of Grand Island across Lake Ontario (Sturrock, *Storyteller*, p. 242).

22 Dahl, *The Collected Short Stories*, p. 160.

23 Nigel Viney, *A Dictionary of Toponyms* (London: The Library Association, 1986), p. 87.

24 I refer the gourmand reader to *Dandy Dutch Recipes* by Mina Baker Roelofs and Carol Von Klompenberg (Iowa City: Penfield Books, 2013).

25 Dahl, *The Collected Short Stories*, pp. 114–15.

26 Dahl, *The Collected Short Stories*, p. 115.

27 Dahl, *The Collected Short Stories*, p. 111.

28 Dahl, *The Collected Short Stories*, p. 115.

29 Sturrock, *Storyteller*, p. 19.

30 Sturrock, *Storyteller*, p. 19.

31 Treglown, *Roald Dahl*, pp. 131–2.

32 Rudd, 'Don't Gobblefunk Around with Words', p. 65.

33 Treglown, *Roald Dahl*, p. 10.

34 Dahl, *The Collected Short Stories*, p. 128.

Works cited

Dahl, Roald, 'The Landlady', *The Collected Short Stories of Roald Dahl* (London: Penguin, 1992), pp. 3–11.

Roelofs, Mina Baker, and Carol Von Klompenberg, *Dandy Dutch Recipes* (Iowa City: Penfield Books, 2013).

Rudd, David, '"Don't Gobblefunk Around with Words": Roald Dahl and Language', in *Roald Dahl* (New Casebooks), ed. Ann Alston and Catherine Butler (Basingstoke: Palgrave Macmillan, 2012), pp. 51–69.

Sturrock, Donald, *Storyteller: The Life of Roald Dahl* (London: HarperPress, 2010).

Treglown, Jeremy, *Roald Dahl: A Biography* (San Diego: Harcourt Brace and Company, 1994).

Viney, Nigel, *A Dictionary of Toponyms* (London: The Library Association, 1986).

Wallis Budge, E. A., *The Babylonian Legends of the Creation and the Fight Between Bel and the Dragon* (London: Harrison and Sons, 1921).

5

Homes, Horizons and Orbits:
Welsh Dahl and the Aerial View

Richard Marggraf Turley

[They] flew through the night for what seemed like hours and hours until they came at last to a gigantic opening in the earth's surface, a sort of huge gaping hole in the ground, and . . . glided slowly round and round above this massive crater and then right down into it . . . Suddenly there was a brightness like sunlight below them.[1]

First aeronautic, then abruptly chthonic, this whimsical fantasy of flight from Roald Dahl's valedictory children's book, *The Minpins* (1991), depicts Little Billy being guided by Swan into the underground refuge of a vast blue lake. At first sight a touching portrayal of serene escape from childhood tormentors, the avian episode is disturbed by the language of ordnance, by the 'massive crater' and 'huge gaping hole' in the earth. The passage might not seem out of place in one of the adult flying stories Dahl wrote in the final years of the Second World War, based on his experiences as a fighter pilot with 80 Squadron. Indeed, troubled by images of night-time bombing raids, the climactic scene in *The Minpins* could almost be describing an aerial perspective on such cities as those reduced to rubble by Bomber Command pilots in Dahl's story, 'Someone Like You' (1944) – cities where women and old men in shelters are as likely to be hit as enemy soldiers.[2] Recalled too, perhaps, in the image of the crater are the ruins of Bexley, Kent, to which Dahl and his family relocated from Llandaff in 1927. When Dahl returned to south-east England in 1941 after flying sorties in the skies of Greece and Syria, the young Pilot Officer was greeted by scenes of bombed-out streets, just as he had predicted to his mother Sofie Magdalene before the outbreak of war. Fearing – rightly – that Bexley's position along the flightpath to London would render it vulnerable, he had issued his mother with a stark warning: 'Go to Tenby otherwise you'll be bombed.'[3] *Going Solo* (1986), the second of Dahl's two creatively autobiographical volumes, is punctuated by the anxiety that his mother and sisters would fall victim to aerial bombardment or invasion, and Wales figures – and is complexly figured – in the book as a place of refuge, both from stray ordnance and psychological disequilibrium.

Also ghosting Little Billy's crepuscular flight and descent towards an explosive 'brightness like sunlight' is a defining event in Dahl's war. On 19 September 1940, his Gloster Gladiator Mk 1 biplane crashed in the Libyan desert, leaving him with burns, serious concussion, temporary blindness and spinal injuries. That Dahl survived the war at all was little short of a miracle. Having received no formal combat training, he was, as his 1991 obituary in *Flying* magazine put it, 'plunked into the fray'.[4] On his return to active duty after his accident, Dahl found himself with the remnants of his squadron pitting superannuated Gladiators – a fixed-wheel survivor of an earlier age, powered by a two-blade wooden propeller – against technologically advanced Messerschmitt Bf 109s. Then on 19 and 20 April 1941, 80 Squadron, with a handful of Mk 1 Hurricanes, fought the Battle of Athens against more than a hundred enemy planes.[5] The loss of squadron members became a regular occurrence. Dahl's letters to his mother during this terrifying period may talk of 'fun' and 'looping the loop', but his wartime correspondence continues the practice of his schooldays in censoring information likely to cause distress. His more candid expectation, shared with other members of 80 Squadron during the Battle of Athens, was 'I think we're going to get killed.'[6]

So intense were these experiences that, as Dahl's first biographer, Jeremy Treglown, points out, '[i]t was inevitable that Dahl's later stories for children would often involve flight.'[7] But whereas flight is traumatic in self-announcing ways in the fabling reconstructions of Dahl's flying stories with their cast of traumatised aircrews, ghostly pilots, grieving mothers and carpet-bombed populations, we tend to read aerial drama in his fiction for children in very different terms as a joyous pursuit, as a vector towards refuge or transcendence. Two prominent recent commentators, Hugo Crago and Dahl's latest biographer,

Donald Sturrock, identify a post-concussive narrative of redemption in the children's books, in which the 'fear, anxiety and dread' that suffuse the wartime flying stories are recuperated in more whimsical or mystical representations of flight.[8] The sky, Sturrock suggests, becomes an 'alternative world', a refuge from the 'cruelties of human behaviour', and stories such as *James and the Giant Peach* (1961) and *Charlie and the Chocolate Factory* (1964) evoke the 'ecstasy of flying'.[9] Similarly, for Crago, the flight of Little Billy and Swan in *The Minpins* resonates with a redemptive symbolism that transforms the 'great sense of loss and damage' in the early work into a 'vision of abundant life and beauty'.[10] Sturrock's concept of post-concussive salvage valuably alerts us to curative modalities in Dahl's *oeuvre*, whose spiky, cynical, sometimes sadistic humour has elicited censure for its supposed 'unhealthy' effects on younger readers. I offer here an alternative, post-*traumatic* (rather than post-concussive) narrative, in which the author's war shocks, complicated by memories of Wales, are carried into the fiction for children. Whereas Sturrock and Crago configure depictions of fantastical flight as a working-through of the fighter pilot's experience of peril and extreme violence, I suggest that Dahl is trapped in cycles of repetition around an aetiology of unexorcised memories of combat. In other words, I am concerned with the layered forms in which traumatic events such as Dahl's flying accident and the Battle of Athens invade the children's stories.

Hollindale suggests that by making his 'life events' available to younger readers in *Boy: Tales of Childhood* (1984) and *Going Solo*, 'Dahl is placing his adult self within reach of children.'[11] I wish to explore this crucial insight within the explicit frame of trauma theory. What follows is in four sections. Starting with a key episode from *Boy* and moving forward (and backward) to the end of *Charlie and the Chocolate Factory*, as well as to the astronomical escape velocities of *Charlie and the Great Glass Elevator* (1972), I develop an engagement with issues of belonging, recollection and orientation; with horizons, parabolas (and parables); and with aerial views (of ground, of home, of targets) in Dahl's life and work. What becomes apparent is that far from being exorcised or accommodated in fantasy settings, irreality and whimsy, the traumas associated by Dahl with war aviation are precisely *exercised* in the aerial geometries and unpowered parabolas of the Charlie books, as well as in his other well-loved children's stories. In many cases, key episodes recalled in the autobiographical volumes and (further) fictionalised in the children's stories exist as what we might term traumatic assemblages: that is, doubled or compacted memories that bring into tense apposition scenes from childhood and subsequent experiences in Greece and Syria. Elevated viewing and horizoning, relocation, mislocation and peripheral vision, together with complex psychological geographies that collapse Kent, Somerset, Glamorgan and the Western Desert, nuance the seemingly easily dichotomised universes of the children's fiction and the stories for adults, allowing us to appreciate the complex ways in which Dahl's imagination thrives on the opposing vectors of troubled homing and aerial escape.

1. Bedtime Stories

My point of departure is also Dahl's: the multiply defining epsiode from *Boy* in which the nine-year-old Roald reflects on his first exile from Wales and on the acts of homing and mental navigation required to return to that country. The vignette, written when Dahl was in his sixties, enacts narratives of rootedness and displacement through the recollection of night-time (re)orientation at St Peter's preparatory school in Weston-super-Mare, Somerset, in 1925. The young boarder had been moved to St Peter's from Llandaff Cathedral School by Sofie Magdalene, outraged by a brutal caning her son had received at the hands of his headmaster, Mr Coombes.[12] In *Boy*, Dahl paints a striking picture of homesickness on his first night away from Wales, which he sought to assuage by calculating the direction in which the family villa, Cumberland Lodge in Llandaff, lay:

> The first miserable homesick night at St Peter's, when I curled up in bed and the lights were put out, I could think of nothing but our house at home and my mother and my sisters. Where were they? I asked myself. In which direction from where I was lying was Llandaff? I began to work it out and it wasn't difficult to do this because I had the Bristol Channel to help me.[13]

From his Weston dormitory, the adept schoolboy deploys the pilot's trick of using rivers and waterways to orient himself. Dahl later described the method in his flying story, 'They Shall Not Grow Old', in which a fighter pilot is sent to Beirut to find two French destroyers:

'I flew over Tyre and Sidon and over the Damour River and then I flew inland over the Lebanon hills, because I intended to approach Beyrouth from the east.'[14] Using the Bristol Channel (seen from his St Peter's 'cockpit') much as his 'flyer' does the Damour River, Roald calibrates his position relative to Llandaff-over-the-horizon:

> If I looked out of the dormitory window I could see the Channel itself, and the big city of Cardiff with Llandaff alongside it lay almost directly across the water but slightly to the north. Therefore, if I turned towards the window I would be facing home. I wriggled round in my bed and faced my home and my family.
>
> From then on, during all the time I was at St Peter's, I never went to sleep with my back to my family. Different beds in different dormitories required the working out of new directions, but the Bristol Channel was always my guide and I was always able to draw an imaginary line from my bed to our house over in Wales.[15]

Dahl's dormitory calculations suggest precocious orientation skills. However, Dahl's 1984 account of his boyish 'pilotage' in 1925 has been sifted through the author's intervening experience as a fighter pilot, conditioned in particular by his *mis*orientation over the Western Desert. Dahl, who had just received his wings, was ordered to take his Gladiator biplane (registration K7911) from RAF Fouka to the forward airfield at RAF Sidi Haneish on the Libyan Plateau, operated by 80 Squadron. The flight was estimated to take fifty minutes. As his logbook records, Dahl took off from Fouka at 18:15 with an hour or so of daylight left. As dusk fell, there was still no sign of the airbase. Running low on fuel, the light failing, Dahl – increasingly desperate now, realising a return to Fouka was out of the question – conned the horizon for sight of his squadron. There was no way home.

> It was nearly dark now. I had to get down somehow or other. I chose a piece of ground that seemed to me to be as boulder-free as any and I made an approach. I came in as slowly as I dared, hanging on the prop, travelling just above my stalling speed of eighty miles an hour. My wheels touched down. I throttled back and prayed for a bit of luck.
>
> I didn't get it. My undercarriage hit a boulder and collapsed completely and the Gladiator buried its nose in the sand at what must have been about seventy-five miles an hour.[16]

Dahl's injuries required extensive surgery, including the reconstruction of his nose, which was pushed back into his skull on impact with
the aircraft's metal reflector-sight. *Going Solo* records how a Harley
Street plastic surgeon rebuilt Dahl's nose using Rudolph Valentino's
as a template, a fantastical reconstruction that no doubt appealed to
the author.[17] Interviewed about his crash in *The Times* in 1983 on the
eve of *Boy*'s publication, Dahl made an explicit link between his terrifying forced landing and subsequent writing career, asserting that his
'monumental bash on the head' had altered his personality, leaving
him with a sudden need to write fiction.[18]

Sturrock recognises the importance of the Gladiator crash to Dahl's
sense of himself as a writer, and argues that representations of flight in
the children's stories may be seen as post-concussive 'epiphanies', as
transcendent refuges from horror.[19] I suggest that episodes of levitation
in books such as *James and the Giant Peach*, *Charlie and the Chocolate Factory*
and *Charlie and the Great Glass Elevator* gesture more urgently at Dahl's
need to re-enact or fantastically to 'reconstruct' – *out of trauma*, and in
often emphatically *non*-transcendent, non-epiphanic forms – key events
from his time in the Mediterranean theatre. Contemporary trauma
theory acknowledges the disjunction between the original traumatic
event and the victim's understanding of it. In the case of writers, as
Roger Luckhurst clarifies, paraphrasing Geoffrey Hartman, the desire
to grasp the meaning of such events gives rise to irrepressible refig-
urings of traumatic incidents, where figurative language constitutes
'a form of "perpetual troping" around a primary experience that can
never be captured'.[20] Dahl's work exhibits precisely such 'perpetual
troping'. Traumatic memories from his war years associated specifically with his career as fighter pilot, the bombing of loved ones and his
own status as a killer (on which the flying stories meditate), together
with the author's complexly signifying Welsh home as both refuge and
site of childhood violence, stage troubling and compacted returns in
his fiction for children.

Not all injuries sustained in the Libyan desert were physical. As a
trainee pilot, Dahl found himself near the top of his class, and the crash
was, as Sturrock points out, a 'humiliating start to a flying career that
had promised great things'.[21] The indignity appears to have been felt
keenly: in *Going Solo*, Dahl disavows all blame for the episode, claiming
the coordinates his Commanding Officer had given him were inaccu-
rate: 'It was revealed at an inquiry into my crash held later that the CO

at Fouka had given me totally wrong information. Eighty Squadron had never been in the position I was sent to. They were fifty miles to the south.'[22] The RAF's accident report makes no such admission, merely noting that 'Pilot Officer Dahl was ferrying an aircraft from No. 102 Maintenance Unit . . . but unfortunately not being used to flying aircraft over the desert he made . . . an unsuccessful forced landing.'[23] Aspects of the crash landing feature in no fewer than three of Dahl's adult flying stories, including his first published tale, 'A Piece of Cake', renamed 'Shot Down Over Libya' on its US publication in the *Saturday Evening Post*.[24] The racy change of title appears to have been made by the newspaper's editors to boost readership; subsequently, however, Dahl promoted the idea that his plane had been downed by enemy fire rather than by faulty navigation. Four decades later in 1984, when alluding on the last page of *Boy* to a second volume of autobiographical material that would become *Going Solo*, Dahl is still lending currency to the myth:[25] 'I shot down some German planes and I got shot down myself, crashing in a burst of flames and crawling out and getting rescued by brave soldiers crawling on their bellies over the sand.'[26] In the introduction to her 1995 collection of essays, *Trauma: Explorations in Memory*, Cathy Caruth suggests that the traumatic event cannot be grasped or assimilated 'fully at the time, but only belatedly, in its repeated *possession* of the one who experiences it'.[27] The recirculation of traumatic material at the end of *Boy* suggests that both the crash and its likely cause (pilot disorientation) remained unexorcised in the author's mind.

In the same passage of *Boy* in which he discusses shooting down German planes, Dahl is eager to draw a clear distinction between events in the Western Desert and memorable incidents in his youth and school-days at Llandaff, Weston and Bexley: 'But all that is another story. It has nothing to do with childhood or school or Gobstoppers . . . It is a different tale altogether.'[28] Despite this assertion, Dahl's memories of 'wriggl[ing] around' in his bed at St Peter's to face his Welsh home and his account of the forced landing in Libya are very much part of the same, entangled story. The account in *Boy* of young Roald's successful display of homing in his Weston dormitory attempts to repair the newly qualified Pilot Officer's defective horizoning over Libya (such temporal effects, or 'disjunction of time', are characteristic of trauma fiction).[29] Whereas Dahl in 1940 was unable to find his squadron's base – whether through bungling inexperience or a superior's misdirection – his school-boy self proves sufficiently resourceful to plot an accurate flight path to his childhood home from multiple coordinates ('Different beds in different dormitories required the working out of new directions').[30] The two events, one in Weston, one in the Western Desert, are mutually embedded (compacted, *impacted*) memories of horizoning and (self-)location. Dahl's account of that first lights out at Weston is troubled by the failed orientation strategies of Dahl the Pilot Officer. The schoolboy's triumphant act of orientation already 'repeats' – as it seeks, but *fails*, to grasp – Dahl-the-fighter-pilot's traumatic disorientation in the desert, his inability to draw an imaginary line home.[31]

2. Skyhooks

> Repetition is not simply the attempt to grasp that one has almost died but, more fundamentally and enigmatically, the very attempt *to claim one's own survival*.[32]

Dahl's studied *sangfroid* when writing to Sofie Magdalene about his dog-fights over Greece in April 1941 should not disguise the fact that daily combat against the Nazi war machine, mounting losses and the likelihood of being killed took an inevitable toll. In a brief but memorable passage from *Going Solo*, Dahl recalls being unable to light a cigarette after flying a sortie because his hands were shaking too much.[33] In the modality of post-Freudian trauma theory pioneered in the 1990s by Cathy Caruth and Shoshana Felman, repetition is recognised as both a symptom of post-traumatic stress disorder and an attempt – always unfulfilled – by the traumatised subject to grasp the meaning of the original traumatic event. As Caruth suggests, such events become accessible only in the moment of their return, in their 'repeated *possession*' of the one who experiences them. To be traumatised, then, 'is precisely to be possessed by an image or event'.[34] In *Trauma Fiction* (2004), Anne Whitehead adds, valuably, that such events act as haunting revenants; writers tend to 'narrativise' this sense of haunting in fictional forms characterised by 'repetition and indirection'.[35] The following two sections of this essay examine recursive effects – in the form of the return of images, motifs and rhetoric – in Dahl's work to argue that aspects of the stories for children may be considered as complex responses to extreme violence. I wish to suggest, in other words, that these stories may be understood as combat fiction.

In their introduction to *Trauma and Romance in Contemporary British Literature* (2014), Susana Onega and Jean-Michel Ganteau argue that a writer's need to represent trauma exerts pressure on traditional 'transparent' modes of realism, which come to be seen as inadequate as ways of giving voice to the unspeakable:

> This urgent and irrepressible need to represent trauma . . . has forced fiction to problematise the traditional conventions of transparent realism by moving toward the pole of non-fictional testimony, while simultaneously incorporating the most salient modal strategies of romance, and so paradoxically moving towards the contrary pole of unabated fictionality and fantasy.[36]

Such compulsive desire for representation is brokered, then, through narratives that exhibit a shift towards nonfictional 'testimony' while simultaneously making use of key romance strategies. While Dahl, who has received surprisingly little attention from literary theorists, does not feature in the essays curated by Onega and Ganteau, in signal respects his work – encountered not as distinct bodies of writing for children and adults, but rather as a series of (traumatically) related adjacencies – exhibits movement between the poles of testimony and romance. I do not simply mean that we can identify stylised verisimilitude in the flying stories, fabling testimony in the autobiographical volumes, and unabashed fantasy in the children's books. Rather, the terrors experienced by Dahl in the Mediterranean, his fears for the safety of his family in Bexley, and his vision of Wales, his country of birth, as a refuge from horror (which at the same time itself signifies as a traumatic site of institutional violence), seek representation through recursive themes, motifs and images associated with flight. The ghostly returns of this material in scenes of flight, I argue, should not be considered redemptive or transcendent, but instead as markers of unassimilated trauma, as sites of worry. What follows is not only an attempt to 'diagnose' Dahl by identifying symptom clusters, or psychopathologies, in his writing, but also an interrogation of conventional distinctions between his adult flying stories and his work for children. Also at stake is the crucial issue of the extent to which an alertness to Dahl as a traumatised writer allows a more attuned appreciation of his relation to Wales.

James and the Giant Peach and *Charlie and the Chocolate Factory* are often regarded as escapist fantasies whose aerial *jouissance* offers ecstatic release from the world of overbearing, bullying adults and stultifying systems. At issue in each narrative, however, is a dilemma: *how to remain aloft*. Both books propose surreal solutions that involve unpowered or else impossibly powered flight, and both culminate in crash landings, albeit ones in which the protagonists receive the 'bit of luck' denied Dahl in the desert.[37] Tempting though it may be to regard James's and Charlie's successful deplanings as, in Sturrock's and Crago's terms, recuperative examples of disaster averted, and the peach, in Catherine Butler's formulation, as figuring a 'retreat from the cruelties and vicissitudes of the world', trauma studies suggest that the traumatic condition allows no final assimilation of the original crisis, no definitive representation of its aporia.[38] That is to say, Dahl's imaginative preoccupation with crash landings is not exorcised by James's successful touch-down on the Empire State Building. Rather, his anxieties are recycled back into a stock of recursive images, ready for reassembly, as we shall see, in *Charlie and the Chocolate Factory*. With their representations of precarious flight and perilous descent, both novels confront Dahl's own near-death experience in the desert, figured through what Cathy Caruth terms a 'double telling', an 'oscillation between a *crisis of death* and the correlative *crisis of life*', in which the latter is bound up with the 'unbearable nature of . . . survival'.[39] In Charlie's case, the struggle with gravity will produce a new danger – that of not landing at all; in *Charlie and the Great Glass Elevator*, the lift's roof-splintering lift-off from Wonka's chocolate factory takes the protagonist into orbit, straight into the Cold War and the space race, back-and-out into conflict between nations. Like all trauma victims, then, Dahl finds himself in a perpetual 'crisis of representation'.[40] In the quotation at the head of this section, Caruth contends that repetition constitutes more than simply the attempt to take in the fact that one has almost died. '[M]ore fundamentally and enigmatically', she notes, 'it is the very attempt *to claim one's own survival*'.[41] As the various scenes of flight in Dahl's fiction for children seem to register, survival is a claim that must be renewed.[42]

It might seem fanciful to suggest that the deep traumas of Dahl's war writing of the 1940s and 1950s are carried over into well-loved children's fantasies. Consider, however, the apparently surreal scene in which the crew of the giant peach attempt to extricate themselves from a shark-infested sea. James (another resourceful schoolboy) concocts a plan of levitation involving hundreds of yards of silk. Miss Spider demands to know what James intends to attach the silk to, prompting Centipede's droll remark: 'Skyhooks, I suppose.' Easily missed is Willy Wonka's identical quip at the beginning of *Charlie and the Great Glass Elevator* in response to Grandma Josephine's similarly incredulous inquiry into the lift's method of propulsion:

> 'What in the world keeps this crazy thing up in the air?' croaked Grandma Josephine . . .
> 'Skyhooks,' said Mr Wonka.

The giant peach, it transpires, is levitated by means of hundreds of tethered seagulls. The secret of Wonka's soaring glass elevator is never shared, but we may assume its power source is equally improbable. Such fantasies of impossible flight present themselves as quintessential whimsy, calculated to appeal to young readers. As cognate *re*-presentations, however, of Dahl's predicament as his fuel gauge fell – that is, as relational returns linked linguistically through Centipede's and Mr Wonka's invocation of 'skyhooks' – they function as a registration of deeper anxiety about remaining airborne. Within the books' fantasy logic, *skyhooks* would appear to be magical fixed points in the sky from which heavy objects can be safely suspended. Dahl, however, probably encountered the term *skyhook* during his flying days as the nickname commonly used for the Airco DH.6, a trainer biplane used during the First World War by the Royal Flying Corps, which remained in service as late as the 1930s. The plane was almost impossible to stall or spin (hence the nickname – it stayed up), and could fly at speeds as low as 30mph – attributes that would probably have saved Dahl in the desert. *James and the Giant Peach* and *Charlie and the Great Glass Elevator* further frame both flying peach and lift in terms of Dahl's wartime experiences – specifically the trauma of forced landing, and Dahl's anxieties that his failure to follow training protocols might have caused it.

In one of the stranger episodes in the peach's transatlantic flight, James and the insect aeronauts encounter hordes of wispy Cloud-Men standing atop fleecy clouds, whose hostile response to the peach directly invokes Dahl's terrifying world of dog-fighting. Hailstones hurled by the Cloud-Men take on the qualities of 'bullets from a machine gun', which smash into peach flesh:

This evidently infuriated the Cloud-Men beyond belief. All at once, they spun around and grabbed great handfuls of hailstones and rushed to the edge of the cloud and started throwing them at the peach, shrieking with fury all the time.

'Look out!' cried James. 'Quick! Lie down! Lie flat on the deck!'

. . . The hailstones came whizzing through the air like bullets from a machine gun, and James could hear them smashing against the sides of the peach and burying themselves in the peach flesh with horrible squelching noises – *plop! plop! plop! plop!* And then *ping! ping! ping!* as they bounced off the poor Ladybird's shell because she couldn't lie as flat as the others. And then *crack!* as one of them hit the Centipede right on the nose . . .

'Ow!' he cried. 'Ow! Stop! Stop! Stop!'[43]

As well as injuring Centipede's nose, the ghostly Cloud-Men – haunting revenants, in Whitehead's terms – also pour quick-drying rainbow paint over him, causing him to exclaim in panic: 'My eyelids won't open! I can't see.' Calibrated from within the context of Caruth's and Whitehead's analysis of traumatic repetition, Centipede's injuries are suggestive. As has already been discussed, Dahl's nose required surgical reconstruction following his desert crash, and as a consequence of cranial swelling the author was unable to open his eyes for several weeks.[44] The encounter with the Cloud-Men, then, collapses – or assembles – two traumas, air combat over Greece in April 1941 (machine-gun bullets smashing into James's 'aircraft') and Dahl's forced landing in September 1940 (during which he sustained injuries mirroring the Centipede's).

The crew wake to find the peach hanging over New York. Like Dahl over the desert, who had 'to get down somehow', they search for a means of safe descent.[45] At that moment, a passenger plane slices through the silk strings attaching the peach to the seagulls: 'the enormous peach, having nothing to hold it up in the air any longer, went tumbling down towards the earth like a lump of lead.'[46] Uncontrolled descent returns us to the traumatic territory of the Libyan desert:

James could see the skyscrapers rushing up to meet them at the most awful speed, and most of them had square flat tops, but the very tallest of them all had a top that tapered off into a long sharp point – like an enormous silver needle sticking up into the sky.

And it was precisely on to the top of this needle that the peach fell!
There was a squelch. The needle went in deep.[47]

The peach's 'successful' crash landing on the spire of the Empire
State Building might present itself as self-healing. (Jeremy Treglown is
insightful in describing Dahl the story-teller as a healer manqué.)[48] But
the unassimilability of forced landing in the Libyan desert is suggested
by the prominent imagery of medical needles, hinting at the months of
pain and recuperation endured in hospital in late 1940 and early 1941
– hinting, that is, at other kinds of bedtime stories.

3. The Biggest Bomb

Dahl abhorred the practice of civilian bombing, and in a letter to *The
Times* in 1983 referred to the 'ghastly RAF raid on Dresden'.[49] It may
have been no more than good fortune that saved Dahl himself from
being given a commission as a bomber pilot. On receiving their wings,
Dahl's trainee group at RAF Habbaniya found itself 'divided up into
fighter pilots or bomber pilots', with no reason given for the division.[50]
Dahl's horror at the bombing of civilian populations is explored in his
first novel, *Sometime Never*, begun in 1946, around the time he read John
Hersey's *New Yorker* article on the atomic destruction of Hiroshima.[51]
When the novel appeared in the US in 1948, it was the first to imagine
the nuclear bombing of a British city, and includes a shocking vignette
of 'scorched and seared and half-melted' Londoners sitting upright in
a double-decker bus:

> all of them had had their hats blown off their heads so that they sat there
> bald-headed, scorch-skinned, grotesque, but very upright in their seats.
> Up in front, the black-faced driver was still sitting with his hands resting
> on the wheel, looking straight in front of him through the empty sockets
> of his eyes.[52]

Dahl had also registered his revulsion at indiscriminate bombing in
'Someone Like You'. The short story engages sharply with the tactic
of saturation bombing, and includes a distinctive 'twist'. Examining
the *mutual* impact of such methods of warfare, Dahl presents an acute
psychodynamic portrait of two carpet bombers:

'You know,' he said, 'you know I keep thinking during a raid, when we are running over the target, just as we are going to release our bombs, I keep thinking to myself, shall I just jink a little; shall I swerve a fraction to one side, then my bombs will fall on someone else. I keep thinking, whom shall I make them fall on; whom shall I kill tonight.'[53]

A sense of the arbitrariness with which he himself escaped becoming a bomber pilot seems to have preyed on Dahl's mind. Perhaps he worried he had an innate propensity for such a role. His diary recounts the glee with which as a child he rigged up a Meccano 'chariot' on wires to carry soup cans filled with payloads of water across the Dahls' two-acre Bexley garden. The intended targets were local women exercising their right to walk their dogs along a public footpath that traversed the bottom of the family's grounds, and the young Roald scored a direct hit. 'For days afterwards', he records, 'I experienced the pleasant warm glow that comes to all of us when we have brought off a major triumph.'[54] The pressure of the realisation that he could easily have been assigned to drop bombs on inhabitants of towns and cities just like Bexley exerts itself at various times in his children's stories, and occasions some striking switches of perspective. One example is the arrival of James's magical peach above New York, which causes panic on the streets below. The formulaic imagery of aerial views, of beetle-like cars and microscopic people, is shockingly interrupted by the language of an air raid:

Far below them, in the City of New York, something like pandemonium was breaking out. A great round ball as big as a house had been sighted hovering high up in the sky over the very centre of Manhattan, and the cry had gone up that it was an enormous bomb sent over by another country to blow the whole city to smithereens. Air-raid sirens began wailing in every section. All radio and television programmes were interrupted with announcements that the population must go down into their cellars immediately.[55]

The scene is manifestly in dialogue with 'Someone Like You' – 'narrated back', as it were, at the flying story's carpet bomber protagonists from the perspective of bombed civilians:

Faster and faster [the peach] fell. Down and down and down, racing closer and closer to the houses and streets below . . . And all the way along Fifth Avenue and Madison Avenue, and along all the other streets in the City, people who had not yet reached the underground shelters looked up and saw it coming, and they stopped running and stood there staring in a sort of stupor at what they thought was the biggest bomb in all the world falling out of the sky on to their heads. A few women screamed. Others knelt down on the sidewalks and began praying aloud. Strong men turned to one another and said things like, 'I guess this is it, Joe,' and 'Good-bye, everybody, good-bye.' And for the next thirty seconds the whole City held its breath, waiting for the end to come.[56]

Amid the whimsy of boot-wearing centipedes and talking silkworms, the passage sets up a tonal confusion. A traumatic singularity has formed in which burgeoning irreality and a psychodynamically veridical portrait of civilian populations caught in the open during an air raid are collapsed into the same time and space.

If the peach's descent condenses two images operating out of trauma – desert crash-landing and air raid (the latter itself condensing the act of being bombed and of being cast as the bomber) – a near-identical traumatic assemblage occurs near the end of *Charlie and the Chocolate Factory*. Treglown suggests the intensity of Dahl's experiences in the skies of Greece made it 'inevitable' that the author's stories for children would 'often involve flight'.[57] Certainly, the aeronautical trajectories of Willy Wonka's lift seem to resonate suggestively with Dahl's time in 80 Squadron. The following passage, for instance, summons the distinctive sound of the Gloster Gladiator, known for the scream of the 'wind in the wires':

> the lift began flattening out again, but it seemed to be going faster than ever, and Charlie could hear the scream of the wind outside as it hurtled forward . . . and it twisted . . . and it turned . . . and it went up . . . and it went down . . . and . . .[58]

But while the lift puts Dahl back in the cockpit of his plummeting Gladiator, it also threatens to become one of the four-engined heavy bombers Dahl narrowly escaped piloting. In the final scenes of *Charlie and the Cholocate Factory*, Mr Wonka's glass elevator drops onto the Buckets' tiny cottage, smashing through the roof like the 4,000lb 'Satan' bombs that destroyed parts of London in the Bliz:

CRASH went the lift, right down through the roof of the house into the old people's bedroom. Showers of dust and broken tiles and bits of wood and cockroaches and spiders and bricks and cement went raining down on the three old ones who were lying in bed, and each of them thought that the end of the world was come. Grandma Georgina fainted, Grandma Josephine dropped her false teeth, Grandpa George put his head under the blanket, and Mr and Mrs Bucket came rushing in from the next room.

. . .

'Just look at our house!' cried poor Mr Bucket. 'It's in ruins!'[59]

The fantasy destruction at the end of *Charlie and the Chocolate Factory* parallels actual bomb damage to the roof of the Dahls' Bexley house, when stray ordnance brought one of the Victorian ceilings crashing down around Dahl's mother and sisters.[60] Again, war trauma is carried into the children's fiction, resonating in complex ways with ideas of both homing and homecoming.

4. Escape Velocities

'Oh, look,' he cried, pointing down, 'there go the other children! They're returning home!'[61]

It is tempting to view the aerial virtuosity of the glass elevator (surely capable of outmanoeuvring the most skilfully piloted Messerschmitt Bf 109) as an embodiment of the 'glory of flight', and the aerobatic ending to *Charlie and the Chocolate Factory* as a joyous, epiphanic conclusion to a story in which Wonka 'hands over his world to the young boy'.[62] Yet Charlie's ballistic exit from the chocolate factory is not, I suggest, pitched towards freedom at all; nor is it (merely, or unproblematically) the prelude to taking possession of the keys to a new home. Rather, the grand inversion of gravity that catapults Charlie into uncertain space can be productively understood as an act of breaking with Roald's Welsh past.

'Corporal punishment', Peter Hollindale notes, often strikes readers of Dahl's creatively autobiographical writings as the 'dominant memory' of the author's school days; certainly, as Treglown and others point out, a large section of *Boy* is given over to recollections of beatings.[63] The flogging episode with perhaps the most far-reaching consequences takes place in the rooms of Dahl's headmaster in Llandaff Cathedral School. Along with four other practical jokers, Dahl claims, he was caned for his part in placing a mouse in a jar of gobstoppers in the local sweet shop. With the shopkeeper supposedly in ghoulish attendance, the school friends were subjected to a sadistic beating. Movingly, and surely not coincidentally, when Dahl narrates his own punishment, the scene slips into, and resonates with, the discourse of downed fighter planes:

> By the time the fourth stroke was delivered, my entire backside seemed to be going up in flames.
> Far away in the distance, I heard Mr Coombes's voice saying, 'Now get out.'[64]

Stationed here, I suggest, is yet another of the traumatic assemblages that form connected nodal points across Dahl's *oeuvre*, linking and collapsing memories as well as time and space. Discursively entangled in this passage are memories of the searing pain inflicted by both the cane and the heat from the exploding fuel tank of Dahl's Gloster Gladiator, which left a fiery wreck from which the semi-conscious pilot had to rouse himself to 'get out'.[65] Another node with which the scene in Mr Coombes's office is linked is located in 'A Piece of Cake', Dahl's fictionalised account of his crash. As the pilot in the story lies injured in the flaming wreckage, his inner voice tells him: 'The – plane – is – burning. Get – out – repeat – get – out – get – out.'[66] Llandaff and the Libyan desert are produced through a process of mutual prisming.

Mr Coombes's injunction that Dahl leave his room also resonates in the context of the young boy's relationship with Wales, which was strongly inflected by the family's Norwegian identity and cultural reference points. Born in Llandaff, Roald held British citizenship (unlike the rest of his family), but spoke Norwegian at home. Sofie Magdalene's strong accent marked her as an outsider all her life, and during the war the family was regarded with suspicion as 'alien nationals'.[67] Coombes's 'get out', then, may also be freighted for Dahl with a cultural agon that was certainly felt, and articulated, by his mother, whose attitudes towards Wales were transparently conflicted. The headmaster's assault on her son prompted her to move Roald not only from his Llandaff school, but also over the border. In Dahl's memory in *Boy* of

Sofie's enraged response (presumably translated from Norwegian) to the caning, she declares: 'I shall find you an *English* school this time.'[68] In September 1925, at the age of nine, Dahl was duly relocated to Weston, Somerset, where he became a boarder, effectively leaving Wales. Two years later, the entire family moved to Kent.

Although Dahl does not express any particular yearnings for Wales after his relocation, the country figures resonantly in his imagination as a place of detached refuge from war, with the Pembrokeshire seaside town of Tenby, in particular, evoked in letters to his mother as a haven from both bombs and invasion.[69] In fact, Wales did not turn out to be as immune from violence as Dahl assumed. In addition to the damage inflicted on larger centres of population in the south, such as Cardiff, Swansea and Newport (each of which suffered its own 'Blitz'), targets in west Wales, including Haverfordwest, Pembroke Dock and Tenby itself, were also hit. The vulnerability of home, and of one's relation to home, features prominently in Dahl's work. It is the act of homecoming, as we have seen, that causes the destruction of the Buckets' cottage and which casts Charlie as both triumphant aerial wizard and malevolent bombardier. Indeed, the elevator's glass construction, seemingly designed with elevated views over cities in mind, hints at the glass-bottomed 'blister' in which Second World War bomb-aimers lay. Charlie's homing instinct also takes us back to Roald's dormitory at St Peter's in Weston. Buried in Dahl's adult recollection of that first wretched night is his (intervening) wartime knowledge, discussed earlier in this essay, that bomber pilots navigated by rivers during blackouts. At some level, perhaps, resenting having been sent away from Wales owing to his Llandaff headmaster's act of violence, Dahl returns some of that violence in the form of a mental bombing run implied in the 'imaginary line' he draws between his new bed and his Welsh home. In the same way as Charlie, heir to Wonka's fabulous riches, destroys the traumatic site of his childhood destitution, Dahl, now a boarder at prestigious St Peter's (a feeder school for Repton), attacks the country that brutally expelled him, the land that told him to 'get out'. The suspicion that the elevator represents an explosive threat is voiced by the US President in *Charlie and the Great Glass Elevator* as the lift nears the USA Space Hotel: '"That's not a bed, you drivelling thickwit!" yelled the President. "Can't you understand it's a trick! It's a bomb. It's a bomb disguised as a bed!"'[70]

The chocolate factory is itself threatened by the elevator in similar terms, the lift's return trajectory again hybridised with the language of the bombing run. The Buckets – squeezed in and around the grandparents' bed – demand to know why Mr Wonka is taking the lift high above the chocolate factory, rather than landing beside it:

'Go down!' yelled Grandpa George.
    'No, no!' Mr Wonka yelled back. 'We've got to go up!'
    'But why?' they all shouted at once. 'Why up and not down?'
    'Because the higher we are when we start coming down, the faster we'll all be going when we hit,' said Mr Wonka . . .
    'When we hit *what?*' they cried.
    'The factory, of course,' answered Mr Wonka . . . 'It's not easy to punch a hole in a roof as strong as that.'[71]

Like Charlie, who brought the lift smashing down through the roof of his parents' cottage, Mr Wonka turns bombardier, aiming his payload at industrial factories (here, his own), calculating speed and trajectory as carefully as the young Roald planned his own bombing run from Weston to Llandaff. The lift's psychic 'payload' is the grandparents' bed, symbol of the family seat – indeed, the bed is the traumatic object that connects the family drama playing out in the elevator to that staged in the homesick Roald's bed at St Peter's. (Just as the young Dahl draws an 'imaginary line' between St Peter's and Cumberland Lodge, so we can draw a line between his Weston bed and the bed carried by the glass elevator.) What is being delivered, or visited on, the chocolate factory – just as it has already been visited on the Buckets' home – is that paradigmatic site of exile, Roald's first dormitory bed.

As well as producing a violent Welsh (re)visitation, Dahl's traumatic dislocation in Weston contributes to imaginative energies that take the schoolboy, finally, all but beyond the pull of Wales, as Wonka's lift – continuing into orbit, into weightlessness – appears to perform a final dissociative act. Wonka reveals the ultimate aerial perspective, 'the countries and oceans of the Earth spread out below' like a map. But as we've seen, the escape velocity and upward trajectory take Charlie into Cold War anxieties. In the President's imagination, the lift – and Charlie himself – are configured as a guided missile. Thus flight in Dahl's fiction for children rarely displays (or seldom solely displays) ecstatic or redemptive characteristics; on the contrary, it is usually accompanied by anxiety and unease. As Charlie observes: 'It was an eerie and frightening feeling to be standing on clear glass high up in the sky. It made you feel that you weren't standing on anything at all.'[72] The children's stories do not 'redeem' or 'heal' Dahl's combat experience, but relive it, traumatically. No less than Dahl, Charlie and James are 'flyers', exiles, survivors of 'eerie and frightening' events, each with an irrepressible need to renew covenant with their survival.

Notes

[1] *The Minpins* (London: Penguin, 2008 [1991]), p. 43.

[2] The pilots describe their helplessness in the face of the fact that the vagaries of their flight path, or a touch of the ball of the foot on the rudder-bar, could easily 'throw the bombs on to a different house and on to other people', causing the bomb-aimers to 'miss getting the soldiers and get an old man in a shelter'; 'Someone Like You', *The Collected Short Stories of Roald Dahl* (London: Penguin, 1992), pp. 318, 319. Staring round at the people in the bar, one of the pilots remarks: 'I've killed more people than there are in this room hundreds of times. So have you . . . Same sort of people. Men and women and waiters. All drinking in a pub' (pp. 322–3).

[3] Letter to Sofie Magdelene, written from Dar es Salaam, dated 19 March 1939; included in *Going Solo* (London: Puffin, 1988 [1986]), p. 29.

[4] *Flying*, February 1991, pp. 29–30.

[5] Dahl worked out that of the fifteen fellow trainees with whom he learned to fly in Nairobi in late 1939, thirteen were killed within two years of the war; see Dahl, *Going Solo*, p. 83.

[6] Dahl, *Going Solo*, p. 154. As Peter Hollindale points out, the accident in the Western Desert may have saved Dahl's life, initially taking him out of action for seven months and ultimately leading to the author being invalided out of the RAF in June 1941. See 'And Children Swarmed to Him Like Settlers. He Became a Land: The Outrageous Success of Roald Dahl', in *Popular Children's Literature in Britain*, ed. Julia Briggs, Dennis Butts and Matthew Orville Grenby (Aldershot: Ashgate, 2008), p. 279.

[7] Jeremy Treglown, *Roald Dahl: A Biography* (London: Faber and Faber, 1994), pp. 46–7.

[8] Donald Sturrock, *Storyteller: The Life of Roald Dahl* (London: HarperPress, 2010), p. 197.

[9] Sturrock, *Storyteller*, pp. 136, 154.

[10] Hugo Crago, *Entranced By Story: Brain, Tale and Teller, from Infancy to Old Age* (London: Routledge, 2014), p. 215.

11 Hollindale, 'And Children Swarmed to Him Like Settlers', p. 279.

12 See Sturrock, *Storyteller*, p. 49.

13 Roald Dahl, *Boy: Tales of Childhood* (London: Puffin, 1986 [1984]), pp. 89–90.

14 Dahl, *The Collected Short Stories*, p. 293.

15 Dahl, *Boy*, p. 90.

16 Dahl, *Going Solo*, p. 100.

17 Dahl, *Going Solo*, p. 113.

18 Interview with Peter Lennon ('A Bumpy Ride to Fantasy'), *The Times*, 22 December 1983, p. 8. Years after the accident, Dahl's writing space in his shed in the village of Great Missenden in Buckinghamshire was shaped by the physical accommodations he made for his spinal injuries.

19 Sturrock, *Storyteller*, p. 136.

20 Roger Luckhurst, *The Trauma Question* (London: Routledge, 2008), p. 7.

21 Sturrock, *Storyteller*, p. 124.

22 Dahl, *Going Solo*, pp. 101, 103.

23 Sturrock, *Storyteller*, p. 126.

24 The episode is also dramatised in 'Only This' and 'Lucky Break', and appears in Dahl's first story for younger readers, *The Gremlins* (1943), in which the protagonist Gus crash-lands his plane and afterwards recuperates, like Dahl, in a 'small, dark' hospital room.

25 When *Going Solo* appeared in 1986, Dahl finally clarified the situation: 'There seems . . . to be an implication that I was shot down by enemy action . . . The fact is that my crash had nothing whatsoever to do with enemy action. I was not shot down'; Dahl, *Going Solo*, p. 97.

26 Dahl, *Boy*, p. 176.

27 Cathy Caruth (ed.), *Trauma: Explorations in Memory* (Baltimore, MD: Johns Hopkins University Press, 1995), p. 4.

28 Dahl, *Boy*, p. 176.

29 See Michelle Balaev, *The Nature of Trauma in American Novels* (Evanston, IL: Northwestern University Press, 2012), p. xvi.

30 Dahl, *Boy*, p. 90.

31 One of Dahl's most accomplished flying stories, 'Beware of the Dog', turns on wrong coordinates. The downed protagonist spends much of the tale believing he is in hospital in Brighton, when in fact he is being held in northern France.

32 Cathy Caruth, *Unclaimed Experience: Trauma, Narrative and History* (Baltimore, MD: Johns Hopkins University Press, 1996), p. 58.

33 Dahl, *Going Solo*, pp. 152–3.

34 Caruth (ed.), *Trauma: Explorations in Memory*, pp. 4–5.

35 Anne Whitehead, *Trauma Fiction* (Edinburgh: Edinburgh University Press, 2004), p. 3.

36 Susana Onega and Jean-Michel Ganteau, 'Traumatic Realism and Romance in Contemporary British Narrative', in *Trauma and Romance in*

Contemporary British Literature, ed. Susana Onega and Jean-Michel Ganteau (London: Routledge, 2014), p. 4.

37 Dahl, *Going Solo*, p. 100.

38 Catherine Butler, 'Introduction', in *Roald Dahl* (New Casebooks), ed. Ann Alston and Catherine Butler (Basingstoke: Palgrave Macmillan, 2012), p. 4.

39 Caruth, *Unclaimed Experience*, p. 7. Dahl's account of his forced landing is recounted in a chapter of *Going Solo* entitled 'Survival'.

40 Luckhurst, *The Trauma Question*, p. 65.

41 Caruth, *Unclaimed Experience*, p. 58.

42 Actor Kenneth Haigh, Dahl's Great Missenden neighbour and friend, referred to Roald as 'Big Daddy Survivor himself'; Treglown, *Roald Dahl*, p. 203.

43 Roald Dahl, *James and the Giant Peach* (London: Puffin, 2001 [1961]), pp. 113–14.

44 Sturrock, *Storyteller*, pp. 128–30.

45 Dahl, *Going Solo*, p. 100.

46 Dahl, *James and the Giant Peach*, pp. 136–7.

47 Dahl, *James and the Giant Peach*, p. 138.

48 Treglown, *Roald Dahl*, p. 125.

49 *The Times*, 19 September 1983, p. 15. Dahl claimed he could not open fire on civilians. In *Going Solo*, he states he would have been unable, if required, to give the command to shoot fleeing German citizens in Dar es Salaam (p. 64). Like the other Hurricane pilots in his squadron, Dahl reports, he did not open fire during the first pass of the ground strafe on the Vichy French planes after they spotted young French women drinking wine with the pilots next to the wings (p. 193). The squadron's 'chivalry' cost them damage to their planes on their second run, when the Vichy ground crews were prepared for the attack. The incident is dramatised in 'They Shall Not Grow Old', *The Collected Short Stories*, pp. 285–99.

50 Dahl, *Going Solo*, p. 93.

51 Sturrock, *Storyteller*, p. 254.

52 Roald Dahl, *Sometime Never* (London: Collins, 1949), p. 158.

53 Dahl, *The Collected Short Stories*, p. 318. Outside the WW2 flying stories, Dahl's anti-bombing sentiments make rare undisguised appearances. The most explicit of these occurs during an exchange between the BFG and Sophie about humankind's propensity for violence against itself: '"human beans is squishing *each other* all the time," the BFG said. "They is shootling guns and going up in aerioplanes to drop their bombs on each other's heads every week"'; Roald Dahl, *The BFG* (London: Jonathan Cape, 1982), p. 100.

54 Sturrock covers the incident in *Storyteller*, p. 59. The incident is perhaps recalled in Dahl's poem 'The Cow' from *Dirty Beasts* (1983). The flying cow, Daisy, drops a cowpat on a man standing beneath her: 'She dived, and using all her power / She got to sixty miles an hour. / "Bombs gone," she cried.

"Take that!" she said, / And dropped a cowpat on his head'; Roald Dahl, *Dirty Beasts* (London: Penguin, 2001 [1983]), p. 22.

55 Dahl, *James and the Giant Peach*, p. 133.
56 Dahl, *James and the Giant Peach*, pp. 137–8.
57 Treglown, *Roald Dahl*, p. 46.
58 Roald Dahl, *Charlie and the Chocolate Factory* (London: Puffin, 2001 [1964]), p. 154. *Charlie and the Great Glass Elevator* includes a comparable passage: 'Everybody clutched hold of everybody else and as the great machine gathered speed, the rushing whooshing sound of the wind outside grew louder and louder and shriller and shriller until it became a piercing shriek and you had to yell to make yourself heard'; Roald Dahl, *Charlie and the Great Glass Elevator* (London: Penguin, 2001 [1972]), p. 12. The description recalls Dahl's memory of first climbing into a Tiger Moth with the engine running, putting his head into the slipstream and getting 'a rush of wind full in the face'; Dahl, *Going Solo*, p. 85.
59 Dahl, *Charlie and the Chocolate Factory*, p. 187
60 See Sturrock, *Storyteller*, p. 159. Dahl's family survived, and moved to Quainton, forty miles north-west of London.
61 Dahl, *Charlie and the Chocolate Factory*, p. 180.
62 Sturrock, *Storyteller*, p. 156.
63 Hollindale, 'And Children Swarmed to Him Like Settlers', p. 278. See also Treglown, *Roald Dahl*, pp. 19–23.
64 Dahl, *Boy*, p. 50.
65 Dahl, *Going Solo*, p. 101.
66 Dahl, *The Collected Short Stories*, p. 224.
67 Sturrock, *Storyteller*, p. 160.
68 Dahl, *Boy*, p. 51.
69 In 1939, Dahl exhorted his mother to move from Bexley back to Wales: 'It's absolute madness to stay anywhere in the East of England now. You'll have parachute troops landing on the lawn if you don't look out'; *Going Solo*, p. 76.
70 Dahl, *Charlie and the Great Glass Elevator*, pp. 25–6.
71 Dahl, *Charlie and the Great Glass Elevator*, pp. 12–13, 14.
72 Dahl, *Charlie and the Chocolate Factory*, p. 180.

Works cited

Dahl, Roald, *The BFG* (London: Jonathan Cape, 1982).
—, *Boy: Tales of Childhood* (London: Puffin, 1986 [1984]).
—, *Charlie and the Chocolate Factory* (London: Puffin, 2001 [1964]).
—, *Going Solo* (London: Puffin, 1988 [1986]).
—, *James and the Giant Peach* (London: Puffin, 2001 [1961]).
—, *The Minpins* (London: Penguin, 2008 [1991]).

—, 'Someone Like You', *The Collected Short Stories of Roald Dahl* (London: Penguin, 1992), pp. 317–23.

—, *Sometime Never* (London: Collins, 1949).

Butler, Catherine, 'Introduction', in *Roald Dahl* (New Casebooks), ed. Ann Alston and Catherine Butler (Basingstoke: Palgrave Macmillan, 2012), pp. 1–13.

Balaev, Michelle, *The Nature of Trauma in American Novels* (Evanston, IL: Northwestern University Press, 2012).

Caruth, Cathy, *Unclaimed Experience: Trauma, Narrative and History* (Baltimore, MD: Johns Hopkins University Press, 1996).

— (ed.), *Trauma: Explorations in Memory* (Baltimore, MD: Johns Hopkins University Press, 1995).

Crago, Hugo, *Entranced By Story: Brain, Tale and Teller, from Infancy to Old Age* (London: Routledge, 2014).

Hollindale, Peter, 'And Children Swarmed to Him Like Settlers. He Became a Land: The Outrageous Success of Roald Dahl', in *Popular Children's Literature in Britain*, ed. Julia Briggs, Dennis Butts and Matthew Orville Grenby (Aldershot: Ashgate, 2008), pp. 271–86.

Lennon, Peter, 'A Bumpy Ride to Fantasy', interview with Roald Dahl, *The Times*, 22 December 1983, p. 8.

Luckhurst, Roger, *The Trauma Question* (London: Routledge, 2008).

Onega, Susana, and Jean-Michel Ganteau, 'Traumatic Realism and Romance in Contemporary British Narrative', in *Trauma and Romance in Contemporary British Literature*, ed. Susana Onega and Jean-Michel Ganteau (Routledge: London, 2014), pp. 1–16.

Sturrock, Donald, *Storyteller: The Life of Roald Dahl* (London: HarperPress, 2010).

Treglown, Jeremy, *Roald Dahl: A Biography* (London: Faber and Faber, 1994).

Whitehead, Anne, *Trauma Fiction* (Edinburgh: Edinburgh University Press, 2004).

6

Dahl and Dylan:
Matilda, 'In Country Sleep' and
Twentieth-century Topographies of Fear

Damian Walford Davies

1. A Complex Cocktail

When Roald Dahl wrote 'Second Draft 4/12/86' at the head of a manuscript that would eventually be published – in a radically different form
– as *Matilda* in 1988, it is likely he was fully aware of the work's structural
and conceptual limitations. In his writing hut at Great Missenden that
winter, as he drew towards him the electric heater he had enterprisingly
strung aloft on two wires, Dahl was wrestling with a tale, provisionally
entitled 'The Six-Year-Old Wonder' (previously 'The Miracle Child'), in
which Matilda was 'born wicked' and in which her teacher, Miss Hayes
– the prototype of Miss Honey – was a gambling addict with a bookie
father.[1] His US editor, Stephen Roxburgh, would play a significant (and
unacknowledged) role in suggesting the major revisions that would yield
the book as we now have it – Dahl's final long story for children.[2] Dahl
was physically exhausted following two operations for diverticulitis the
previous year; indeed, although he had stolidly borne the chronic back
pain caused by his crash in the Western Desert in September 1940, by
1967 – as Donald Sturrock observes – 'the complex cocktail of pain-
killers that comprised his medication was no longer able to deal wth
his worsening spinal and sciatic pain', and he had been in poor health
throughout the 1970s.[3] The evidence of the manuscripts reveals that as
he drafted and redrafted *Matilda*, Dahl in the second half of 1986 was
preoccupied with others' physical vulnerability, too, and was seeking a

purchase, late in life, on the tragedies that had beset his family, almost like a curse, since the early 1960s.

Focusing in this essay on early drafts of *Matilda*, and offering an engagement with Dahl's little-known work of fantasy, *Sometime Never* (1948), I explore for the first time Dahl's complex registrations of his lifelong anxieties concerning his own health, the welfare of his family and his fears concerning the future of humankind, first in the age of the atom bomb and subsequently in the age of global, mutually assured thermonuclear destruction. I attend in particular to the uncanny irruption into the second draft of *Matilda* – at a moment of crucial connection between Matilda and Miss Hayes/Honey – of a late poem by Dylan Thomas, Dahl's compatriot, fellow celebrity and, as I will suggest, troubling second self. This invocation of Thomas marks a nodal site of fear that gathers to itself nearly half a century of disquiet, pain and trauma. It also maps Dahl's topographies of fear, bringing Great Missenden, the landscapes of a layered Welsh pastoral, Hiroshima and Nagasaki, and New York into suggestive alignment. Behind Dahl's unprecedented struggle with the writing and revision process in *Matilda* is his need to comprehend and represent the ways in which he had been deeply marked by a series of personal calamities and by fear of the mushroom cloud.

The first draft of *Matilda* reveals Dahl in the summer of 1986 to have been much preoccupied by accidents and death. Having already displayed her miraculous telekinetic power in school, Matilda accompanies Miss Hayes to the latter's cottage – a paradigmatic site of Dahl's complex of fears, as we shall see – remarking blithely on the way:

> I'm going to be a doctor, a doctor who . . . saves children's lives and I would like to discover a great medicine and all you have to do is take one dose when you're a baby and you'll never be ill again in your life! . . . I will invent good-behaviour pills and everyone in the world will take two of them once a year and they will make it impossible for you to be bad or to be a burglar or a murderer or to shoot anybody so there would never be any more wars . . . [4]

In the context of the narrative ecology of this first draft, it is an incongruous statement (the 'good-behaviour pills' are a disturbing amalgam of philanthropic idealism, state regulation and the oral carnivalesque of *Charlie and the Chocolate Factory* (1964)) that seems to gesture at a need on the part of the author himself to believe in miracles – here, the protective power of medical science. Later in the same draft, as Miss Hayes accompanies Matilda home from the cottage, the child's precocious outpouring of love ('perhaps I can make miracles happen and people will learn to be kind to one another . . . kindness is the only thing') is interrupted by police and ambulance sirens.[5] They encounter a 'nightmare scene' on the by-pass, where a 'container truck' has crushed a minibus full of school children. It is clear that some of the children are dead; others remain trapped: 'You could hear the kids screaming inside it', an onlooker observes.[6] The incident did not survive revision, but one might suggest that this highway carnage is gathered into the unnerving detail, introduced in the third draft, that stands at the beginning of the chapter 'Miss Honey's Cottage' in the published novel, in which Matilda and her teacher, en route to her cottage, pass 'the butcher with bloody lumps of meat on display and naked chickens hanging up'.[7] Both Matilda's telekinetic powers and her philanthropic conversion (akin to a spiritual convincement) are figured in this first draft in terms of a massive release of hidden force, at once devastating and creative: 'It seemed as though a valve had burst open somewhere inside her and a great gush of intense stored-up energy was being released from her body and brain.'[8] With only minor inflections, the description appears in the book as published. I suggest these unnerving motifs of child death, accident, theft, murder and energy discharge are registrations, late in Dahl's writing career, of the series of catastrophes that befell him and his family and of his own fear of nuclear destruction, precipitated, of course, by the dropping of atom bombs on Japan in 1945 and never fully exorcised by the author. These calamities, and Dahl's response to the possibility of megadeath (a term that entered the language around 1953, the year of Dylan Thomas's death), need to be rehearsed in order to provide the full context in which the introduction, into the second draft of *Matilda*, of a 1947 poem by Thomas is to be understood. That poem – a richly dense and paradoxical prayer for his daughter and address to his wife – is implicated in Thomas's own private and public fears.

2. Malignant Spells

Dahl was not, it seems, a superstitious man, but as Sturrock notes, it was difficult for him not to believe that he and his family were plagued

by some 'malignant neurological spell'.[9] Famously, Dahl himself suffered massive head injuries in September 1940 – what he termed (with
a hint of understatement proper to his officer class and its English values) 'a monumental bash on the head' – when he crashed his Gloster
Gladiator in the Western Desert of Libya.[10] His spinal injuries would
result in debilitating, chronic pain, and it has been persuasively argued
that the accident's neurological consequences – part of what might
now be diagnosed as 'postconcussive syndrome' – involved a significant alteration in personality and an augmented 'sense of fantasy'.[11] In
complex but convincing ways (Dahl himself certainly believed so), Dahl
the writer was born in the buckled, flaming cockpit of his Gladiator (a
space of both comfort and terror, insight and blindness, earthfast rootedness and aerial acrobatics he sought to replicate in his writing hut
at Great Missenden, which was partly modelled on Thomas's writing
shed in Laugharne).[12]

In 1960, on the corner of Madison and 85th Street in New York,
'the pram carrying Roald's sleeping four-month-old baby, Theo, was
hit by a cab' and was 'propelled 40 feet through the air' and 'crushed
against the side of a bus'.[13] Theo was diagnosed with a 'terrific neurological deficit', and sustained multiple fractures of the skull. A number
of invasive surgical procedures, initially only intermittently successful, were needed to drain fluid from Theo's brain – fluid that at one
point caused him to go blind. Pitifully, Theo 'would be rushed back
into hospital after convulsing, leaving his parents to face once more
his "huge, desolate, bewildered eyes" when he awoke in the emer-
gency room'.[14] Theo recovered, but his health kept Dahl and his wife,
Patricia Neal, 'on the jump constantly'.[15] Since the cerebral valves
designed to relieve the pressure of fluid on the brain that were then
in use functioned less than optimally, Dahl collaborated with a preci-
sion metal turner, Stanley Wade, and a neurosurgeon, Kenneth Till,
to produce the 'Wade-Dahl-Till Valve', which helped save the lives of
over 3,000 children. The burst 'valve' in Matilda's brain both registers
and euphemises that neurological horror of 1960.

In 1962, in an uncanny repetition of his own father's experience
(Harald Dahl had lost his seven-year-old daughter Astri to peritonitis in 1920), Dahl's seven-year-old daughter Olivia contracted
measles encephalitis – a brain inflammation arising from measles –
and was rushed to hospital, Dahl following the ambulance through
the Buckinghamshire lanes. Olivia died in hospital; her death left

her father 'limp with despair' and precipitated what Patricia Neal referred to as 'the landslide of danger and frustration' that came close to breaking the family and which was one of the many elements that contributed to the couple's estrangement and, ultimately, their divorce in 1983.[16] Sturrock remarks that Dahl felt plagued by 'sinister forces': having believed himself and his family to be protected from these malign energies in his 'rural enclave' in Buckinghamshire – seemingly a world away from the death-haunted corners of Manhattan – he had found that they had pursued him even there.[17] Neither Dahl's valorisation of the rural from the late 1940s – to which I shall return – nor any fatherly effort on his part could offer a bulwark against harm. Neal remarked that she felt 'as if the family were living through the Book of Job'.[18] Driven always by a need to protect and provide for his family, Dahl was left wretchedly aware of the limits of parental care in the face of accident and illness. The Matilda of the novel's first draft – who, as we have seen, imagines a world in which 'all you have to do is take one dose when you're a baby and you'll never be ill again in your life!' – is, I suggest, Olivia returned, crying out for vaccination and for the immunisation of the world's children, as Dahl himself did publicly following Olivia's death, his most robust communication to parents being the letter he issued in 1986, the year of the drafting of *Matilda*.[19]

The Dahls' misfortune continued, and America once again became the site of family trauma. In 1965 in Hollywood, where she was filming John Ford's *Seven Women*, Patricia Neal experienced a 'terrific pain' in her head, which suddenly 'jerked back'; Dahl, who was present in the house in Pacific Palisades, knew she was suffering a stroke and immediately telephoned one of Los Angeles's most distinguished neurosurgeons.[20] Pat had suffered two cerebral haemorrhages; in hospital she suffered a third, massive rupture, 'caused by an aneurysm'. '[B]esieged by tubes', she lay for three weeks in a coma.[21] *Variety* prematurely announced the death of the Oscar-winning actress. She woke to find herself without movement or speech. As is widely known, so began the long and painful process of Neal's astonishing recuperation, in which Dahl played a vigorously practical and unsentimental role.[22]

The series of cranial catastrophes and neurological nightmares was not yet over, however. In 1978, Charlotte, the daughter of Llandaff-born Felicity ('Liccy') Crosland, with whom Dahl had been in a relationship since the early 1970s and whom he was to marry in 1983, was involved in a car accident that resulted in a 'severely fractured skull' and a coma.[23] Jeremy Treglown notes that during the final two decades of Dahl's life, 'the lives of his daughters, particularly Tessa and Lucy, were to be characterized by an emotional storminess for which he felt partly responsible [and] which he couldn't calm.'[24] As we shall see, in 1986 Dahl would turn to Dylan Thomas to help articulate a prayer for daughters both dead and living. Dahl's fatherly and spousal instincts, his self-identification as paterfamilias and as robust guardian of the Dahl clan, had already sustained multiple shocks when appallingly, in February 1990, nine months before Dahl's own death, Liccy's twenty-six-year-old daughter Lorina died of an aneurysm caused by a 'tumour on her brain'.[25]

3. Atomic Fears: *Sometime Never*

Bound up in drafts of *Matilda* and its published version alongside imaginative inscriptions of the traumas outlined above are Dahl's deep-seated fears concerning nuclear holocaust – fears in which Dylan Thomas's post-1945 work is also saturated. Posted to the British Embassy in Washington in 1942 as Assistant Air Attaché, tasked with securing the support of America's political elite and its public for the British war effort, Dahl seems from the first to have been involved in covert intelligence work. Certainly, by April 1944 he was an employee of William Stephenson's British Security Coordination (BSC), whose remit was to counteract anti-British interests in the US and cultivate pro-British feeling through the manipulation of the American media.[26] Dahl was at BSC's installation, Camp X, on the shores of Lake Ontario when the mushroom clouds rose over Hiroshima and Nagasaki in August 1945. Inured as he must have been by then to the moral murkiness of espionage and of wartime geopolitical strategy, his shock when the *Enola Gay* dropped 'Little Boy' and the *Bockscar* dropped 'Fat Man' was profound. The name of the former forever ironised Dahl's own persona, 'Boy' – which is how he had signed his schoolboy letters to his mother, and which was to be the title of his first fabling autobiography, published in 1984. Dahl returned to England in the summer of 1946 haunted by a new fear; as Sturrock remarks, 'even as his ocean liner steamed across the Atlantic, he saw both his own and his family's futures blighted by a sinister new threat: the mushroom cloud of imminent nuclear holocaust.'[27]

First at Grendon Underwood, at the heart of the Buckinghamshire countryside, then at nearby Grange Farm, Great Missenden, nuclear peril became his fixation throughout 1946. Sturrock confirms that Dahl was at this time 'haunted' by the power of the atomic weapon and the threat it posed to humanity – indeed, 'preoccupied . . . to the point of obsession'.[28] Terrified and imaginatively stirred by the atomic – and later, thermonuclear – threat, both Dahl and Dylan Thomas were to intervene in post-war debates concerning 'the meaning of the atomic bomb', contributing vitally to the already dense store of images in cultural circulation, drawing on (and inflecting) the motifs and generic expectations of science fiction inherited from the 'future war stor[ies]' that magazines, films and radio programmes had imagined.[29] It was in late summer 1946 that Dahl read John Hersey's stunning 31,000-word article on Hiroshima, to which *The New Yorker* had devoted an entire issue on 31 August. As Patrick B. Sharp has emphasised, in its focus on the effects – immediate and lingering – of US superscience on six individuals in Hiroshima, Hersey's article contested and undermined both the long-established 'Yellow Peril stories of science fiction' and the version of the Hiroshima narrative that had been carefully curated by the American government and military since 6 August 1945.[30] In its early forms, that official narrative elided the effects of the explosions on humans in favour of an account that emphasised justified retribution, the need to terminate the war, and the effect of the blasts on the built environment. In contrast, Hersey's intervention foregrounded 'the subjective experience of the victims' and relegated the 'objective language of blast effects' to 'parenthetic comments'.[31] Much of the power of Hersey's *Hiroshima*, which has been seen as a forerunner of the 'New Journalism' and which was the product of on-the-ground research, lies in the uncanny effects generated by its conflation of fiction and reportage and their mutually ironising interplay. Profound horror, revulsion and pity are all the more forcefully communicated for being always held at bay in the article's innovative (and disconcerting) hybrid discourse. Dahl felt the need to discuss his fear of nuclear holocaust with his friend Dennis Pearl and with his American mentor, the newspaper mogul Charles Marsh. Hersey's article did not engender atomic terror in Dahl; it confirmed it.

Having published *Over to You* in 1946, an expertly controlled and psychologically acute collection of short stories that fictionalised his own wartime experience, Dahl responded to the nuclear threat of

the immediate post-war years in the form of a generically and stylisti-
cally hybrid fantasy that had the distinction of being 'the first novel to
address the destructive power of the atom bomb' – *Sometime Never*, published in Britain in 1949 after its appearance in the US under the title
Some Time Never: A Fable for Supermen in April the previous year.[32] The
novel sought to exploit the cultural capital surrounding the machine-
age (and specifically British air force) folklore of the 'gremlins'. These
were the imp-like 'saboteurs' (complete with tails, horns and green
bowler hats), bent on wreaking mechanical havoc on aircraft, that had
been part of RAF mythology since the 1920s, and which Dahl had
popularised in the 1943 story, *The Gremlins* (published with the assistance of Walt Disney, with whom a Gremlins film had been planned).[33]
That the gremlins were an externalisation by RAF pilots of the profound terror of aerial combat is clear.

Treglown sees in *Sometime Never* an 'unsuredness of style', arguing
that the novel 'cannot decide whether it is for adults or for children'
and that 'the resulting clashes of tone are bizarre.'[34] Certainly, fabu-
lism, phantasmagoria, motifs from fairy tales and from science fiction
(both pulp and literary), 'cartoon-strip satire', political lampoon and
'anal humour' cohabit dislocatingly with lyrical pastoral, inhabitations
of the psychology of fighter pilots, Hersey-influenced reportage, and a
self-conscious modality of anti-nuclear polemic and historiography.[35]
Dahl's American literary agent (and surrogate parent), Ann Watkins
(at this time also Dylan Thomas's agent), had offered suggestions for
revisions, and it is true that a somewhat nervous Dahl went out of his
way to seek others' reassurance concerning the bold moves of *Sometime
Never*.[36] When the novel appeared, *The Saturday Review* drew attention
to what it regarded as the 'cumbrousness' of the book's 'supernatural
machinery', while the *Times Literary Supplement* found 'the whimsical
Gremlins mythology . . . an irritating imposition'.[37] I suggest, however,
that the work's generic and stylistic hybridity is the result, not of any
artistic 'confusions' (Treglown's word again) on Dahl's part, but rather
of a carefully calibrated decision to communicate the 'confusions',
horrific absurdity and irrationality of the atomic mindset itself, and
the destabilising sense that sci-fi literary and celluloid fantasy – at the
moment of Little Boy's detonation in freefall at 08:16 Japan Standard
Time, 44.4 seconds after release – had actually come true. To argue,
as Treglown does, that the book's main interest lies 'in its revelation
of Dahl's volatile mood at the time' is to refuse to contest both the

wounded (in all senses) Dahl's response to its lukewarm reception – he described it as a 'bad book' – and to miss the novel's daring conflation of contemporary folklore, apocalyptic narrative, atomic trauma and ecological parable, together with its complex acts of mapping.[38]

I argue that *Sometime Never* offers a series of cartographies of atomic terror comprising multiple topographies of fear: a Neo-Romantic Kentish landscape of burgeoning hops, oast houses and aerodromes, from which the three airmen Peternip, Stuffy and Progboot operate in Part 1 (and which in the light of what follows functions as an act of memorialisation, a Domesday chorography); the blasted, post-World War III nuclear landscapes of Greece, France and America; and the global network of underground tunnels in which the Gremlins await the 'Great Day' when humans, 'doomed to disappear', commit self-murder on a planet that is referred to at one point as 'the War Star'. Most impressive among these mappings is the *tour de force* post-apocalyptic psychogeographical *dérive* that the confounded and irradiated Stuffy takes from the darkness of Piccadilly Street underground station through obliterated, ground zero central London (the spectral, layered, 'unreal city' of high Modernism here in its razed atomic death) out into the fields at the city's margins:[39]

'Jesus Christ Almighty,' whispered the man beside him. 'Lord God Jesus Christ Almighty.' Then he leaned forward and vomited quietly between his legs.

. . .

He moved on across Oxford Circus and up Regent Street toward the Queen's Hall, still thinking, in a vague and dreamy way, about Peternip . . .

. . .

Then he saw him. He knew him at once by the size and shape of his body and by the way he lay there on the ground. He knew for certain it was Peternip and he strolled slowly over to the body and stood beside it, looking down at it and seeing the way the hands were clasped together with the skin hanging loosely from them like two gloves half taken off, seeing the red-black face, the scorched and melted flesh upon the face, the empty eyes, the hair burnt off, and seeing now the knees drawn up close under the stomach and the grey suit half-burnt, half-singed, lying in fragments over the pale blue shirt which showed clean and untouched underneath.

. . .

It is very perfect, this London of ours, and the people too are perfect,
which is a comforting thing to consider when one walks alone in a big city
at eventide.[40]

It is an expertly choreographed episode. In such descriptions of the
effects of a nuclear strike on a major city, its prescient envisioning of
the deployment by 'medical humans' of chemical and biological warfare and the use of drones ('small and incredibly swift pilotless planes'),
and its considered diagnosis of the debilitating existential 'fear of the
future' engendered by the atomic age, *Sometime Never* taps into what the
shifting narrator-persona describes as a horror 'secretly harboured in
the heart', which lies 'half visible, half out of sight somewhere between
the seven layers of skin'.[41] It is clear from *Sometime Never* that Dahl's
fear of the future operated on two, uncannily linked, scalar levels, and
that his horror of a nuclear cataclysm was allied *from the first* with a
fear of deadly neurological harm – which, as we have seen, so tragi-
cally came to pass. In Dahl's novel, following World War III and the
further proliferation of nuclear and bacterial weaponry, a Chinese sci-
entist isolates a cerebral virus drawn from 'a rare deep-sea fish known
as Piscortes Vulmen', subjects it to radiation, and injects it into human
subjects who die horribly of an 'encephalitis' (a type of the acute brain
inflammation that killed Dahl's beloved Olivia). Thus 'Virus Mists' are
developed, to be carried by drones as weapons of war.[42] Dahl dared
to imagine 'the pleasant possibilities of the future' in scenarios that
conflated megadeath and deadly neurological damage at the level of
the individual.

Such horror would be harboured throughout Dahl's career, and
would issue, I argue, in euphemised, but unmistakably tagged, forms
such as the giant peach at the end of its transatlantic flight above New
York in *James and the Giant Peach* (1961). The peach is taken by a panicked nation to be 'the biggest bomb in the history of the world' (the
image resonates anew post-9/11).[43] It is no coincidence that the novel
appeared at the high-water mark of the debate concerning 'the moral-
ity of possessing nuclear weapons' and in the very same year as the
detonation (here one repeats Dahl's own words) of the biggest bomb
in the history of the world, the Soviet Union's *Tsar Bomba*. This was a
thermonuclear device that yielded 1,500 times the combined energy of
the two bombs dropped on Japan.[44]

In *The Rise of Nuclear Fear*, Spencer R. Weart contends that during the 1940s and 1950s, cultural critics clearly recognised that the raft of radioactive creatures that populated contemporary sci-fi magazines and films 'were personifications of nuclear bombs'. Weart emphasises that, more accurately, 'in the popular imagination the creatures filled vacant space where the public declined to look at real bombs'.[45] As various histories of nuclear fear have reminded us, by the late 1950s and early 1960s, when anti-nuclear feeling began to be debated and conceptualised in the world press, when '[d]isarmament activism' was being mobilised, and when the 'image of the victimized child' had become a powerful element of anti-nuclear protest, the public was certainly looking squarely at the prospect of nuclear holocaust and its horrific aftermath of 'death dust'.[46] In this context, the bomb-peach with its payload of giant ('magically' irradiated mutant) creatures is the ghost of pre-bomb pulp fiction, appearing now above Manhattan's skyscrapers in a new culture of fear. The artificial distinction between adult fiction and children's fantasy that has hitherto prevented Dahl from being seen whole should not occlude the fact that *James and the Giant Peach* is just as much a 'novel of [atomic age] ideas' as *Sometime Never* (which, as already noted, is itself intimately related to Dahl's 1943 children's tale, *The Gremlins*). James's peach is Dahl's 'personalized Bomb', the product of a Dahlian 'angst' concerning World War that Ann Watkins had described a decade before as 'melodramatic and bloody'.[47]

4. Back to the Future: *Matilda*, Dark Pastoral, Dylan Thomas

It is the same angst – new only in the ways in which it is conditioned by the particular geopolitical and technological realities of the early 1980s and the second great upsurge in nuclear fear to which they gave rise – that saturates the late chapter, 'Miss Honey's Cottage', in *Matilda*, to which we can now return to calibrate the precise uses to which Dahl puts Dylan Thomas's own atomic anxiety and post-apocalyptic imaginings. As I have already established, the manuscript evidence reveals the difficulty Dahl was having as he formulated the unorthodox relationship between the precocious Matilda and the teacher who, in the published novel, is in crucial ways herself a child, in need of protection and deliverance. At this point in his drafting, Dahl drew into suggestive alignment – within an ambiguous 'fairy-tale deep structure' that was intimately related to the values of the rural – his chronic disquiet concerning thermonuclear destruction, the trauma of personal loss, and reflections on his relationship with his adult children.[48] Dylan Thomas provides both a text and a parallel experience through which Dahl's culturally and psychologically complex bundle of fears achieves expression. Further, invoking Thomas involves triangulating Japanese, English, American and Welsh topographies of fear. While this may seem an impossible weight for a touching episode in a children's book to bear, the continuum that is Dahl's hybrid writing career, together with the profound dread of nuclear holocaust that fuelled his apocalyptic imagination, argue otherwise.

The early 1980s was a period of 'war fever revival' following the multiplication of intercontinental and shorter-range nuclear weapons by both superpowers in the late 1970s and the intermediate-range weapons face-off between eastern Europe and NATO states. As David Cortright argues, the Soviet invasion of Afghanistan in December 1979 catalysed 'a renewed Cold War response in the United States which paved the way for the election of Ronald Reagan' (alongside whom Patricia Neal had performed more than once), whose early administration, trumpeting a perceived American 'window of vulnerability', was committed to military spending and clung 'to the option of "first use"'.[49] In response, campaigns for a 'nuclear freeze' and for disarmament again gained widespread publicity and support, becoming once more – as it had done in the late 1950s and early 1960s – 'radically democratized' as 'nuclear fear reached unprecedented levels' in the early 1980s.[50] At Greenham Common, in major European cities and across the United States, massive 'antinuclear peace mobilizations' were a reflection of a traumatic fear that the present writer himself remembers experiencing only too vividly as a child and young adult. Calling for a 'guarantee of existence for the unborn' and an acknowledgement of 'the honor and the humanity of the living', Jonathan Schell's era-defining nonfiction work, *The Fate of the Earth* (1982), crystallised that fear and conceptualised the ethical argument against nuclear weapons in formulations that brought past, present and future into a living ethical relationship.[51] Though more than three decades apart, Schell's entreaty – at once muscular and lyrical – and Dahl's *Sometime Never* are driven by the same moral, ecological, philosophical and psychological analyses:

By acting to save the species, and repopulating the future, we break out of the cramped, claustrophobic isolation of a doomed present, and open a path to the greater space – the only space fit for human habitation – of past, present, and future . . . By threatening life in its totality, the nuclear peril creates new connections between the elements of human existence – a new mingling of the public and the private, the political and the emotional, the spiritual and the biological.[52]

Schell emphasised that a decision to 'open a path' to the future would amount to 'a form of love' that would 'bear a resemblance to the generative love of parents'; once again, it was the figure of the vulnerable child, and the love of her parents and guardians, that most powerfully focused the issue.[53] Dahl would have seconded George F. Kennan's appeal in 1982: 'Surely there is among us . . . a sufficient health of the spirit, a sufficient affirmation of life . . . to permit us to slough off this morbid preoccupation, to see it and discard it as the illness it is.'[54] But thermonuclear fear was itself a 'morbid preoccupation' that Dahl could not exorcise. Though the superpowers were 'frightened enough' by 1984 'to seek an accommodation', Dahl would have to wait until the signing of the Intermediate-range Nuclear Forces Treaty at the Washington Summit of December 1987 before a measure of that anxiety lifted.[55] As he wrote and revised *Matilda*, however, the lack of a substantive breakthrough between the Reagan and Gorbachev administrations at summits in Geneva (November 1985) and, 'in the shadow of Chernobyl', in Reykjavík (October 1986) would have only confirmed his fears.[56]

This climate of renewed dread in the early 1980s, together with the data conceptualised so far in this essay, form the background against which the complex evolution of *Matilda* and the invocation of Dylan Thomas can illuminatingly be seen. In the chapter entitled simply 'The Cottage' in the novel's first draft, Dahl has Miss Hayes walk with Matilda to a space that would in the second draft be significantly more layered, both physically and symbolically. In the first draft, the teacher's modest but 'wonderfully cosy' home is 'a tiny white cottage with a thatched roof' that stands 'alone in its garden surrounded by green meadows' down 'a narrow lane' beyond the busy by-pass.[57] Revisions that belong to a second draft amplify the evocation of rural topography – initial work towards establishing the context in which Dahl would soon feel the need to invoke Dylan Thomas:

They came finally to a <five-barred> gate on the left-hand side of the road. 'This way,' Miss Hayes said and she opened the gate and led Matilda through and closed it again. They were now walking along a narrow <lane that was no more than a> rutted cart-track. There was a high hedge of hazel-nut on either side and could [*sic*] see clusters of nuts up among the leaves. The nuts were still green but they were beginning to ripen and soon the squirrels would have them. The bank below the hedge on the left was yellow with celandines.[58]

Further work towards a second full draft adds seasonal specificity – 'It was a golden early summer's afternoon and there were splashes of white hawthorne [*sic*] on the hedge-Tops' – that unmistakably keys this landscape into the contingent, vulnerable pastoral with which *Sometime Never* had begun:

> That year the warm weather came at the beginning of March and almost at once the leaf-buds on the hedges and on the trees swelled and began to burst before their time. Soon there was a pale powdering of green over all the countryside . . . Then suddenly the blackthorn blossomed, shining white along the tops of the hedges, primroses made splashes of yellow in the long grass . . . In August the Germans came.[59]

It is likely Dahl is drawing in both instances on the local topography of Great Missenden and the Misbourne valley in the Chiltern Hills – the enclave he had embraced in the late 1940s as seeming to offer protection against the world's malign forces, but which had proved to be just as much a place of fear and accident as the corner of Madison and 85th (a memory gathered into the account of the calamity on the English by-pass in the second draft of *Matilda*) and the bedroom of the rented house in Los Angeles into which he had rushed to find his wife wretchedly 'covered in vomit' and 'unable to recognize her own children' following her stroke.[60]

Sturrock emphasises the strength of Dahl's lifelong commitment to a 'pastoral ideal' and a 'gipsy ideal'.[61] Described by his second wife Liccy as a 'countryman through and through', Dahl cultivated the persona of an 'eccentric Arcadian' who was regarded by metropolitan arbiters of taste as a 'rural maverick'.[62] It is clear that his valorisation of the rural can be traced to his boyhood at the farm estate of Tŷ Mynydd, Radyr, north-west of Cardiff, which 'came to embody a kind of paradise, irretrievably taken from [him] at a very young age' following the death of his father.[63] However, Dahl always understood the pastoral ideal to be a fragile and ambiguous affair, a fantasy whose darker human and non-human ecologies he exposed in short stories published in *Someone Like You* (1953) and *Kiss, Kiss* (1960). Smartly referencing Jacqueline Susann's 1966 novel of sex(ism), neurological and psychological damage, cancer, barbiturate dependence and abortion, *Valley of the Dolls*, the description Dahl's daughter Tessa offered of the family settlement in and around Great Missenden – 'The Valley of the Dahls' – captures her father's own acknowledgement of pastoral's pathologies.[64]

It is in Dahl's work towards a second draft of *Matilda* that Miss Hayes's cottage and the co-dependent relationship between adult and child begin to take on the ambiguous resonances of fairy tale. Miss Hayes leads Matilda to a 'farm labourer's cottage' of red brick that looks 'more like a doll's-house'; at the gate, Matilda 'hung back', though nothing in this draft accounts for her apprehension, other than the description of the garden, perhaps, which was 'now a wilderness of nettles and blackberry bushes and long brown grass'.[65] Subsequent drafting introduces a feature that emphasises the embowered, secret nature of the dwelling: the oak tree whose 'massive spreading branches seemed to be enfolding and embracing the tiny building, and perhaps hiding it as well from the rest of the world'.[66]

It is at this point – an uneasy intertextual pastoral now established – that Dahl calls on the work of Dylan Thomas, and does so in ways that enhance our understanding of the former's negotiation of 'folk and fairy tale conventions'.[67] Dahl had long been an admirer of Thomas; although there is no evidence to confirm the supposition, it is entirely possible that Dahl, resident in New York between 1951 and 1954, saw Thomas on one of his American tours. There is no explicit surviving reference by Dahl to Thomas's death in the city on 9 November 1953 from the infamous 'insult to the brain' (that deathly neurological spell once more); however, I suggest that the chapter of *Matilda* Dahl was drafting in the latter part of 1986 constitutes a point of intense engagement with Thomas as fellow-Welshman, husband and father, and as a writer whose horror of atomic apocalypse had matched his own. On BBC radio's *Desert Island Discs*, Dahl's choice, in October 1979, of Thomas reading 'Fern Hill' is significant, not only since it took Dahl back to the swallow-thronged lofts of his own lost Welsh country upbringing at Tŷ Mynydd, but also because of his realisation, in a climate of heightened nuclear tension at the close of the 1970s, that Thomas's poem articulated a post-atomic pastoral, haunted by the central concern of his own *Sometime Never*: 'fear of the future'. It is on similar ground that Thomas is summoned again in the imaginative space of *Matilda* in the autumn of 1986.

Following the description of the spreading oak in the second full draft, Dahl begins his act of embedding Dylan Thomas in this nascent fairy tale topography of fear. It is worth citing the layers of drafting at some length:

> <Miss Hayes, with one hand on the gate which she had not yet opened, turned to Matilda and said,>
> 'A poet called Dylan Thomas once wrote some lines that I think of every time I walk up this path,
>
> To eat your heart in the house in the lovely [lonely?] wood.[68]

The evidence of the holograph suggests that Dahl then added, above the (misquoted) line of verse, 'Matilda waited, and Miss Hayes', before proceeding on a fresh sheet of his yellow American legal pad:

> in a rather wonderful slow voice, began reciting the poem:
>
> 'Never and never, my girl riding far and near
> In the land of the hearthstone Tales, and spelled asleep,
> Fear or believe that the wolf in the sheepwhite hood
> Loping and bleating roughly and blithely shall leap,
> My dear, my dear,
> Out of a lair of [*sic*] in the flocked leaves in the dew dipped year
> To eat your heart in the house in the rosy wood.'
>
> There was a moment of silence, and Matilda, who had never before heard great romantic poetry spoken aloud, was profoundly moved. 'It's like music,' she whispered.
> 'It is music,' Miss Hayes said.[69]

Keying the addition back, mid-sentence, to the previous sheet (and drafting further additions on another, separate page), Dahl's draft proceeds in substantially the form in which the text was finally published:

> And then, as though embarrassed at having revealed such a secret part of herself, she quickly pushed open the gate and walked up the path. Matilda hung back. She was a bit frightened of this place now. It seemed so unreal and remote and fantastic and so totally away from this earth. It was like an illustration in Grimm or Hans Andersen. It was the house where the poor woodcutter lived with Hansel and Gretel and where Red Riding Hood's grandmother lived and it was also the house of The Seven Dwarfs and The Three Bears and all the rest of them. It was straight out of a fairy-tale.[70]

Here, it is the implications of Thomas's poem, teased out below, that cause Matilda to hang back. Further, it is clear from the evidence cited above that it is the introduction of Thomas's lines that prompts Dahl's explicit invocation, in the section quoted above, of the fairy tale frame.

It is Dahl as well as Miss Hayes/Honey who at this point reveals 'such a secret part' of himself. The lines quoted are those of the first stanza of Thomas's 'In Country Sleep', written in a 'peasant's cottage' (as Thomas informed John Davenport) in the grounds of the Villa del Beccaro in the hills above Florence over a period of three months in the summer of 1947, and published in both *Horizon* and *The Atlantic Monthly* in December of that year.[71] The *Atlantic* had served as an outlet for Dahl's short story, 'Smoked Cheese' (alongside an article by Albert Einstein on the atom bomb) in November 1945, and thus it is certainly possible that Dahl read Thomas's poem on its initial magazine publication; equally, Dahl may have first encountered it as the title poem of the slim volume Thomas published in the US in 1952.[72]

James J. Balakier reads 'In Country Sleep' as a 'meaningfully ambiguous reenactment of the deep-seated psychological tensions between a father-husband and his daughter-wife', addressed 'just after story-telling bedtime to the sleeping child'.[73] (As his daughter Aeronwy recalled, Thomas used to read to her from Grimm, enacting 'the main characters', and impersonating both 'wolf' and 'child'; 'We both relished the thrill of horror and fear.')[74] In John Goodby's formulation, it is a poem of 'conflicted paternal and spousal affections'.[75] Addressed as 'my girl' in the poem's first section, in which fairy tale motifs are conflated with religious iconography, and as 'my love' in the more mythic, more sexualised second part (in which, as Goodby argues, 'a kind of magic realism uncovers the latent sexual content of the fairy tales'), the poem's compound subject is both girl and woman, both young Aeronwy and Caitlin Thomas.[76] Clearly, this poetic diptych (a third section was envisaged but never completed) also articulates a father's complex response to the sexual world his young daughter – who is 'an amalgamation of fairy tale heroines such as the "haygold haired" Goldilocks, Sleeping Beauty, and Little Red Riding Hood' – will one day have to negotiate.[77] Thomas offered multiple, seemingly contradictory, responses to readers' interpretations of the identity of the addressee and of the poem's central antagonist, the 'Thief'. He wept when the critic William York Tindall told him he believed the poem was about 'how it felt to be a father' ('but whether from vexation, beer or sentimental agreement', Tindall couldn't say). Thomas informed a female admirer of the poem that it was addressed to Caitlin (and that the 'Thief' was 'jealousy'); and, in reply to a reporter in New York, he identified 'alcohol', 'fame', 'success', 'exaggerated introspection or self-analysis' and 'anything that robs you of your faith, of your reason for being' as the poem's creeping adversary.[78]

In the poem's first section, the speaker repeatedly urges his young charge not to fear the traditional bugbears and hazards of fairy tale and folklore – wolf, witch, ghost and various metamorphosed males with questionable designs on her 'honeyed' heart (an adjective that may have suggested to Dahl the change of name from Miss Hayes to Miss Honey at the moment he incorporated 'In Country Sleep' into the second draft of *Matilda*). Rather, the child is enjoined to believe in the benevolence of a rural order – 'that country kind', 'the greenwood keep', 'the green good' – whose environments and cycles of predation (the 'pastoral beat of blood', 'The sermon / Of blood') may seem perturbing, but which should be understood, the speaker insists, as sacramental:

> Sleep, good, for ever, slow and deep, spelled rare and wise,
> My girl ranging the night in the rose and shire
> Of the hobnail tales . . .
> . . .
> Never, my girl, until tolled to sleep by the stern
>
> Bell believe or fear that the rustic shade or spell

Shall harrow and snow the blood while you ride wide and near . . .
. . .
A hill touches an angel. Out of a saint's cell
The nightbird lauds though nunneries and domes of leaves

Her robin breasted tree, three Marys in the rays.
Sanctum sanctorum the animal eye of the wood
In the rain telling its beads, and the gravest ghost
The owl at its knelling.[79]

But this is not a space evacuated of threat and dread. The speaker emphasises the crucial need for the girl to fear the inevitable and obligatory coming, not of some 'wolf in his baaing hood', intent on assaulting her virginity, but of 'the Thief as meek as the dew'. In traumatised, recursive syntax towards the end of the poem, the speaker insists that this entity – proclaimed by the very natural order that serves as a bulwark against it – will, every night, 'seek a way sly and sure' to steal the girl's belief in the very vulnerability of her faith, *which is the precise ground of that faith*.[80]

In the second full draft of *Matilda*, Miss Hayes quotes the first stanza of 'In Country Sleep' at the gate of her cottage as a protective mantra against fears that, at this point in the development of the novel, are not convincingly contextualised, plot- or character-wise. It is clear that at some level, Thomas's poem is recalled and summoned into the narrative under the satiric pressure – as a complex intertextual extrusion – of three of the revisioned fairy tales (those of Snow White, Little Red Riding Hood and The Three Little Pigs) that Dahl had published four years previously in his book of verse, *Revolting Rhymes*. There, the evil stepmother eats what she believes to be Snow White's heart (compare Thomas's 'To eat your heart in the house in the rosy wood'); the dwarfs, like Miss Hayes, bet compulsively on horses; and the traditional horror of the wolf is neutralised by a gun-toting, murderous Little Red Riding Hood.[81] The interplay between received fairy tale, dissenting revision, the imaginatively subpoenaed poem and its unstable new narrative context in *Matilda* is a choice example of the uncanny, transgressive blurring of generic boundaries practised by Dahl. As suggested above, however, at the moment it is introduced into *Matilda*, 'In Country Sleep' sits somewhat ex-centrically within what I have called the narrative ecology of this second draft. Yet as far as the subsequent revisions to *Matilda* are concerned, it is clear that the invocation of Thomas was nothing short of transformative. The ensuing exchange in the second full draft between Miss Hayes and Matilda in which Miss Hayes confesses her gambling addiction – an exchange that is, significantly, brought *inside* the cottage (now an intimate, paradoxical Thomasian space), having in the previous draft occurred later, in a nearby wood – for the first time configures Matilda as 'not really a child at all' but rather 'both child and grown-up all rolled into one'. 'So I suppose we might call you a grown-up child', ventures the compromised Miss Hayes, placing herself, now, in the role of a child in need of Matilda's intervention.[82] At work here, I suggest, is the influence of the hybrid subject and speaker of 'In Country Sleep', in which the personae of adult and child, father and husband, daughter and wife are challengingly conflated by a poet whose aim is to excavate the psychology of fatherhood. Further, I suggest that the intensity of the speaker's fatherly and spousal watchfulness in 'In Country Sleep' significantly shaped both the new narrative of Matilda's *neglect* by her parents in the next draft of *Matilda*, and the wholesale change in the history of Miss Hayes/Honey, who becomes an orphan, her father a suicide (more likely murdered). Thus in the published novel, Miss Honey's recitation of 'In Country Sleep' achieves a convincing emotional and psychological coherence: here is an adult-child, robbed of her father, enslaved by her tyrannous aunt, intoning both for herself and for an abandoned child-adult a poem of profound paternal concern.

Dahl's negotiation of the fairy tale frame, refracted through Dylan Thomas, is highly sophisticated. Referring to the published novel, Deborah Cogan Thacker suggests that the fairy tale element in Thomas's poem 'allows us to see [Miss Honey's] own sense of herself as a child in a fairy tale' and that it 'triggers [Matilda's] own reaction to Miss Honey's cottage', which serves to 'forewarn the reader of Miss Honey's threatened situation'.[83] But Thomas's poem is precisely about educating the young subject *out of* fairy tale fear (and thus out of the 'improving', regulatory ideology (and its gendered norms) of which the fairy tale, at least in its written form, has traditionally been an agent).[84] The first stanza of 'In Country Sleep' radically ironises the perception – Matilda's, by implication – that the cottage is 'like an illustration in Grimm or Hans Andersen'. Here, however, we must attend carefully to the ambiguous modality of the narration. Dahl is scrupulous not

to identify this perception definitively as Matilda's; rather, the statement 'It was straight out of a fairy-tale' hovers between subjectivities,
unowned, emphasising that it is part of a mindset that the precocious
Matilda, having listened attentively to what the speaker of Thomas's
poem is actually urging, has already begun to resist. Matilda hangs
back from the path to the cottage since Thomas's poem has made her
aware of the reality of more authentic threats (including that of nuclear
destruction) to her own and Miss Hayes's well-being. If Matilda
remains in the position of a fairy godmother, helping Miss Hayes kick
her gambling habit in the second draft, and restoring her to her patri-
mony in the revenge comedy of 'retributive justice' and 'fantasy class
justice' of the published version, she does so only to find her telekinetic
powers spent utterly at the end.[85] The fairy tale must be put by.

Miss Hayes's commodification of Thomas's poem is, of course,
Dahl's also. How did it serve him at this moment in the latter half of
1986, only four years before his death? I suggest that his quoting of the
first stanza of 'In Country Sleep' marks the psychological need he felt
to rehearse his family's vulnerability – and that of the species. It was
also an interpretive act deriving from the realisation that Thomas's
poem is one of a series of 'Cold War pastoral[s]' in Thomas's late *oeuvre*
that articulate, in 'annihilatory' imagery, both public and private anxieties – enunciations over which, as John Goodby has argued, falls 'the
shadow of the bomb'.[86] Dahl would have recognised in the poem what
Balakier calls 'the catalog of falling objects to which the Thief's arrival
is compared – snow, rain, hail, dew, leaves, winged seeds, a falling star',
together with the images in the final lines of each section – the 'cyclone
of silence' and 'the outcry of the ruled sun' – as what they are (and what
critics have taken them to be): figurings of hubristic superscience issu-
ing in atomic destruction, 'the manmade sun of the nuclear fireball'.[87]
Thus the presence of Thomas's poem in *Matilda* enabled Dahl to register in multilayered, intertextual form a fear he had already encoded
in the first draft's description of the 'intense stored-up energy' that was
released 'from [Matilda's] body and brain' – 'mysterious forces that
we know nothing about'.[88] Further, Dahl may well have been aware
of the wider project within which Thomas conceptualised 'In Country
Sleep' – the projected long poem entitled 'In Country Heaven', begun
most probably in the spring of 1947.[89] It exists in a 43-line *ur*-version
and a briefer revision; it also clearly feeds the ambiguous pastorals of
the poems 'In Country Sleep', 'In the White Giant's Thigh' and 'Over

Sir John's Hill'. Announced in a BBC broadcast of 25 September 1950 and in a note appended to 'In the White Giant's Thigh' in *Botteghe Oscure* in November of that year, 'In Country Heaven' was directly motivated by Thomas's nuclear fear as he contemplated 'the next lunatic war'.[90] It was to be a poem about the 'self-killed' earth ('black, petrified, wizened, poisoned, burst'), delivered by 'countrymen of heaven' or 'heavenly hedgerow men' who recall aspects of a world now 'gone for ever'. Thomas emphasised that the poem was meant to be 'an affirmation of the beautiful and terrible worth of the earth'.[91]

Dylan Thomas's 'Thief' is a personal test, a personal terror. For Dahl, it was the thief in the night that had invaded the 'country kind' and 'greenwood keep' of The Valley of the Dahls (it should be noted that 'Dahl' itself means 'valley') in the form of the 'malignant neurological spell' that had injured Theo and Pat and robbed him of Olivia. Struggling with the drafting of *Matilda*, he was himself in constant pain. 'In Country Sleep' occupies a pivotal position in Dahl's career, serving as a complex node in which memories of rural Radyr are bound up with the terrors of war, fear of nuclear apocalypse, the trauma of personal loss and Dahl's recognition of fellowship – both tragic and joyful – with another Welsh writer. When Dahl, now on his own sad height, called on Dylan, he did so not to achieve any resolution of these issues but rather to keep their dislocations and their topographies of fear linked and painfully in focus. As Treglown remarks, when Thomas's address to his dying father, 'Do not go gentle into that good night', was read at Dahl's funeral, the assembled company realised that

> The lines spoke for Dahl's children, and also reminded everyone, especially his sisters, of the father Roald himself had missed for seventy of his seventy-four years . . . But the most moving words . . . were Peter Mayer's . . . 'in the passing and crossing over, just as my people say on our Day of Atonement, we are all children united with our parents'.[92]

Notes

1   The first two substantive (holograph and typescript) drafts of *Matilda* are preserved in the Roald Dahl Museum and Story Centre, Great Missenden (hereafter RDMSC) as RD/2/27/1–2 and RD/2/27/3–4. I am grateful to Rachel White, collections manager and archivist at The Roald Dahl Museum and Story Centre, Great Missenden, for her invaluable advice.

2   See Jeremy Treglown, *Roald Dahl: A Biography* (London: Faber and Faber, 1994), pp. 242–5 and Donald Sturrock, *Storyteller: The Life of Roald Dahl* (London: HarperPress, 2011), pp. 541–2.

3   Sturrock, *Storyteller*, p. 451.

4   RDMSC, RD/2/27/2, p. 34, typescript of the first draft of *Matilda*.

5   RDMSC, RD/2/27/2, p. 43, typescript of the first draft of *Matilda*.

6   RDMSC, RD/2/27/2, pp. 45–6, typescript of the first draft of *Matilda*.

7   Roald Dahl, *Matilda* (London: Puffin, 2013 [1988]), p. 171.

8   RDMSC, RD/2/27/2, p. 43, typescript of the first draft of *Matilda*.

9   Sturrock, *Storyteller*, p. 412.

10 See Sturrock, *Storyteller*, pp. 122–38.

11 Sturrock, *Storyteller*, pp. 135–6.

12 See Sturrock, *Storyteller*, pp. 135, 154. Information on the link between the writing sheds at Laugharne and Great Missenden is from Rachel White, collections manager and archivist at the Road Dahl Museum and Story Centre, Great Missenden, who reveals that the archive holds 'photographic negatives of Thomas's work hut taken by Roald Dahl while on holiday in Wales in 1966' (email correspondence, 13 April 2015).

13 Sturrock, *Storyteller*, p. 368.

14 Sturrock, *Storyteller*, p. 373.

15 Sturrock, *Storyteller*, p. 375.

16 Sturrock, *Storyteller*, pp. 387, 388.

17 Sturrock, *Storyteller*, pp. 391, 19.

18 Sturrock, *Storyteller*, p. 392.

19 For this letter, see *http://roalddahl.com/roald-dahl/timeline/1960s/november-1962*, accessed 15 January 2016.

20 See Sturrock, *Storyteller*, pp. 409–10.

21 Sturrock, *Storyteller*, p. 411.

22 Sturrock, *Storyteller*, p. 414.

23 Sturrock, *Storyteller*, p. 476.

24 Treglown, *Roald Dahl*, p. 192.

25 Sturrock, *Storyteller*, p. 550. For an engagement with *Charlie and the Chocolate Factory* as a response to the tragedies discussed above, see William Todd Schultz, 'Finding Fate's Father: Some Life History Influences on Roald Dahl's *Charlie and the Chocolate Factory*', *Biography*, 21/4 (Fall 1998), pp. 463–81. Schultz suggests the proliferation of 'claustral' spaces in Dahl's work (and life) proceed from trauma.

26 See Sturrock, *Storyteller*, pp. 163–8, 206–9, 221, 224–5, 226–30, 232, and Jennet Conant, *The Irregulars: Roald Dahl and the British Spy Ring in Wartime Washington* (New York: Simon & Schuster, 2009).

27 See Sturrock, *Storyteller*, p. 247.

28 Sturrock, *Storyteller*, pp. 247, 256.

29 See Patrick B. Sharp, 'From Yellow Peril to Japanese Wasteland: John

Hersey's "Hiroshima"', *Twentieth-century Literature*, 46/4 (Winter 2000), p. 435.

30 See Sharp, 'From Yellow Peril to Japanese Wasteland', pp. 439, 440.

31 Sharp, 'From Yellow Peril to Japanese Wasteland', p. 446.

32 Sturrock, *Storyteller*, p. 252 and Treglown, *Roald Dahl*, p. 81.

33 See Sturrock, *Storyteller*, p. 175.

34 Treglown, *Roald Dahl*, p. 82.

35 Treglown, *Roald Dahl*, p. 83.

36 For Watkins, see Sturrock, *Storyteller*, pp. 201–2, and for Dahl's 'trepidation', pp. 266–7.

37 Sturrock, *Storyteller*, pp. 272, 273.

38 Sturrock, *Storyteller*, p. 272.

39 Roald Dahl, *Sometime Never* (London: Collins, 1949), pp. 177, 133, 119.

40 See Dahl, *Sometime Never*, pp. 148–63.

41 Dahl, *Sometime Never*, pp. 216, 35, 141–2.

42 Dahl, *Sometime Never*, pp. 219–23.

43 Roald Dahl, *James and the Giant Peach* (London: Puffin, 2013 [1961]), p. 129.

44 Spencer R. Weart, *The Rise of Nuclear Fear* (Cambridge, MA: Harvard University Press, 2012), p. 148.

45 Weart, *The Rise of Nuclear Fear*, p. 106.

46 See the chapters 'Death Dust' and 'The Imagination of Survival' in Weart, *The Rise of Nuclear Fear*, pp. 110–22 and 123–37 and David Cortright, *Peace: A History of Movements and Ideas* (Cambridge: Cambridge University Press, 2008), pp. 126, 133.

47 Weart, *The Rise of Nuclear Fear*, p. 129; Sturrock, *Storyteller*, p. 253.

48 Peter Hunt, 'Roald Dahl and the Commodification of Fantasy', in *Roald Dahl* (New Casebooks), ed. Ann Alston and Catherine Butler (Basingstoke: Palgrave Macmillan, 2012), p. 184.

49 Cortright, *Peace*, p. 139; Weart, *The Rise of Nuclear Fear*, pp. 230–1; George F. Kennan, *The Nuclear Delusion: Soviet-American Relations in the Atomic Age* (London: Hamish Hamilton, 1984), p. 185.

50 See Cortright, *Peace*, pp. 140–1.

51 Jonathan Schell, *The Fate of the Earth* (London: Picador, 1982), p. 173.

52 Schell, *The Fate of the Earth*, pp. 172, 173.

53 Schell, *The Fate of the Earth*, pp. 174, 175.

54 Kennan, *The Nuclear Delusion*, p. 200.

55 Weart, *The Rise of Nuclear Fear*, p. 238.

56 Weart, *The Rise of Nuclear Fear*, p. 241.

57 RDMSC, RD/2/27/2, p. 35, typescript of the first draft of *Matilda*.

58 RDMSC, RD/2/27/3, MS pages (no pagination), second draft of *Matilda*.

59 Dahl, *Sometime Never*, p. 11.

60 Sturrock, *Storyteller*, p. 409.

61 Sturrock, *Storyteller*, pp. 250, 359.

62 Sturrock, *Storyteller*, pp. 250, 251, 492.
63 Sturrock, *Storyteller*, p. 45.
64 Sturrock, *Storyteller*, p. 19.
65 RDMSC, RD/2/27/3, MS pages (no pagination), second draft of *Matilda*.
66 RDMSC, RD/2/27/4, MS pages (no pagination), second full draft of *Matilda*.
67 See Deborah Cogan Thacker, 'Fairy Tale and Anti-Fairy Tale: Roald Dahl and the Telling Power of Stories', in Alston and Butler (eds), *Roald Dahl*, p. 15.
68 RDMSC, RD/2/27/4, MS pages (no pagination), second full draft of *Matilda*.
69 RDMSC, RD/2/27/4, MS pages (no pagination), second full draft of *Matilda*. In a July 1970 interview, 'Bedtime Stories to Children's Books', preserved on cassette in the archive at Great Missenden (RD/12/1/2), Dahl states that he wished he had Thomas's reading prowess and described Thomas's voice as 'the most beautiful thing you've ever heard'.
70 Dahl, *Matilda*, p. 180.
71 Dylan Thomas, *The Collected Letters*, ed. Paul Ferris, new edn (London: J. M. Dent, 2000), p. 705.
72 *The Atlantic Monthly*, 176/5 (November 1945), pp. 43–4 and 115–16.
73 James J. Balakier, 'The Ambiguous Reversal of Dylan Thomas's "In Country Sleep"', *Papers on Language and Literature*, 32/1 (Winter 1996), p. 43.
74 Quoted in John Goodby, *The Poetry of Dylan Thomas: Under the Spelling Wall* (Liverpool: Liverpool University Press, 2013), p. 402.
75 John Goodby (ed.), *The Collected Poems of Dylan Thomas: The New Century Edition* (London: Weidenfeld & Nicolson, 2014), p. 406.
76 Goodby (ed.), *The Collected Poems of Dylan Thomas*, p. 406.
77 Balakier, 'The Ambiguous Reversal', p. 23.
78 See Dylan Thomas, *The Collected Poems, 1934–1953*, ed. Walford Davies and Ralph Maud, rev. edn (London: J. M. Dent, 1996), p. 250.
79 Thomas, *The Collected Poems*, pp. 139–40.
80 See *The Collected Poems*, p. 251 for Thomas's (comparably recursive) prose MS paraphrase of these lines: 'If you believe (and fear) that every night, night without end, the Thief comes to try to steal your faith that every night he comes to steal your faith that your faith is there – then you will wake with your faith steadfast and deathless. If you are innocent of the Thief, you are in danger. If you are innocent of the loss of faith, you cannot be faithful.'
81 Roald Dahl, *Revolting Rhymes* (London: Puffin, 1984 [1982]), pp. 24, 26, 40, 47.
82 RDMSC, RD/2/27/4, MS pages (no pagination), second full draft of *Matilda*. For a reading of Matilda's complex role as both agent and antagonist of patriarchal power, see Kristen Grant, 'The Good, The Bad, and The Ugly: Resistance and Complicity in *Matilda*', *Children's Literature Association Quarterly*, 33/3 (Fall 2008), pp. 246–57.

83 Thacker, 'Fairy Tale and Anti-Fairy Tale', p. 23.
84 See Thacker, 'Fairy Tale and Anti-Fairy Tale', p. 16.
85 See Clémentine Beauvais, 'Child Giftedness as Class Weaponry: The Case of Roald Dahl's *Matilda*', *Children's Literature Association Quarterly*, 40/3 (Fall 2015), p. 277 and Thacker, 'Fairy Tale and Anti-Fairy Tale', p. 28.
86 See Goodby, *The Poetry of Dylan Thomas*, pp. 400–10.
87 Balakier, 'The Ambiguous Reversal', p. 29; Goodby (ed.), *The Collected Poems*, pp. 407, 408; Goodby, *The Poetry of Dylan Thomas*, pp. 405, 408. The resonance of these images of atomic power would have been amplified in the poem's original publication contexts. In *Horizon*, 'In Country Sleep' conducts a dialogue with Cyril Connolly's editorial, which reflects on the superpowers' belief that 'they are about to fulfil an historical mission, even though it be only to destroy each other' (*Horizon*, 16/96 (December 1947), p. 3). Likewise, when 'In Country Sleep' appeared in the *Atlantic*, Thomas's imaging of atomic apocalypse would have been more legible than it is now, given that the previous issue had carried Einstein's article entitled 'Atomic War or Peace' (*The Atlantic Monthly*, 180/5 (November 1947), pp. 29–32).
88 RDMSC, RD/2/27/2, pp. 43, 41, typescript of the first draft of *Matilda*.
89 See Thomas, *The Collected Poems*, pp. 155, 259–63 and Goodby (ed.), *The Collected Poems*, pp. 403–5.
90 See Thomas, *The Collected Poems*, p. 254.
91 *Botteghe Oscure*, 8 (1950), pp. 337–8. See also 'Three Poems', *On the Air with Dylan Thomas: The Broadcasts*, ed. Ralph Maud (New York: New Directions, 1992), pp. 223–6.
92 Treglown, *Roald Dahl*, pp. 256–7.

Works cited

Roald Dahl Museum and Story Centre, RD/2/27/2, first draft of *Matilda*.
—, RD/2/27/3, second draft of *Matilda*.
—, RD/2/27/4, second full draft of *Matilda*.

Dahl, Roald, *James and the Giant Peach* (London: Puffin, 2013 [1961]).
—, *Matilda* (London: Puffin, 2013 [1988]).
—, *Revolting Rhymes* (London: Puffin, 1984 [1982]).
—, *Sometime Never* (London: Collins, 1949).

Balakier, James J., 'The Ambiguous Reversal of Dylan Thomas's "In Country Sleep"', *Papers on Language and Literature*, 32/1 (Winter 1996), pp. 21–44.
Beauvais, Clementine, 'Child Giftedness as Class Weaponry: The Case of Roald Dahl's *Matilda*', *Children's Literature Association Quarterly*, 40/3 (Fall 2015), pp. 277–93.

Cortright, David, *Peace: A History of Movements and Ideas* (Cambridge: Cambridge University Press, 2008).

Conant, Jennet, *The Irregulars: Roald Dahl and the British Spy Ring in Wartime Washington* (New York: Simon & Schuster, 2009).

Goodby, John, *The Poetry of Dylan Thomas: Under the Spelling Wall* (Liverpool: Liverpool University Press, 2013).

Grant, Kristen, 'The Good, The Bad, and The Ugly: Resistance and Complicity in *Matilda*', *Children's Literature Association Quarterly*, 33/3 (Fall 2008), pp. 246–57.

Hunt, Peter, 'Roald Dahl and the Commodification of Fantasy', in *Roald Dahl* (New Casebooks), ed. Ann Alston and Catherine Butler (Basingstoke: Palgrave Macmillan, 2012), pp. 176–89.

Kennan, George F., *The Nuclear Delusion: Soviet-American Relations in the Atomic Age* (London: Hamish Hamilton, 1984).

Schell, Jonathan, *The Fate of the Earth* (London: Picador, 1982).

Schultz, William Todd, 'Finding Fate's Father: Some Life History Influences on Roald Dahl's *Charlie and the Chocolate Factory*', *Biography*, 21/4 (Fall 1998), pp. 463–81.

Sharp, Patrick B., 'From Yellow Peril to Japanese Wasteland: John Hersey's "Hiroshima"', *Twentieth-century Literature*, 46/4 (Winter 2000), pp. 434–52.

Sturrock, Donald, *Storyteller: The Life of Roald Dahl* (London: HarperPress, 2011).

Thacker, Deborah Cogan, 'Fairy Tale and Anti-Fairy Tale: Roald Dahl and the Telling Power of Stories', in *Roald Dahl* (New Casebooks), ed. Ann Alston and Catherine Butler (Basingstoke: Palgrave Macmillan, 2012), pp. 14–30.

Thomas, Dylan, *The Collected Letters*, ed. Paul Ferris, new edn (London: J. M. Dent, 2000).

—, *The Collected Poems, 1934–1953*, ed. Walford Davies and Ralph Maud, rev. edn (London: J. M. Dent, 1996).

—, *The Collected Poems of Dylan Thomas: The New Century Edition*, ed. John Goodby (London: Weidenfeld & Nicolson, 2014).

—, 'Three Poems', *On the Air with Dylan Thomas: The Broadcasts*, ed. Ralph Maud (New York: New Directions, 1992), pp. 223–6.

Treglown, Jeremy, *Roald Dahl: A Biography* (London: Faber and Faber, 1994).

Weart, Spencer R., *The Rise of Nuclear Fear* (Cambridge, MA: Harvard University Press, 2012).

7

'There is Something Very Fishy about Wales': Dahl, Identity, Language

Ann Alston and Heather Worthington

1. Exile

In the book bearing his name, the BFG tells Sophie 'there is something very fishy about Wales.'[1] Even allowing for Dahl's well-known delight in wordplay (particularly apparent in *The BFG*), it seems there is more to this seemingly throwaway line than a mere joke for children. Taking its cue from Dahl's play on 'Wales' and 'whales' in the context of the piscine, this essay examines the ways in which Wales in Dahl's fiction is associated with the word 'fishy' both in its colloquial sense of 'questionable' or 'suspicious' and in its more literal sense, betokening slipperiness, otherness, that which is submerged and apprehended only in flashes. The BFG's declaration is further layered by the fact that whales are, of course, not fish at all. Dahl's Wales, like whales, suffers from misprision, from being carelessly (and often wrongly) labelled, subsumed into dominant categories. The BFG's comment can be read as configuring Wales as a site of uncanny linguistic play and difference, tall tales and elusive origins, and as a marker of (slippery) memory – or of its absence or elision. Dahl, who spent his early childhood years in Radyr and Llandaff on the outskirts of Cardiff, rarely engages in a sustained and explicit way with Wales in his writing, yet we suggest that his Welsh experience can be seen to be inscribed in his wordplay, his interest in the marginalised and often disempowered, and in his acknowledgement of the contingent, elusive and hybrid nature of identity and belonging.

Dahl is culturally situated in a myriad locations. Forever divided between his Norwegian ancestry and his upper-middle-class English education, Dahl was a man of many parts, his cultural, national and political affiliations shaped both by the patina of colonial imperialism acquired through his wartime experiences and, from 1942, by his complex relationship with America. While he may not have been fully cognizant of the impact his Welsh childhood had on him and of the ways in which Wales remained part of his fluid identity, and while memories of any (Anglo-)Welsh acculturation may well be difficult to capture, they are nonetheless formative and remain operative, conditioning his modes of representation in important ways. Dahl's elusive Welsh heritage is obliquely apprehended in the opening chapter of *James and the Giant Peach*:

> They lived – Aunt Sponge, Aunt Spiker and now James as well – in a queer ramshackle house on the top of a high hill in the south of England. The hill was so high that from almost anywhere in the garden James could look down and see for miles and miles across a marvellous landscape of woods and fields; and on a very clear day, if he looked in the right direction, he could see a tiny grey dot far away on the horizon, which was the house that he used to live in with his beloved mother and father. And just beyond that, he could see the ocean itself – a long thin streak of blackish-blue, like a line of ink, beneath the rim of the sky.[2]

Wales is not explicitly mentioned here, but reference to Dahl's quasi-autobiographical *Boy: Tales of Childhood* clearly shows the personal memories on which Dahl drew in his representation of James as a lonely child taken from his home and family and of his orientation vis-à-vis 'home'. Dahl's own account of his childhood removal from Llandaff to St Peter's School in Weston-super-Mare resonates suggestively with the opening paragraph of *James*:

> St Peter's was on a hill above the town. It was a long three-storeyed stone building that looked rather like a private lunatic asylum, and in front of it lay the playing-fields with their three football pitches . . . [The headmaster] shook me by the hand and as he did so he gave me the kind of flashing grin a shark might give to a small fish just before he gobbles it up . . . The first miserable homesick night at St Peter's, when I curled up in bed and the lights were put out, I could think of nothing but our house

at home and my mother and my sisters. Where were they? I asked myself.
In which direction from where I was lying was Llandaff? . . . I wriggled
round in my bed and faced my home and my family . . . I was always
able to draw an imaginary line from my bed to our house over in Wales.
Never once did I go to sleep looking away from my family. It was a great
comfort to do this.[3]

Like the aunts' house in *James*, St Peter's School represents a prison on
top of a hill from which the child can draw 'an imaginary line' to home.
The description of the English Channel in *James and the Giant Peach* – 'a
long thin streak of blackish-blue, like a line of ink' – seems powerfully
to key this fictional world into Dahl's memories of school. There is an
act of triangulation here between England and Wales, between past
and present, between fiction and fact. The world between James and
home is 'lovely but forbidden'; the intervening woods and fields – and
in the case of *Boy*, the Bristol Channel – represent the (inaccessible)
route to home and happiness and to the idealised childhood to which
neither Dahl nor James can return. If, as the BFG suggests, whales and
Wales are fishy and slippery, in England the piscine imagery is more
threatening, as Dahl configures the headmaster as sharklike in relation
to Dahl the Welsh minnow. Such marine motifs saturate *James and the
Giant Peach*, in which the aunts are respectively spongy and spiky, and
where the crew of the peach will have to fend off, mid-Atlantic, their
own shark attack, en route to America.

For Dahl, the prep school and its headmaster, with his potential to
'gobble up' a small child, mark the beginning of the end of his (Welsh)
childhood as the English educational establishments his parents so
valorised consume the child and deliver him, transmogrified, into an
adult world. James's experience is different; fiction enables him to create a new, if unusual, family as he escapes from his aunts' prison-house.
In both fiction and fact, James and the young Dahl are initially at the
mercy of those in power, but in the course of their adventures – and
this is the dominant theme in Dahl's fiction, whether for adults or for
children – they will become empowered, if in complex ways. Central
to this empowerment is the creation of their own stories: Dahl and
James are the tellers of their own tales (*James and the Giant Peach* ends
in a metafictional move that identifies James himself as the author of
the book 'you have just finished reading').[4] The identification of child
narrator-protagonist as author suggests how strongly Dahl's (Welsh)

childhood memories and emotions, his own early sense of identity, consciously or unconsciously inflect the text.

2. Conscription

The conscious Dahl, however, is always dominant – the adult, angli-cised Dahl who, while apparently siding with the disempowered, is himself a regulatory presence in his narratives. In seeking to enable the child reader to identify with the child protagonist, whether in *Boy* or in his stories for children, Dahl offers himself as the reader's confidant. Speaking of *Boy* (in whose introductory note Dahl, referring to the memories about to be related, states 'All are true'), Catriona Nicholson observes that

> The confidential voice of Dahl, the big, friendly, child-wooing author, continues to preside within the text through a recurring device which is both assuring and pedantic. As if in vindication of his 'all are true' guar-antee, the endorsement of 'I promise you', or 'I must tell you', used at strategic intervals throughout the book, serves as an interpellatory device to hail and alert the reader. Each confiding phrase usually precedes or emphasises the disclosure of a significant 'secret' or it provides a further endorsement to revelations of how Dahl, the playful boy-trickster, and his friends managed to outwit a hostile grown-up or some adult in authority.[5]

That Dahl takes the side of the child against the oppressive adult world has been forcibly argued elsewhere, with Christine Hall and Martin Coles describing his alignment with the child as a 'two fingered gesture to the adult world'.[6] Yet this straightforward classification is reductive; his texts are as complex – as slippery – as his psyche. As Peter Hunt suggests, 'appearing' to be on the side of the child is the 'central trick in Dahl's writing bag', while Catherine Butler describes Dahl as adopting 'a kind of saloon-bar rhetoric which works to put readers in an effect-ive arm lock, conscripting them to the views of the narrator in a way that can feel coercive'.[7] Certainly, Dahl's 'empowerment' of the child, be that the reader or protagonist, is in fact its opposite. His concerted acts of hailing leave no room for independence; readers' responses are channelled and controlled within an illusion of freedom. There is, then, a constant tension between Dahl's apparent identification with the child and his adult identity, between anarchy and authority; his 'script' is really a 'con'. The young reader, whose identification with Dahl is also an act of submission, is unknowingly conscripted into sharing the author's own social and cultural mindset. The empowerment of the child may be illusory, but it is a powerful and convincing illusion, crucial to which is the location of the child as marginal – as other to and oppressed by the adult world.

3. Dahl-as-Other: *The BFG*

The BFG is the text that most clearly embodies (and reflects on) Dahl's own 'otherness', his acculturation into the dominant culture, his commitment to wordplay as a tool of resistance (even to his own interpellation of the reader) and his acknowledgement of the role of language in the construction of identity. The eponymous protagonist is, unusually, an adult, albeit an 'uncivilised' giant, which reverses the norm of child as other. Indeed, the BFG is trebly othered: by his size, by his lack of education and by his (mis)use of language, all of which are more usually perceived to be attributes of the child. In *The BFG*, the child-eating giants are extreme representations of cruel adults seen from the child's perspective; from Dahl's own perspective, they may represent the oppressive adults who metaphorically consumed his childhood and young adulthood. The adult hostility he encountered at that time clearly influenced his writing and coloured his perceptions of the world.

The BFG also shares with Dahl a sense of otherness consequent on not belonging. The fictional figure is an outcast from his giant 'family' and clearly cannot be part of human society either. While he can speak the language of his tribe, he yearns to learn how to speak normatively. Born in Wales of Norwegian parents, educated in England and from 1942 formatively influenced by America, Dahl was exposed to a range of nationalities, languages and cultural and political world views. His 'Englishness' was always a complex matter. His schoolmasters may well have been surprised by Dahl's later success as a writer, as his school reports criticised his grasp of the structures of the English language: 'A persistent muddler . . . sentences mal-constructed. He reminds me of a camel'; '[an] illiterate member of the class'.[8] As David Rudd points out, although Dahl may have 'cultivated his Received

Pronunciation he always seems wary of, if not antagonistic towards, the British Establishment'.[9] It was of course, the British Establishment's celebrated school system that inflicted beatings on the vulnerable young Dahl, and it is arguably his perception of the unjustness of those punishments that ignited his lifelong drive to empower the weak and vulnerable (complex as that process was) and to puncture authority. Linguistic play – indeed, the disruption of language as a system of control – is central in his armoury. It can also be read as a rejection of a fixed English identity. Rudd convincingly argues that

> Dahl had a particular animosity towards what he saw as the Great Grammatizator, which can be seen to represent the language of the establishment, of a Great Britain that, reluctantly, he found himself a part of. He learned its ways, certainly, but kept himself on its margins, both geographically and mentally. His stories clearly reflect this notion of being a bit of an outsider, both in the modes in which he chose to write (tales of fantasy and the macabre, tales for children) and in the style of his writing.[10]

Nationality and identity are not fixed entities but socially and linguistically constructed phenomena, and Dahl was very much a conflation of cultures: Norwegian, Welsh, American, English – perhaps most powerfully Anglo-Welsh. From a position that always seems to be peripheral, Dahl appears to ridicule Establishment codes while also seeking to 'civilise' the reader. As Peter Hunt observes, 'when it was pointed out to Dahl that his authoritarian self should disapprove of his own books, he agreed: "It's a tightrope act".'[11] In his fiction for children, Dahl's voice can often be heard in the persona of narrator and in the vocalisation of (aspects of) the child protagonist, but rarely in the guise of an adult character. In *The BFG*, Dahl clearly inhabits the persona of the eponymous – literally monstrous – protagonist. The BFG struggles with language, its structure and order, as did young Dahl; he is explicitly declared to be the author of the text, which is published under a pseudonym – 'Roald Dahl'; and there are other indicators of Dahl's identification with the figure – even Quentin Blake's illustrations mark the similarity. The BFG has a recognisably human (Dahlesque) physiology, but has a rather different psychology and certain supernatural physical abilities. When Sophie – who is to some extent his translator and later his tutor – first encounters him, he is a figure of both fairy tale and nightmare:

In the silvery moonlight, the village street she knew so well seemed completely different. The houses looked bent and crooked, like houses in a
fairy tale. Everything was pale and ghostly and milky-white . . .

The tall black figure was coming her way. It was keeping very close to
the houses across the street, hiding in the shadowy places where there was
no moonlight.[12]

At this point in the narrative, this literally liminal figure (it cleaves to
thresholds) has no name, no recognisable shape ('It wasn't a human. It
couldn't be'), no nationality, and seems to exist beyond the pale of the
known; the absence of markers of identity reinforces a sense of monstrosity. By inhabiting the persona of the BFG, Dahl locates himself as
other or in-between, neither English nor Welsh, but a possibly monstrous combination of the two.

4. *The BFG*: Assimilation and Resistance

The BFG's otherness resides less in his appearance than in his
language, which is comprehensible but characterised by grammatical
solecisms and onomatopoeic portmanteau neologisms. Writing for
children enabled Dahl to resist linguistic and thus cultural nationalist
assimilation. As David Rudd has argued, Dahl's linguistic play is
an instrument of resistance to 'the language of the powerful',
which 'defines a particular society's reality, making the ruling class's
version seem natural and transparent' – merely 'how things are'. He
goes on:

It is only when things do not fall within their allotted semantic categories
that they become troublesome, 'out of order', and need addressing. Seen
in these terms, Dahl's obsession with the scatological and violent becomes
a way of fighting back, drawing on a tradition – often linked to the working class, to the masses – whose energy derives precisely from upsetting
the status quo, and which, furthermore, thereby seems to satisfy deep-
seated desires in many readers, too.[13]

While the narrative structure of *The BFG* conforms largely to the
grammatical and syntactical requirements of 'the language of the
powerful', the BFG is 'out of order', represented as one of the working

class in his clothing as well as in his 'uncultured' speech. His language is erratic, playful, troublesome. However, while Dahl celebrates the BFG's otherness and what Hall and Coles term his 'deviant' speech, it seems that the plot structure requires that the BFG must master 'proper' language in order to be able to write his story.[14] As Hall and Coles observe,

> There is a great sense of pleasure and fun in the giant's use of language, but ultimately the structure of the text as a whole validates conformity and learning the correct use of language (the giant becomes the author of the successful book we've just read) . . . the giant's language is creative, comprehensible, and imaginative, the child is bound by good manners and her own intelligence to accept the giant's language, but in the end his language won't do.[15]

The observation is perhaps reductive: the text may seem to validate conformity as described, but nonetheless the book retains and celebrates the giant's language. That the BFG taught himself the basics of reading and writing from Dickens's *Nicholas Nickleby* before progressing to read the rest of Dickens (and indeed Shakespeare) suggests a thoroughgoing linguistic and cultural assimilation. Equally, however, in order to resist assimilation, it is necessary to know the rules. One might suggest that Dahl's own otherness, his resistance to Establishment protocols and to assimilation, can be mapped onto a Welsh resistance to anglicisation. While Dahl conformed in superficial ways to English culture, he did so – as Rudd suggests – 'reluctantly'. Once he has read Dickens, the BFG – Dahl's doppelgänger – no longer (alas) refers to him as 'Dahl's Chickens'; however, despite learning to speak 'properly', the BFG-as-author has not lost what the text suggests Dahl admires most – difference, individuality, idiosyncrasy. As already noted, much of the BFG's identity lies not in his size or origin or nocturnal activities, but in the way he speaks. Readers' attention is constantly focused on his constant disruption of meaning:

> 'Words,' he said, 'is oh such a twitch-tickling problem to me all my life. So you must simply try to be patient and stop squibbling. As I am telling you before, I know exactly what words I am wanting to say, but somehow or other they is always getting squiff-squiddled around.'
> 'That happens to everyone,' Sophie said.

'Not like it happens to me,' the BFG said. 'I is speaking the most terrible wigglish.'
    'I think you speak beautifully,' Sophie said.[16]

Here, early in the narrative, grappling with the fluidity of language, the
BFG seemingly cannot order its flux. Nonetheless, the BFG's speech
makes sense; as in literal translation from one language to another, his
language is comprehensible but energisingly non-standard, defamiliar-
isingly ex-centric.

5. Wigglish/Wenglish

'[T]he most terrible wigglish': we are back in slippery cultural territory. 'Wigglish' is clearly to be understood as a slippery, dubious kind
of English. In the context of Dahl and Wales, however, the term resonates with another compound word, used to describe a hybrid dialect:
'Wenglish'. Robert M. Lewis notes that Wenglish emerged in the
nineteenth and early twentieth centuries as 'a distinctive new form
of English' – 'primarily a spoken medium', with its own distinctive
grammar and lexis – from the 'fusion of native South Wales Welsh
(Gwenhwyseg) and the various forms of English' spoken by those who
migrated to the industrial centres of south Wales, 'notably from the
West Country, from the West Midlands, and to a lesser extent from
Ireland'.[17] Dahl's father Harald was of course part of that same inward
migration. 'Retain[ing] for the most part the phonology and intona-
tion of South Wales Welsh' together with aspects of its syntax, this 'new,
emergent speech' incorporated over a period of time 'a large number
of words and expressions from Welsh', some 'with their pronunciation
or meaning slightly modified', together with literally translated Welsh
idioms (such as '"to keep a noise" – a direct translation of the Welsh
"cadw stŵr"'), 'hybrids containing both Welsh and English elements',
words from a variety of English dialects, and loans from standard
English.[18] The development of Wenglish coincided with the steady
weakening of the Welsh language, such that by 1921 when Dahl was
five, only around a third of Glamorgan's population of 1.2 million
spoke both Welsh and English.[19] By 1900, Lewis remarks, 'Wenglish
had reached a plateau of development' and had become 'a formidable
medium for the expression of matters relating to family and home life,

to work and to the local community'.[20] Dahl cannot have known the term 'Wenglish' as a child (it seems to have been coined in the 1980s) and his upper-middle-class upbringing in Radyr and Llandaff would have insulated him to a significant degree from daily exposure to it. However, his obviously close relationship with 'Joss Spivvis' – the former miner from the Rhondda Valley who was the Dahls' gardener at Cumberland Lodge, Llandaff – provides one likely point of contact.[21] Certainly, the concept of a hybrid language particularly associated with (Anglo-)Welsh identity that serves as a mark of distinctiveness and as a site of resistance to assimilation (even as it betokens the decline of Welsh itself) resonates with the ways in which Dahl uses 'wigglish' in *The BFG* and indeed elsewhere in his fiction for children. In the same context, however, the BFG's education into Standard English can be seen as submission to a dominant culture and as a loss of distinctive identity. The BFG is already separated from his savage brother giants by his refusal to eat human flesh and by his attempt to educate himself. To speak properly is suddenly to become empowered; once an agent of power, the BFG can imprison the other giants and deny them their 'normal' diet, forcing on them the values of their captors. It seems that, at the end of the tale, the BFG's brother giants face a lifetime of captivity (and a diet of 'repulsant' snozzcumbers) as punishment for refusing to 'learn the language' and conform to the dominant culture. The BFG, and implicitly Dahl, prefer to infiltrate that culture and subvert it from the inside, surreptitiously seizing power. In *The BFG* it is not the child Sophie who is empowered, but the Big F[oreign] Giant.

The response of the implicitly English Sophie to the BFG's lament about his language is twofold – or two-faced: she celebrates the imaginative colour of the giant's speech by claiming it to be 'beautiful' while simultaneously agreeing to tutor him out of it into conformity and normativity. (It is significant that she shares her name with Dahl's mother, Sofie Magdalene, whose valorisation of the English education system Dahl is careful to note in *Boy*.) Indeed, the BFG masters the Queen's English so precisely that the Queen of England herself, having read his book 'about his own past life', is so impressed she commissions its publication, telling the BFG: 'I think we ought to get this book printed properly and published so that other children can read it.'[22] Significantly, this is the moment when Dahl inserts himself openly into the text. The reader is told that 'because the BFG was a very modest giant, he wouldn't put his own name on it. He used somebody else's name instead' – that is, Roald Dahl's.[23] Placing himself into the text as the BFG's *nom de plume*, Dahl takes control of the text and its contents. Ultimately, then, the Queen's English seems to prevail and yet, as ever with Dahl, the dissident element remains: the book is published with the BFG's 'terrible wigglish' eternally preserved between its covers. Dahl's text celebrates linguistic difference and hybridity while paradoxically also insisting on linguistic normativity and cultural conformity.

Hope Howell Hodgkins argues that linguistic play in *The BFG*, and the portmanteau words in particular, teach children about the complexities of a 'patched up world', and concludes that 'semantic instability is both terrifying and funny.'[24] The concept of the 'patched-up' is suggestively aligned with Dahl's multiple identities: Norwegian, Anglo-Welsh, American, English. Frightening too are the strangeness and opacity of some of the BFG's pronouncements. In homage to Prufrock, and in an echo of his own summer 1930 Repton school report, which ran 'I have never met a boy who so persistently writes the exact opposite of what he means', Dahl reminds the reader in the voice of the BFG that 'what I mean and what I say is two different things.'[25] The statement differentiates sharply between complex identity and speech: what the BFG/Dahl are and what they say are not necessarily the same. Dahl's text may pay lip service to the dominant culture and language, but the unexorcised otherness of the BFG and his prominence in the closing pages of the narrative suggest a privileging of the marginalised – brought within the bounds of convention, certainly, and yet hardly domesticated.

Dahl's own unfixed identity drives his commentary on and critique of cultural homogenisation. It is an identity the BFG shares. He is tortured and isolated, looking on from the margins of both human and giant civilizations. He does not belong in the wasteland with the blood-thirsty, 'human bean'-gobbling giants, who 'were all naked except for a sort of short skirt around their waists' and whose skins are 'burnt brown by the sun'.[26] His own attire – 'a sort of collarless shirt and a dirty old leather waistcoat' and 'faded green' trousers, 'far too short in the legs' – resembles that of a Dickensian hero fallen on hard times.[27] Nik Coupland suggests that 'speakers project different social identities . . . through their style choices'; the BFG does this both linguistically and in his physical appearance (as did Dahl).[28] At his introduction to the Queen, the BFG appears in wholly different couture:

Just then, there was a rustle in the bushes beside the lake.

Then out he came!

Twenty-four feet tall, wearing his black cloak with the grace of a nobleman, still carrying his long trumpet in one hand, he strode magnificently across the Palace lawn towards the window.[29]

But once again, what the BFG means is not necessarily what he may say or how he may appear. Noble as he appears on the palace lawn (a masterless man turned courtier), the BFG brings his own 'wigglish' and manners to the Queen's very bedroom, talking of 'whizzpoppers' while breakfasting with her, and indeed releasing one into the Great Ballroom. His language, his very flatus, fill the Queen's space as he physically dominates the room. This dominance is further enhanced as he takes on the role of saviour, leading the Air Force to the 'great yellow wasteland' that is his home and that of the man-eating giants – territory so foreign it 'isn't in the atlas'. The fact that the BFG is 'always able to gallop there' despite the fact that he has not 'the foggiest idea where the Giant Country is in the world' is a version of young Dahl's and the fictional James's unerring homing instinct.[30] Given the close association between Dahl and his BFG persona, it is hard not to align the Wales of Dahl's childhood with the giants' territory – space beyond Establishment maps that exerts a powerful gravitational pull and which retains an ability to disturb the centre (itself being one).

The BFG shares the 'foreign' and 'savage' origins of the other giants, but ends the story as hero, with his own newly built house in Windsor Great Park, next door to the Queen. Dahl would surely have known that the name of the historic house occupied after the Restoration by the 'Ranger of the Great Park' is Cumberland Lodge – the name of the Dahl villa in Llandaff. The BFG is given the title of 'Royal Dream Blower' and is ensconced at the centre of the very Establishment Dahl professed to despise.[31] While this seems a happy ending, the thoughtful reader might question the methods through which the BFG has gained his noble position and royal sinecure – theft and betrayal of his origins. Thus we return to Dahl's slipperiness. He was at once the protector and celebrator of the underdog – defying convention, embracing the postmodern – and one who craved the Establishment's endorsement.[32] He is an adult who colonises the child world, empowering young readers but retaining power over them. It is significant in this regard that Sophie herself is elided from the text at the end of *The BFG*. As Deborah Thacker suggests:

> [Dahl's] method of 'performing' the storytelling event – allowing his child characters to ask questions that his child readers might ask – shows the pleasure of the experience of mutual engagement in the making of a story. The pleasure of this experience, for both teller and told, is at once subversive and liberating, but it is in the *act* of telling that the power resides.[33]

The BFG tells his own story, and while Sophie is free to interrupt, she is ultimately silenced, and the narrative concludes with Dahl's self-insertion into and control over the text.

In the context of the appropriation and consumption of the small nation by the larger, Dahl's incorporation of his childhood experience of Wales into his fiction can be seen as a complex act of resistance, a refusal to be fully assimilated into the dominant culture. His time in Wales may have been short, but it was a period that left deep impressions. Dahl's Welsh experience is the silent facilitator of his narrative strategies. Given his fame and popularity, and the global dissemination of his work, it can surely be argued that in his layered acts of telling Dahl has taken elements of his Anglo-Welsh identity to the world.

Notes

1   Roald Dahl, *The BFG* (Harmondsworth: Puffin, 1986 [1982]), p. 28.
2   Roald Dahl, *James and the Giant Peach* (Harmondsworth: Puffin, 1985 [1961]), p. 8.
3   Roald Dahl, *Boy: Tales of Childhood* (Harmondsworth: Puffin, 1986 [1984]), pp. 78–9, 89–90.
4   Dahl, *James and the Giant Peach*, p. 111.
5   Catriona Nicholson, 'Dahl, The Marvellous Boy', in *A Necessary Fantasy? The Heroic Figure in Children's Popular Fiction*, ed. Dudley Jones and Tony Watkins (New York: Routledge, 2000), p. 311.
6   Christine Hall and Martin Coles, *Children's Reading Choices* (London and New York: Routledge, 1999), p. 53.
7   Peter Hunt, 'Roald Dahl and the Commodification of Fantasy', in *Roald Dahl* (New Casebooks), ed. Ann Alston and Catherine Butler (Basingstoke: Palgrave Macmillan, 2012), p. 181; Catherine Butler, 'Introduction', in the same volume, p. 3.

8 In 'Lucky Break', Dahl quotes four of the unflattering school reports he received between the ages of 14 and 17; see Roald Dahl, *The Wonderful Story of Henry Sugar and Six More* (London: Jonathan Cape, 1977), p. 216.
9 David Rudd, '"Don't Gobblefunk Around with Words": Roald Dahl and Language', in Alston and Butler (eds), *Roald Dahl*, p. 53.
10 Rudd, 'Don't Gobblefunk Around with Words', p. 65.
11 Hunt, 'Roald Dahl and the Commodification of Fantasy', p. 181.
12 Dahl, *The BFG*, pp. 10–11, 12.
13 Rudd, 'Don't Gobblefunk Around with Words', pp. 53–4.
14 Hall and Coles, *Children's Reading Choices*, p. 148.
15 Hall and Coles, *Children's Reading Choices*, p. 148.
16 Dahl, *The BFG*, p. 53.
17 See Robert M. Lewis, 'Wenglish, The Dialect of the South Wales Valleys, as a Medium for Narrative and Performance' (unpublished Ph.D. thesis, University of Glamorgan, 2010), pp. 12, 45, 11–12; *http://dspace1.isd.glam.ac.uk/dspace/bitstream/10265/531/1/lewisphd.pdf* (accessed 2 January 2016).
18 Lewis, 'Wenglish', pp. 12, 48, 49.
19 See Lewis, 'Wenglish', Appendix 1.10.
20 Lewis, 'Wenglish', p. 28. Lewis writes that contemporary Wenglish is 'best conceived of as a continuum of speech, with "broad" Wenglish, using many specifically Wenglish lexical, syntactic, grammatical and phonological features, at one end of the continuum, and a mildly accented approximation to Standard English at the other' (p. 39).
21 See Roald Dahl, 'Joss Spivvis', in *When We Were Young: Memories of Childhood* (Newton Abbot: David & Charles Publishers, 1987), pp. 13–16.
22 Dahl, *The BFG*, p. 207.
23 Dahl, *The BFG*, p. 207.
24 Hope Howell Hodgkins, '"White Blossoms and Snozzcumbers": Alternative Sentimentalities in the Giants of Oscar Wilde and Roald Dahl', *Critic*, 65/1 (2002), p. 47.
25 Dahl, *The Wonderful Story of Henry Sugar*, p. 216; Dahl, *The BFG*, p. 49.
26 Dahl, *The BFG*, p. 34.
27 Dahl, *The BFG*, p. 24.
28 Quoted in Lewis, 'Wenglish', p. 59.
29 Dahl, *The BFG*, p. 157.
30 Dahl, *The BFG*, p. 180.
31 Dahl, *The BFG*, p. 205.
32 Treglown notes that Dahl longed to be included on the honours list; see Jeremy Treglown, *Roald Dahl: A Biography* (London: Faber and Faber, 1994), pp. 231, 248.
33 Deborah Cogan Thacker, 'Fairy Tale and Anti-Fairy Tale: Roald Dahl and the Telling Power of Stories', in Alston and Butler (eds), *Roald Dahl*, p. 28.

Works cited

Dahl, Roald, *Boy: Tales of Childhood* (Harmondsworth: Puffin, 1986 [1984]).

—, *James and the Giant Peach* (Harmondsworth: Puffin, 1985 [1961]).

—, 'Joss Spivvis', in *When We Were Young: Memories of Childhood* (Newton Abbot: David & Charles Publishers, 1987), pp. 13–16.

—, *The BFG* (Harmondsworth: Puffin, 1986 [1982]).

—, *The Wonderful Story of Henry Sugar and Six More* (London: Jonathan Cape, 1977).

Butler, Catherine, 'Introduction', in *Roald Dahl* (New Casebooks), ed. Ann Alston and Catherine Butler (Basingstoke: Palgrave Macmillan, 2012), pp. 1–13.

Hall, Christine, and Martin Coles, *Children's Reading Choices* (London and New York: Routledge, 1999).

Hodgkins, Hope Howell, '"White Blossoms and Snozzcumbers": Alternative Sentimentalities in the Giants of Oscar Wilde and Roald Dahl', *Critic*, 65/1 (2002), pp. 41–9.

Hunt, Peter, 'Roald Dahl and the Commodification of Fantasy', in *Roald Dahl* (New Casebooks), ed. Ann Alston and Catherine Butler (Basingstoke: Palgrave Macmillan, 2012), pp. 176–89.

Lewis, Robert M., 'Wenglish, The Dialect of the South Wales Valleys, as a Medium for Narrative and Performance' (unpublished Ph.D. thesis, University of Glamorgan, 2010).

Nicholson, Catriona, 'Dahl, The Marvellous Boy', in *A Necessary Fantasy? The Heroic Figure in Children's Popular Fiction*, ed. Dudley Jones and Tony Watkins (New York: Routledge, 2000), pp. 309–26.

Rudd, David, '"Don't Gobblefunk Around with Words": Roald Dahl and Language', in *Roald Dahl* (New Casebooks), ed. Ann Alston and Catherine Butler (Basingstoke: Palgrave Macmillan, 2012), pp. 51–69.

Thacker, Deborah Cogan, 'Fairy Tale and Anti-Fairy Tale: Roald Dahl and the Telling Power of Stories', in *Roald Dahl* (New Casebooks), ed. Ann Alston and Catherine Butler (Basingstoke: Palgrave Macmillan, 2012), pp. 14–30.

Treglown, Jeremy, *Roald Dahl: A Biography* (London: Faber and Faber, 1994).

8

Dahl-in-Welsh, Welsh Dahl: Translation, Resemblance, Difference

Siwan M. Rosser

To translate is to express and reimagine an 'original' text in another language with different ways of seeing and articulating the world. Roald Dahl, of course, had his own particular way of seeing, which has proved sufficiently captivating to have been rendered into fifty-eight languages, including that spoken on the periphery of his own childhood on the outskirts of Cardiff. Although an early-twentieth-century upbringing in Llandaff and Radyr could remain in large part untouched by the Welsh language, Dahl would have noticed a land-scape of unfamiliar spellings and would have tuned in, briefly, to the frequencies of the different tongue spoken on the street. The language surrounded his childhood. A century later, Welsh childhoods (located, as Dahl's was, in an all-encompassing anglophone literary and popular culture) are surrounded by Dahl.

Dahl is an English cultural marker, but his Norwegian heritage invests his work with a complex hybridity that is heightened as his novels migrate into a minority language. In Welsh versions of novels such as *The BFG*, *James and the Giant Peach* and *George's Marvellous Medicine*, he addresses a young readership that is, after all, already well versed in navigating between at least two languages and cultures. Encountering Dahl in Welsh translation, readers will be aware of the linguistic distance of the author himself but also of the cultural closeness of familiar characters and textual references. This essay explores how Welsh versions of Dahl's most popular novels articulate this linguistic and cultural slippage and act of navigation; how Englishness is rendered uncanny – both foreign and familiar – in the process of translating Dahl; and how translation necessarily equivocates between resemblance and difference, creating a text that is both 'Dahl-in-Welsh' and 'Welsh Dahl'.

To date, seventeen of Roald Dahl's books for children have been translated into Welsh. *The Enormous Crocodile* (1978) was translated as *Y Crocodeil Anferthol* by Emily Huws in 1989, and Gwynne Williams translated *Revolting Recipes* (1983) and *Revolting Rhymes* (1982) as *Ych-a-fi* (1993) and *Ffi Ffai Ffiaidd* (1996). Then, in 2002, Rily Publications commissioned Elin Meek to begin an ambitious programme of translating Dahl's children's novels, the most recently published work being *Y Bys Hud* (*The Magic Finger*), which appeared in 2013. The titles, although in a new tongue, are familiar; the illustrations by Quentin Blake instantly recognisable. Yet Dahl in translation appears not quite himself. He is more than a mere reflection. Just as Dahl's social and cultural make-up were creatively refracted through fiction, so the translator reconfigures the original texts' orientations according to her cultural, linguistic and personal expressive resources.

In order to examine these Welsh reconfigurations, I will draw on the work of the French sociologist, Pierre Bourdieu, and interpret the act of translation as a 'socially-situated practice' of textual transfer and transformation in which cultural goods are relocated and invested with new symbolic meaning.[1] Bourdieu envisaged the relationship between the individual and society as structured by various overlapping fields of production in which power is culturally and symbolically created, conserved or transformed by rules, knowledge and the accumulation of capital. Cultural capital is created and defined by various fields of cultural production, including the literary field, and texts are considered cultural goods. These goods do not simply convey the social characteristics of their authors or intended readers, but are also creative manifestations of complex, functional and often confrontational interrelationships between the social, economic and ideological dispositions of various structures, institutions and individuals (or agents) jostling for position within the field.[2] Seeing 'competition and conflict' as being 'at the core of human activity' within fields of production, Bourdieu often employed sports imagery to illustrate how people related to one another and their social surroundings, as if they were players in 'the "game" of human life'.[3] Despite appearing to be guided by free will, all human activity, for Bourdieu, is the result of a dynamic interplay between inherited dispositions and lived experiences, which means that the outcome of the game is never predetermined. This emphasis on play, positioning and power seems to be well suited to an examination of Dahl, whose novels for children appear to revel in rule-breaking playfulness and the empowerment of the disenfranchised. Yet, despite the saturation of Dahl's work in the fantastical, subversive and revolting, his 'slyly satirical commentary' is underpinned by an affirmation of mainly conservative moral values.[4] This implies that Dahl wrote through the lens of what Bourdieu would term a *habitus* or a 'feel for the game' – an ingrained, mainly unconscious, understanding and awareness of the rules and conventions governing the production of children's literature. This understanding led him to take up a position that both challenged contemporary sensibilities as to what was considered respectable for children and conserved the moral impulse embedded from the outset in writing for children.

The resulting texts have, of course, become modern classics, invested with a canonical status that has, in turn, provided the stimulus for translation into dozens of languages, including Welsh. Certainly, Dahl's lexical inventiveness and satirical humour are considerable challenges for any translator. However, this essay will argue that Welsh reconfigurations of Dahl's children's novels do more than showcase the translator's linguistic dexterity. The contours of particular acts of translation are determined not only by the mechanics of any given translation strategy but also by the constantly evolving, dynamic socio-cultural ecology of the target literary field and its agents' *habitus*. Literary texts are the creative expression of a culture's *habitus*, glossed by Edward Said as 'the coherent amalgam of practice linking habit with inhabitance'.[5] They are also a manifestation of the writer's own *habitus*, his incorporated, unconscious (yet acting and uncodified) dispositions and behaviours that are conditioned by social, cultural and individual experiences. As Bourdieu (himself mediated through translation) notes:

> The *habitus*, which is the generative principle of responses more or less well adapted to the demands of a certain field, is the product of an individual history, but also through the formative experiences of earliest infancy, of the whole collective history of family and class.[6]

This *habitus* is never a fixed state simply acquired in childhood; '[b]etween the child and the world', Bourdieu remarks, 'the whole group intervenes . . . with a whole universe of ritual practices and also of discourses, sayings, proverbs, all structured in concordance with the principles of the corresponding habitus', from which creativity is born.[7] Indeed, Dahl and his brand are powerful examples of what Bourdieu terms 'the active, inventive and "creative" capacities of the habitus and the agent'.[8] However, although Dahl is acknowledged as the originator of the translated texts, he no longer has agency in his new literary surroundings. It is now the translator who acquires agency, mediating the text according to her own *habitus*, submitting the original 'to the logic of a target literary field, and to its mechanisms of recognition'.[9] Resulting Welsh translations – neither exactly the same as, nor completely different from, the original – compel the translator and reader to address the impact of their own bilingualism on the texts and contest the dispositions of the target language's literary field. The translations are also players in an unbalanced struggle between a dominant and a minority language, in which the reader's social reality is in constant negotiation. Roald Dahl's inflection from global English to minority Welsh offers resistance to anglophone assimilation. Yet his very presence in the field of Welsh-language children's literature may itself challenge that field's identity as a separate, culturally differentiated and viable creative space, as this essay will show.

1. Translation and the Field of Welsh Children's Literature

Lacking in prestige and cultural or economic capital, emerging or minority children's print culture has always relied on translation as a means of corpus creation. As soon as minority-language communities in the nineteenth and early twentieth centuries recognised how crucial the construction of children's print culture was to the survival of their language, it was always a race to keep up with demand. This remains the case in the context of Welsh-language children's publishing. Translation provides inspiration and solutions for a literary field that occupies a 'dominated position' – a field that is unable to sustain professional writers and commercial independence, and which cannot avoid being 'traversed by the necessity of the fields which encompass [it]: the need for profit, whether economic or political'.[10] Such a dependent field cannot achieve the autonomy and differentiation that marks, for Bourdieu, a fully realised field. Bourdieu writes that '[a]t the very foundation of the theory of fields is the observation . . . that the social world is the site of a process of progressive differentiation.'[11] Once a field reaches a fully formed and autonomous state, it is subject to its own rules and standards and is not subordinate to the demands of other fields.[12] By contrast, children's literature in minority languages – state-sponsored and shaped by concerns regarding education and the cultural politics of language decline and revival – will always be conditioned by the hegemony of other fields, both in Welsh and anglophone contexts, and is thus culturally and economically attracted to the ingrained view of translation as a vehicle for cultural survival.

Welsh children's publishing has historically been dependent on translation. Welsh translations of Dahl are implicated in a long tradition of translation that began in earnest with the first published story-book for children, *Anrheg i Blentyn* (1816) by the prominent Methodist, Thomas Jones of Denbigh. It was an adaptation of the popular seventeenth-century Puritan text, *A Token for Children, being an exact account of the conversion, holy and exemplary lives and joyful deaths, of several young children* (1671–2), by James Janeway, still widely distributed during the first half of the nineteenth century, but the Welsh version makes no reference to its English source or author, as was typical of nineteenth-century translations of popular and children's genres.[13] *Anrheg i Blentyn* reflects the religious and moral imperatives that stimulated the emergence of Welsh children's literature at the time. Other translations reflected the improving imperative (also bound up with a patriotic ideology) of bringing the best of European literature within the reach of young Welsh readers. The first Welsh translation of *Robinson Crusoe* was published in 1795, with subsequent editions and translations appearing over the course of the next two centuries. By the beginning of the twentieth century, the fables and tales of Aesop, the Brothers Grimm, Andersen and Perrault were considered to be essential translation material throughout Europe for an emerging nation, and they appeared regularly in Welsh, as in many other minority languages. The first text published for children in the Basque language, for instance, was *Ipui onac* in 1804, a translation of Aesop's fables by Bizenta Mogel, while *Gelukkig Hansje*, a translation of Grimm's *Hans in Luck*, was the first children's book to be published in West Frisian in 1846 (despite its Dutch title).[14]

Such translations catalysed new enterprises: as Rita Ghesquiere remarks, 'by confronting authors with the best from elsewhere, they stimulated the production of literature in the national language.'[15] However, the translation agenda was driven by more than literary or aesthetic aspirations. Translators were often consciously involved in the ideological project of nation-building, believing that translations would earn their threatened tongues 'the status of a cultivated language, able to carry a national literature'.[16] As Venuti remarks, 'Translating in minor languages is often a calculated political move designed to pre-serve them, to enhance their expressive capacities, and to stimulate cultural development.'[17] Viewed in this context, translation in the field of Welsh-language children's literature is afforded considerable sym-bolic value as a practice informed by the belief (or for Bourdieu, the 'illusio', or 'belief in the game and the value of its stakes') that failure to translate would hasten the language's demise.[18] As Michael Cronin warns: '[i]f a language in a dependent position fails to translate, then the language itself loses its *raison d'être* as it absorbs the dominant lan-guage in a wholly unassimilated fashion.'[19]

2. Translating Dahl

According to Cronin's reasoning, not to translate Roald Dahl would be to undermine the robust survival of the Welsh language. Dahl would exist beyond the boundaries of Welsh, enticing readers away from the minority culture to the dominant literature that is already, or fast becoming, part of their personal *habitus*. Through translation, Welsh publishing aims to capitalise on the symbolic and commercial value of the Dahl brand and other well-known franchises, and recent research suggests that translations outsell original works (a cause of concern for publishers of the latter) and that they achieve high bor-rowing rates from public libraries (which is welcomed by librarians).[20] In the field of Welsh children's literature, translations are fast-tracked to prominence: internationally recognised texts and authors often go hand-in-hand with more appealing commercial design and associated merchandise, together with the promise of a higher turnover and the opportunity to persuade a Welsh-speaking audience to read for pleas-ure in its native language.[21]

Dahl plays his part well in this commercial and cultural game to secure readers, sales and esteem, and it may appear that the target literary field can only gain from his translated presence. As authorised translations, the Welsh texts partake of the status and prestige that has brought the combined sales of Dahl's books, in English and other languages, to approximately 100 million.[22] However, the game is conspicuously one-sided. Faced with such a presence – baleful from a particular cultural perspective – original Welsh novels struggle to compete. Concerns are regularly voiced about this unequal power dynamic, and the argument that translation encourages cultural and commercial viability in a minority literature is not accepted uncritically. That literary translation is necessary for a minority language can be said to be a taken-for-granted ('doxic') belief ('illusio') held by the majority, but the degree to which a culture should depend on translation has always been disputed. Indeed, translation is often perceived by many – as it was in the case of the Irish Free State's translation programme of the 1920s and 1930s – as 'promoting a derivative culture, dependent on foreign literary products (mainly in English), cultivating a cultural cringe rather than native creativity and autonomy'.[23] Competing dispositions at the heart of the literary field both encourage and deprecate the value of translation in an attempt to define the field as differentiated and free from the cultural domination of the majority language. Dahl's presence in Welsh emphasises the fact that translation is not an unambiguously beneficial transfer of cultural capital from one language to another; Welsh translations of his novels work to expose, rather than remedy, the precarious position of a minority language such as Welsh that is both attracted by, and resistant to, a dominant language and culture.

A measured response to translation was articulated by the Welsh publisher Roger Boore, who was involved with an ambitious programme of co-producing books in non-state languages throughout Europe in the 1970s with Gwasg y Dref Wen. He believed that evading translation would create a narrow, introspective culture; at the same time, he acknowledged that too much translation could 'drown' a fragile culture such as Welsh.[24] He proposed that 35 per cent would be a reasonable proportion of translated books within a minority-language market. The percentage in Wales at present is nearer 50 per cant, and children's books account for the clear majority of all translations into Welsh.[25] This has led writers and some publishers to call for a public debate on the issue of translation in Welsh children's literature and on the level of state-supported funding given to translation in comparison with support for original work.[26]

Key figures in the field of children's literature who voice such concerns – writers, publishers and parents (ironically, little attempt has hitherto been made to engage young readers in this debate) – are often denounced, however, as 'benighted essentialists waving the banner of difference and replacing one "master" language with another'.[27] But this resistance to translation is a necessity in that it compels a re-evaluation of the reasoning behind and methodology employed in literary translation into minority languages. Translation's role is, after all, ambiguous at best, being both (in Cronin's formulation) 'predator and deliverer, enemy and friend' of languages in decline.[28] Ghesquiere asks: 'do [Enid Blyton and J. K. Rowling] stimulate new productions or do they curb the growth of children's books in the target system and disturb the market because they overshadow the other books?'[29] The market in Wales is undoubtedly 'disturbed' by an overwhelming dependence on English-language literature, which accounts for almost all source texts translated into Welsh. Only one publisher (Dalen Books) currently translates graphic novels from other European languages; books sourced from non-Western languages are unheard of.

This produces what Cronin terms 'unidirectional' translation, an asymmetrical relationship that limits the ability of the minority language to negotiate the diversity of global culture on (and in) its own terms.[30] By contrast, the culture of English-language children's literature is famous for its reluctance to translate.[31] A bibliography of Welsh literature in English translation, compiled in 2005, indicated that only one Welsh novel for children had been translated into English in nearly two centuries of children's publishing, namely T. Llew Jones's *Tân ar y Comin*, translated as *Gypsy Fires* in 1994.[32]

Literary translation in a minority language such as Welsh is problematised by the cultural politics of language, and when unchecked can lead to an assimilation of the dominant culture, with limited space for negotiation and mediation. Indeed, when it is an exercise in 'mere citation' and imitation, then translation offers very little for the target language in respect of creativity or orientation.[33] But translation that can open a dialogue between the target language and the source text is a necessary and vivifying practice, affirming difference by subjecting the transitional text to the cultural and linguistic *habitus* of the target language, thus allowing its literary field to enlarge and develop.

3. Dahl-in-Welsh

It is in this context of conflict and unease that the notion of 'Dahl-in-Welsh' should be interrogated. Would an unmodified reproduction of the original – for which I propose the term 'Dahl-in-Welsh' – threaten the recognisable separateness of the target language and pose the question: why bother to translate Dahl at all when young Welsh readers are, or soon will be, able to read him in the original English?

At first sight, Dahl-in-Welsh appears to strive for a formal (rather than functional, or dynamic) equivalence in translation – a complete correspondence between the source text and its translation in terms of structure and content, leaving little space for negotiation or reorientation. Dahl-in-Welsh is, after all, culturally (and contractually) obliged to be a direct reproduction, page-by-page, of Penguin's/ Puffin's editions of Dahl-in-English. With no sanctioned domestication of personal or place names, no abridgements or elaborations, the titles, characters and storylines are easily recognised, from the front covers and the typeface to Quentin Blake's trademark, immediately identifiable, illustrations. *Charlie a'r Ffatri Siocled* (2002), *Moddion Rhyfeddol George* (2008), *Y Gwrachod* (2008) and *James a'r Eirinen Wlanog Enfawr* (2011) could not be anything but *Charlie and the Chocolate Factory* (1964), *George's Marvellous Medicine* (1981), *The Witches* (1983) and *James and the Giant Peach* (1961).

The only ambiguous title is *Yr CMM* (2003). Its shape and style implies that it is a Welsh version of *The BFG* (1982), but its unfamiliarity is discordant in the Dahl-in-Welsh repertoire. Furthermore, it also requires the addition of a subtitle on the title page (not the front cover), placed within parentheses – '(Yr Éc Ém Ém)' – to aid articulation (i.e. /ər ɛk ɛm ɛm/). Without this guide, a phonetic pronunciation of the individual letters would produce an awkward-sounding and grammatically incorrect /ər kə m m/ (a /kə/ pronunciation, rather than the prescribed /ɛk/ would render the definite article 'yr' /ər/ – the form used before vowels – a solecism). Furthermore, unless the reader has spotted the reference to the CMM's *full* name in the blurb on the back page, she will have to wait until the end of chapter five to learn that he is 'Y Cawr Mawr Mwyn' or The Big Gentle (rather than Friendly) Giant. With translations that are evidently attempting to render the Welsh and English versions indistinguishable at first glance, the

'Éc Ém Ém' are big, if gentle, reminders of the impossibility of *complete* formal equivalence in translation.

When personal names are descriptive, such as the names of the monstrous giants in *The BFG*, they are translated literally in *Yr CMM*. Thus their Welsh names still convey their unique, grotesque method of devouring people; for example, 'Bloodbottler' becomes 'Y Potelwr Gwaed'; 'Fleshlumpeater' is rendered as 'Y Bwytäwr Talpiau Cnawd'; and 'Manhugger' is 'Y Cofleidiwr Dynion'. Such literal translation is seen in many other translations of *The BFG* such as the Finnish and Swedish versions, although there appears to be a greater degree of creative latitude in some of the Scandinavian names: 'Maidmasher' is reimagined as 'Lastenlyttääjä' ('childmasher' in Finnish) and 'Hjärtekrossaren' ('heartmasher' in Swedish), for instance.[34] All non-descriptive personal names are reproduced in their original form in the Welsh translations, and locations remain the same. 'Welsh' Matilda's imaginative peregrinations still take her from her *English* home to the four corners of the earth: 'Teithiodd dros y byd i gyd tra eisteddai yn ei hystafell fach mewn pentref yn Lloegr' ('She travelled all over the world while sitting in her little room in an English village'); James still travels from England to America in his giant peach, and Sophie and the CMM still visit the Queen at Buckingham Palace.[35] As Sophie and the CMM approach their destination, we can be in no doubt as to the geographical and cultural landscape evoked by the corresponding Welsh and English descriptions:

> Er ei bod hi'n dywyll, gallai Sophie weld eu bod mewn gwlad o gaeau gwyrdd gyda chloddiau taclus rhwng y caeau.

> Dark though it was, Sophie could see that they were in a country of green fields with neat hedges in between the fields.[36]

In the novels that are situated in actual locations, England is always home, Englishness always familiar and comforting. Thus first impressions suggest that the Welsh translations are mostly unchanged from their English originals. While this seems to confirm the symbolic capital and canonical status of Dahl's children's novels, the lack of what Venuti calls 'domestication' (or cultural relocation) might be considered a positive contribution to the target literary field rather than a negative influence, since it extends the use of Welsh beyond its traditional borders.[37] In the opening chapter of the Welsh *Matilda*, the eponymous heroine, the gifted but neglected four-year-old daughter of a bingo-addict mother and an unscrupulous used-car-salesman father, discovers the joy of reading at the local public library, under the watchful gaze of the librarian, Mrs Phelps. Although the geographical location has not yet been specified (there is a later reference to Aylesbury, Buckinghamshire – home territory for Dahl), the English names of the characters and the reading material devoured by Matilda leave us in little doubt as to the language implied by the characters' direct speech. English is clearly the language of conversation in the following exchange, for instance:

Edrychodd Mrs Phelps, oedd yn dal iawn, i lawr ar Matilda, ac edrychodd Matilda'n ôl i fyny arni hithau.

'Ro'n i'n meddwl bod rhai [llyfrau plant yn] wael iawn,' meddai Matlida, 'ond roedd eraill yn hyfryd. Fy hoff lyfr i o'r cyfan oedd *The Secret Garden*. Roedd e'n llawn dirgelwch . . .'

Roedd Mrs Phelps wedi'i syfrdanu. 'Faint yn union yw dy oedran di, Matilda?' gofynnodd.

'Pedair blwydd a thri mis oed,' meddai Matilda.

Roedd Mrs Phelps wedi'i syfrdanu hyd yn oed yn fwy, ond roedd hi'n ddigon call i beidio â dangos hynny. 'Pa fath o lyfr hoffet ti ei ddarllen nesa?' gofynnodd.

Dywedodd Matilda, 'Hoffwn i ddarllen llyfr rhyfeddol o dda y mae oedolion yn ei ddarllen. Un enwog. Dw i ddim yn gwybod am unrhyw enwau.'
. . .

'Rho gynnig ar hwn,' meddai [Mrs Phelps] o'r diwedd. Mae'n enwog iawn ac yn dda iawn. Os yw e'n rhy hir i ti, rho wybod i mi ac fe ddof i o hyd i rywbeth byrrach ac ychydig yn haws.'

'*Great Expectations*,' darllenodd Matilda, 'gan Charles Dickens. Fe fyddwn i wrth fy modd yn rhoi cynnig arno.'

Rhaid fy mod i'n wallgof, meddai Mrs Phelps wrthi ei hun, ond meddai wrth Matilda, 'Wrth gwrs y cei di roi cynnig arno.'

Mrs Phelps looked down at Matilda from her great height and Matilda looked right back up at her.

'I thought some [children's books] were very poor,' Matilda said, 'but others were lovely. I liked *The Secret Garden* best of all. If was full of mystery . . .'

Mrs Phelps was stunned. 'Exactly how old are you, Matilda?' she asked.

'Four years and three months,' Matilda said.

Mrs Phelps was more stunned than ever, but she had the sense not to show it. 'What sort of a book would you like to read next?' she asked.

Matilda said, 'I would like a really good one that grown-ups read. A famous one. I don't know any names.'

. . .

'Try this,' [Mrs Phelps] said at last. 'It's very famous and very good. If it's too long for you, just let me know and I'll find something shorter and a bit easier.'

'*Great Expectations*,' Matilda read, 'by Charles Dickens. I'd love to try it.'

I must be mad, Mrs Phelps told herself, but to Matilda she said, 'Of course you may try it.'[38]

In adult fiction, the suspension of disbelief involved in accepting that Welsh can be spoken by non-Welsh speakers in cultural environments beyond (and in certain contexts, within) Wales is often criticised as too taxing, too far removed from sociolinguistic reality.[39] However, it is an uncontested norm in children's literature. From an early age, Welsh-speaking children are accustomed to the use of Welsh in interlingual fictional encounters, be they in anthropomorphic or international contexts. This linguistic phenomenology – the acclimatisation to what one might call the bilingual uncanny – enables an understanding of the arbitrary relationship between signifier and signified and generates an impulse towards creative linguistic play that was part of the experience of the young bilingual (English and Norwegian) Dahl himself, as Ivana Marinić and Željka Nemet have suggested.[40] However, most original Welsh-language fiction for children above seven years of age is, unsurprisingly, predisposed to indigenous Welsh geographies and social scenarios in which Welsh is naturally spoken, demonstrating the embeddedness of Welsh children's literature in 'the collective imagining of nations' that characterises children's literature as part of a cultural nationalist agenda in many countries.[41] However, such a practice runs the risk of essentialising language and the cultural contexts of its use in ways that reject the vivifying potential of the uncanny. By rejecting domestication and maintaining characters' English (and other) identities, the Welsh translations of Dahl contribute to an expansive and uncanny discourse that contests the use of Welsh as the

expression of exclusively Welsh-located experience. The close correspondence between certain elements of original and translated texts
may well be the product of cultural and contractual constraints that
limit the translator's ability to submit the source texts to a more radical
reimagining; however, as Venuti contends, 'by submitting the majority
[culture] to variation, minor translating also increases the heterogeneity of minor culture, often with unpredictable effects.'[42]

4. Readings of Difference: 'Welsh Dahl'?

Though closely mapped onto their originals, the Welsh translations
of Dahl do not allow the 'full otherness of the dominant language to
emerge'.[43] Despite the aspiration and requirement to appear as similar to the original as possible, these translations inevitably inflect the
source material in vital ways, undermining an essentialised conception of the cultural and linguistic identity of the text. Whereas the
resemblance of Dahl-in-Welsh to the original is maintained through
names, locations, structure and content, difference is established once
the characters begin to speak, allowing an uncanny 'Welsh Dahl'
to emerge.

In direct speech, the translator, Elin Meek, is afforded space to
domesticate as Dahl's verbal innovations and intonations invite her
to adopt a more malleable style of translation, aimed at achieving
functional (or dynamic) rather than formal equivalence. Dialogue, for
instance, is interspersed with an array of traditional exclamations such
as 'Nefoedd wen' (*White heavens*, corresponding to 'good heavens'); 'O'r
annwyl' (*Oh dear*); 'Caton pawb' (*God preserve all*); and 'Arswyd y Byd'
(*Terror of the world*, corresponding to 'heavens above'). Her choice of
expressions, however, understood in Bourdieusian terms, 'has little to
do with conforming to norms through the deliberate use of specific
strategies'; Meek's are 'more or less subjective and random choices'
effected by 'her specific *habitus*, as acquired in the target literary field'.[44]
By evoking verbal interjections that belong, not to the contemporary
speech of young Welsh speakers but to a quasi-historical register, Elin
Meek is (perhaps unconsciously) investing the translated text with
markers of symbolic capital that would be recognised by the target
literary field. In Welsh children's literature, these expressions would
be most commonly found in the historical fiction of the most widely

read children's writer, T. Llew Jones, whose adventure stories regularly require the addition of such dramatic exclamations.[45] Alluding to T. Llew Jones and traditional storytelling in general allows the translated texts to resonate with their new literary and social surroundings.

A further example of the way the translator submits the original to the *habitus* of the target literary field is found in the verbal cruelty of Miss Trunchbull, the odious headmistress who terrorises her pupils and teachers in *Matilda*. The source text has Miss Trunchbull spouting a torrent of abuse whose inventiveness and exaggeration render them, and the dominance of the headmistress, ridiculous and humorous. In English, Miss Trunchbull's expressive imagination knows no bounds; in one tirade she bellows 'You ignorant little slug! . . . You witless weed! You empty-headed hamster! You stupid glob of glue!'[46] In Welsh, however, it is the target language's traditional store of idiomatic vehemence that is showcased by Miss Trunchbull, rather than linguistic invention. Thus, she bawls 'Y twmffat bach twp! [*You stupid little funnel!*] . . . Y pen dafad disynnwyr! [*You dumb sheep's head!*] Y penci gwirion! [*You daft blockhead!*] Y pen meipen! [*You turnip head!*]'[47] These are all expressions associated with spoken Welsh, and demonstrate the impulse of many writers in the field of Welsh children's literature, as Speller remarks of Quebecois writers, 'to define themselves against the bordering Anglophone space . . . [and] to identify themselves with everything that can distinguish them from their more powerful literary and political neighbours'.[48] Although translating Dahl is an acknowledgement of the cultural dominance of the Dahl brand and of the English language, here the translator infuses Welsh Dahl with a type of language that can be clearly differentiated both from the linguistic resources of the source text and from the less aggressive register of traditional storytelling exemplified by T. Llew Jones. Dahl gives licence to a cacophony of verbal abuse rarely seen in Welsh children's literature, validating once more Venuti's claim that 'the heterogeneity of minor culture' is increased, 'often with unpredictable effects', by translation.

Welsh Dahl strives for difference. It is a process that presents the translator with considerable challenges, especially when negotiating particular sections of *The BFG*, *Matilda* and *Charlie and the Chocolate Factory*, as the following discussion will demonstrate. Indeed, the language-muddling BFG exemplifies Dahl's inventiveness at its most challenging: Dahl's innovative word play, neologisms and nonsense deliberately defamiliarise the English language in the original novels, and so must be reinvented in Welsh translation. The BFG's Welsh incarnation, Yr CMM, must speak a version of Welsh that is recognisable, but which at the same time must innovatively disturb the ecology of the language. Grammar is altered and lexicons defied to create a giant that is of this world, yet linguistically other. In the original English, the BFG explains to Sophie that the giants eat 'human beans' (his version of 'human beings'); in Welsh the CMM calls them 'blodau dynol', playing on the similarity of 'blodau' (flowers) and 'bodau' (beings). He then explains that each nation has its particular taste. Turks taste of turkeys in both Welsh and English versions, and those native to Panama taste of hats. But the taste of the Welsh is quite a different matter:

> 'The human bean,' the Giant went on, 'is coming in dillions of different flavours. For instance, human beans from Wales is tasting very whooshey of fish. There is something very fishy about Wales.'
> 'You mean whales,' Sophie said. 'Wales is something quite different.'
> 'Wales is *whales*,' the Giant said. 'Don't gobblefunk around with words.'

> 'Y blodau dynol,' aeth y Cawr yn ei flaen, 'sy'n dod â blas diliynau o wahanol bethau arnyn nhw. Er enghraifft, mae blodau dynol o Gymru'n blasu o giwcymbrau. Mae rhywbeth ciwcymbrog iawn am Gymru [*human flowers from Wales taste of cucumbers. There is something very cucumbery about Wales*].'
> 'Cymreig rych chi'n meddwl [*You mean Welsh*],' meddai Sophie. 'Mae ciwcymbrau'n bethau cwbl wahanol [*Cucumbers are quite different things*].'
> 'Ciw*cym*brau yw Cymru [*Wales is Cucumbers*],' meddai'r Cawr. 'Paid â llowcwincio o gwmpas â geiriau [*Don't gobblewink around with words*].'[49]

The BFG's quip that there is 'something very fishy about Wales' is lost as the lexical similarity of 'Wales' and 'whales' is replaced with 'cucumbers' and 'Cymru'. The implications of Dahl's (seemingly) ludic reference to the slippery inheritance of the land of his birth (explored by Ann Alston and Heather Worthington in this volume) become an inevitable casualty of translation: an allusion that was lexically and culturally impossible to reproduce or appropriate is simply erased. Welsh Dahl reminds us, abruptly at times, of its difference – in *Yr CMM* by omitting a feature that was lexically impossible and perhaps culturally unpalatable in the target literary field, and in *Matilda* by resisting translation altogether.

In the scene involving Matilda's first visit to the home of Miss Honey, the translation adheres to the exact wording of the source text, introducing an unfamiliar and destabilising bilingualism to the text. As indicated earlier, Welsh children's literature usually renders foreignness unproblematic by creating a monolingual space within texts, even in scenes involving English characters where a bilingual reader has the necessary linguistic resources to switch from one language to another. The use of English in Welsh literature, however, especially Welsh children's literature, is discouraged by the literary field's drive towards defining and maintaining linguistic difference. Viewed in this context, the following passage from the Welsh translation of *Matilda* appears unusual to say the least. As Miss Honey and Matilda meander their way to Miss Honey's cottage, the teacher explains that she always thinks of lines written 'by a poet called Dylan Thomas' every time she walks up the path to the house. Matilda waits; then Miss Honey recites the lines in a 'slow wonderful voice':

'Ryw dro ysgrifennodd bardd o'r enw Dylan Thomas rai llinellau y bydda i'n meddwl amdanyn nhw bob tro dw i'n cerdded i fyny'r llwybr hwn.'

Arhosodd Matilda, a dechreuodd Miss Honey adrodd y gerdd mewn llais araf digon rhyfeddol:

'Never and never, my girl riding far and near
In the land of the hearthstone tales, and spelled asleep,
Fear or believe that the wolf in the sheepwhite hood
Loping and bleating roughly and blithely shall leap, my dear, my dear,
Out of a lair in the flocked leaves in the dew dipped year
To eat your heart in the house in the rosy wood.'[50]

Elin Meek's decision to reproduce the source text, an excerpt from Dylan Thomas's 'In Country Sleep', exposes the conflict recognised by Bourdieu to be at the heart of every field of production. This extended passage in English challenges a common conception held in the field of Welsh children's literature that literature should be preserved as a monolingual space. Despite – more precisely because of – young readers' bilingual social reality, it is generally held that literary monolingualism is a means of consolidating native language skills in the very process of acquiring wider cultural knowledge. Literary monolingualism is thus legitimised as a specific language practice with cultural-political and pedagogical justifications, similar to the parallel monolingualism employed in Welsh-medium education, where education is delivered primarily in the minority language to bilingual pupils. However, this protectionist ideology is increasingly challenged by the changing sociolinguistic landscape. A growing number of readers of Welsh children's literature will encounter Welsh only in school and will not develop full proficiency in the language until their secondary school years, with many not utilising the language in their adult life. According to recent figures, 53 per cent of children in Welsh-medium primary schools are not fluent in the language in their parents' opinion (a figure that decreases to less than 8 per cent in Welsh-medium secondary schools).[51] Acknowledging the difficulties facing Welsh-medium education as the sole vehicle for language acquisition in some parts of Wales, educationalists such as W. Gwyn Lewis have questioned the feasibility and benefits of language separation within Welsh-medium education, enquiring whether a more dynamic approach to bilingualism could bring advantages to lesser-used languages such as Welsh.[52]

Quoting Dylan Thomas in a Welsh-language children's novel, therefore, is at odds with the target field's preoccupation with maintaining identity and difference, yet it is a very real expression of the hybrid, bilingual culture in which all Welsh speakers operate. *Matilda* invites us to acknowledge and explore (be it to contest or reaffirm) the reasons behind the evasion of readers' bilingualism in original Welsh-language children's fiction. Translation, in this instance, defamiliarises the target culture, challenging the dominance of monoglossia within the Welsh field. However, despite the inclusion of the original English poetic text, the passage from the translated *Matilda* cannot be said to exemplify a Dahl-in-Welsh act of Venuti's 'foreignisation' (that is, the translation method that acknowledges the source text's original cultural setting); the poet quoted in *Matilda* was, after all, a Welshman. Allowing Dylan Thomas to emerge in his own words indicates a slippery, even contentious, Welsh Dahl who elects to claim Dylan Thomas as a defining feature of the reader's bilingual literary heritage.

The invocation of poetry in *Matilda* complicates the linguistic make-up of Welsh Dahl. In *Charlie a'r Ffatri Siocled* (2002), however, poetry is used to achieve a very different effect. Generic shifts within the novel give rise to a cultural slippage that works to affirm not the conditions of a bilingual literary *habitus*, but rather a distinct Welsh-language literary identity. This is enabled by the unfixed location of Dahl's tale. In the Welsh translation, one might entertain the possibility that Charlie Bucket and his family live in a Welsh industrial town (Swansea, perhaps, Dylan Thomas's own 'ugly, lovely town', and home of Elin Meek, the translator). The language spoken, we are told, is Welsh: Willy Wonka explains that he had to communicate with the natives of Loompaland in 'Wmpalwmpeg', not in 'Cymraeg' (Welsh), when he explained to them their terms of resettlement in his chocolate factory. However, he can then proudly boast to Charlie that they now all speak Welsh ('Maen nhw i gyd yn siarad Cymraeg nawr').[53] And it is these strange beings, sanitised of the racist associations that were attached to them, in the eyes of certain readers, in the first published edition of *Charlie and the Chocolate Factory*, who fully embrace the difference of the Welsh language. While the narrative reproduces the characters' names as they are in the original (with the exception of some orthographical changes), in the Oompa-Loompas' songs – sung to bid farewell to the spoilt children who accompany Charlie on the factory tour – the names undergo translation: Veruca Salt is 'Ferwca Hallt' (Salty), and Violet Beauregarde becomes 'Fioled Mireinwedd', a translation of her French surname. Further, the song that accompanies the disappearance of Mike Teavee into a television set is the most extended example of domestication found in the translated novels. Deprecating the fact that children throughout Wales (not England) are glued to their television sets, the song articulates a desire to see little ones 'o Fôn i Fynwy' (from Anglesey to Monmouthshire) poring instead over books, as children did in days gone by. And to evoke the reading pleasures of the past, the song refers, not to the English classics invoked in the original (such as Beatrix Potter and *The Wind in the Willows*), but to Welsh children's titles: *Llyfr Mawr y Plant*, *Teulu Bach Nantoer*, *Twm Sion Cati*, *Nedw* and *Mops*.[54]

Thus it is in the songs of the Oompa-Loompas, a tribe who have acquired Welsh as a second language, that we see, to paraphrase Cronin, the full otherness of the minority language emerging. The shift from prose to poetry/song subjects the text to further variation as the demands of metre and rhyme release a playful domestication, an articulation of the translator's own literary *habitus*. Elin Meek's decisions to reproduce, inflect or reinvent the source text may seem to be based on feeling or instinct; for Bourdieu, however, such seemingly subjective responses are acts of 'position-taking' prompted by 'social imperatives'.[55] To understand translation as practice – a dynamic action conditioned by, and impacting on, the interplay of *habitus* and field – is to recognise that it is 'neither a consequence of mere mechanical reproduction nor the working out of the seed of inspiration', but rather a result of forces both preservationist and transformational within the target literary field.[56]

5. Dahl-in-Welsh and Welsh Dahl

Like the author himself, the Welsh translations of Roald Dahl's iconic novels for children are culturally and linguistically hybrid. While they appear to be Dahl-in-Welsh – one might say contractually compliant – they in fact represent an uncanny 'Welsh Dahl', establishing difference by identifying with *both* literary languages of Wales. Rather than being the product of a particular translation strategy, this new orientation emerges from the socio-cultural forces that structure and are structured by the inherited and inhabited norms, values and tensions of the target literary field, namely the symbolic capital of the Dahl brand, minority language dependence on translation, concerns regarding cultural and linguistic dominance and the requirement to articulate difference. In the act of translation, the translator is positioned – as Bourdieu positions authors – 'in the space of possibles' within literary fields – a creative space defined 'in short, [by] all that one must have in the back of one's mind in order to be in the game'.[57] The translator appropriates Dahl, creating a text that extends the circumference of the target language, prompting linguistic playfulness and innovation rarely seen in original Welsh children's fiction and establishing a subversive, fantastical '"conspiratorial" engagement with children [that] interrupt[s] the educational and improving qualities of much contemporary children's literature'.[58]

Yet translating Dahl also reveals the conflict and competition implicit in minority-language translation, including its role in the homogenisation of cultural products through the commercialisation of cultural fields. For Bourdieu, 'the grip of the holders of power over the instruments of circulation' creates a 'blurring of boundaries' that 'constitutes the worst threat to the autonomy of cultural production'.[59] Bourdieu is describing the boundaries between experimental literature and bestsellers, but his argument can be applied with equal force to the boundary between marginal and dominant literatures. Few would doubt the distinctiveness and literary inventiveness of Dahl, or indeed the ability of translations of his work to offer target literary fields new orientations and dynamic cultural expressiveness; however, the dependence of Welsh translations for children on one dominant source language should not be an undisputed practice within a minority language. Translation is both 'enemy and friend'. But the field's response to that reliance need not necessarily involve embracing the currents of anglophone culture without a reflective, critical consideration of their effect on the viability of the target language.

The contingent position of the Welsh language and its readers' bilingualism are complicating factors that impact on the transition of Dahl, as symbolic capital, from one language to another. The value of symbolic capital 'is related to the time a product lasts or its felt durability, criteria which are intricately linked to the distinction of either producers or consumers'.[60] Canonised by the durability of his commercial success and by acts of institutional accreditation, Dahl-in-English is essential childhood reading. But his status in the Welsh literary field is more ambivalent. The brand recognition of the translations affords them a prominent position, yet the cultural politics of the target literary field are such that the dominance of translations is robustly challenged. Further, defamiliarising interjections of Welsh idiomatic language or literary references in translations that otherwise adhere to the form and structure of the original can be uncannily *destabilising* for a bilingual reader who has, or will soon, encounter Dahl-in-English. An uncanny Welsh Dahl will generate contrasting responses depending on readers' dispositions and their experiences of Dahl, literature more generally, and their lived social reality. For some, the translations will be their formative encounters with Dahl, and uncanny features of the text, such as the linguistic hybridity of Miss Trunchbull (the fierce English headmistress who is able to spout a torrent of traditional Welsh insults) may heighten their enjoyment. For others, the linguistic and cultural slippage between the Welsh translations and their previous experience of the Dahl brand in English may lead to confusion, even disappointment. Whatever their first language, all readers of Welsh versions of Dahl will also be proficient readers of English. Bilingualism is a feature of their personal *habitus* – the means by which they construct meaning from their surroundings – and as such can be revisioned in the light of Said's description of exiles:

Most people are principally aware of one culture, one setting, one home; exiles are aware of at least two, and this plurality of vision gives rise to an awareness of simultaneous dimensions, an awareness that – to borrow a phrase from music – is contrapuntal.[61]

A bilingual subject can also be said to have a plurality of vision and a contrapuntal awareness of language and culture, and in evoking Dylan Thomas, the Welsh translation of *Matilda* (for example) unexpectedly highlights the contrapuntal dynamics of bilingualism. Yet the very decision to translate Dahl confuses those dynamics, placing Welsh and English versions in competition, asking many readers (children, parents, teachers) to choose between the familiarity of English Dahl and his defamiliarising Welsh incarnations.

Returning to Wales through translation, Roald Dahl crosses a linguistic boundary that would have been familiar to him in his formative years. He returns, not as a naughty schoolboy, but as a global bestseller, and the adherence of the translations to the structure of the source texts indicates the reverence in which the canonised author is held, and the commercial capital of the Dahl brand. However, no translation can avoid the necessary reorientation and repositioning that occur when a text in one literary field is subjected to the *habitus* of another. Thus in his new literary surroundings, Dahl finds himself both foreign and familiar, welcomed and resisted.

Notes

1 Moira Inghilleri, 'The Sociology of Bourdieu and the Construction of the "Object" in Translation and Interpreting Studies', *The Translator*, 11/2 (2005), p. 126.
2 Pierre Bourdieu, *The Field of Cultural Production*, ed. Randal Johnson (Cambridge: Polity Press, 1992), p. 180.
3 Inghilleri, 'The Sociology of Bourdieu', p. 136.
4 See Jackie E. Stallcup, 'Discomfort and Delight: The Role of Humour in Roald Dahl's Works for Children', in *Roald Dahl* (New Casebooks), ed. Ann Alston and Catherine Butler (Basingstoke: Palgrave Macmillan, 2012), p. 31.
5 Edward Said, *Reflections on Exile and Other Essays* (Cambridge, MA: Harvard University Press, 2000), p. 176.
6 Pierre Bourdieu, *In Other Words: Essays Towards a Reflexive Sociology* (1990), quoted in Jean-Marc Gouanvic, 'A Bourdieusian Theory of Translation, or the Coincidence of Practical Instances', *The Translator*, 11/2 (2005), pp. 158–9.

7 Pierre Bourdieu, *Outline of a Theory of Practice*, trans. Richard Nice (Cambridge: Cambridge University Press, 1977), p. 167.

8 Pierre Bourdieu, *The Rules of Art: Genesis and Structure of the Literary Field*, trans. Susan Emanuel (Cambridge: Polity Press, 1996), p. 179.

9 Gouanvic, 'A Bourdieusian Theory of Translation', p. 162.

10 Bourdieu, *The Rules of Art*, p. 216.

11 Quoted in John R. W. Speller, *Bourdieu and Literature* (Cambridge: Open Book Publishing, 2011), p. 80.

12 In his sociologically informed analysis of Flaubert in *The Rules of Art*, Bourdieu refers to the bohemian French literary field of the nineteenth century as an example of such an autonomous field.

13 See Gouvanic, 'A Bourdieusian Theory of Translation', p. 155: '[The] abundance of translations was not governed by any strict respect for authorship rights; publishers could simply appropriate the work of a foreign author without restriction and have her or his work translated, even from a pirate edition.' For an analysis of *Anrheg i Blentyn*, see Siwan Rosser, 'Thomas Jones, Dinbych, a'i *Anrheg i Blentyn*', *The Journal of the Calvinistic Methodist Historical Society*, 32 (2008), pp. 44–73.

14 See Naroa Zubillaga, 'A Corpus-based Descriptive Study of German Children's Literature translated into Basque: Preliminary Results', in *Translating Fictional Dialogue for Children and Young People*, ed. M. B. Fischer and M. W. Naro (Berlin: Frank & Timme, 2012), p. 82, and Jant van der Weg-Laverman, 'West Frisian Children's Literature', in *Handbuch des Friesischen/Handbook of Frisian Studies*, ed. H. H. Munske *et al.* (Tübingen: Niemeyer, 2001), p. 223.

15 Rita Ghesquiere, 'Why Does Children's Literature Need Translations?', in *Children's Literature in Translation: Challenges and Strategies*, ed. J. Van Coillie and W. P. Verschueren (Manchester: St. Jerome, 2006), p. 25.

16 Turid Sigurðardóttir, 'Translation in Faroese Children's Literature', in *Northern Lights: Translation in the Nordic Countries*, ed. B. J. Epstein (Oxford: Peter Lang, 2009), p. 185.

17 Lawrence Venuti, 'Introduction', *The Translator*, 4/2 (1998), p. 138.

18 Bourdieu, *The Rules of Art*, p. 228.

19 Michael Cronin, *Translation and Globalization* (London: Routledge, 2003), p. 162.

20 See Mairwen Jones, *Publishing Children's Books in Welsh: Report to the Welsh Books Council* (2014), pp. 15 (4.14), 33 (9.6).

21 Translations of series such as *Diary of a Wimpy Kid* and *Tom Gates*, for example, were reportedly welcomed by teachers for their potential to inspire reluctant young Welsh readers; see Jones, *Publishing Children's Books in Welsh*, p. 76.

22 See Catherine Butler, 'Introduction', in Alston and Butler (eds), *Roald Dahl*, p. 1: 'At the last count, Dahl's books were available in 54 languages [58 is the number quoted by *http://www.roalddahl.com/global/in-translation*, accessed

15 January 2016] . . . with combined sales of approximately 100 million worldwide.'

23 Cronin, *Translation and Globalization*, p. 38.

24 Roger Boore, *Llyfrau Plant Mewn Ieithoedd Lleiafrifol* (Caerdydd: Gwasg y Dref Wen, 1978), p. 10: 'Y gwir yw bod lle trosiadau mewn unrhyw ddiwylliant yn bwnc dyrys, amlwynebog. Yn un peth, os cyhoeddwch ormod o drosiadau, byddwch yn boddi eich diwylliant eich hun . . . Ond os na chyhoeddwch ddigon o drosiadau, byddwch yn creu diwylliant mewnsyllgar, cul' ('The truth is that the place of translations in any culture is a complex, multifarious issue. For one thing, if one publishes too many translations, one will drown one's own culture . . . But if one publishes too few, one will create an introspective, narrow culture').

25 157 Welsh children's titles (fiction and poetry) were published during 2014, seventy-four of which were translations (data obtained from *http://www.gwales. com*, accessed 1 July 2015). 89 per cent of the translations published between 1965 and 1995 were for children. See Catrin V. Huws and Hywel E. Roberts, 'Addasu, Cyfaddasu a Chyhoeddi yn y Gymraeg 1965–1995: Peth o Ffrwyth Ymchwilio'r Maes', *Y Llyfr yng Nghymru/Welsh Book Studies*, 3 (2000), p. 73.

26 The prominent children's writer and novelist Bethan Gwanas has repeatedly used her Twitter feed and blog to air such concerns. She has approached the Welsh Government's Education and Skills department directly on behalf of fifteen other authors to petition for a review of commissioning rates that result in a situation where a writer can earn as much for a translation as for an original novel. See Jones, *Publishing Children's Books in Welsh*, pp. 71–3.

27 Cronin, *Translation and Globalization*, p. 90.

28 Cronin, *Translation and Globalization*, p. 142.

29 Ghesquiere, 'Why Does Children's Literature Need Translations?', p. 29.

30 Cronin, *Translation and Globalization*, p. 147.

31 See Kristine J. Anderson, 'Children's Literature in English Translation', in *Encyclopaedia of Literary Translation into English: A–L*, ed. O. Classe (London and Chicago: Fitzroy Dearborn, 2000), p. 277.

32 Rhian S. Reynolds, *A Bibliography of Welsh Literature in English Translation* (Cardiff: University of Wales Press, 2005), p. 225.

33 See Cronin, *Translation and Globalization*, p. 38: 'Translation without change is not translation but mere citation, leading only to the barren fields of subjection.'

34 See Hanna-Mari Sorvari, 'Domestication and Foreignisation in the Finnish and Swedish Translations of *The BFG* by Roald Dahl' (unpublished MA thesis, University of Jyväskylä, 2014), pp. 34–5.

35 Roald Dahl, *Matilda*, trans. Elin Meek (Hengoed: Rily Publications, 2008), p. 15; Roald Dahl, *James a'r Eirinen Wlanog Enfawr*, trans. Elin Meek (Hengoed: Rily Publications, 2011), p. 132; Roald Dahl, *Yr CMM*, trans. Elin Meek (Hengoed: Rily Publications, 2003), p. 154.

36 Dahl, *Yr CMM*, pp. 127–8; Roald Dahl, *The BFG* (London: Puffin, 2013), pp. 127–8.
37 Lawrence Venuti, *The Translator's Invisibility* (New York: Routledge, 1995), p. 18.
38 Dahl, *Matilda*, trans. Meek, pp. 7, 9; Dahl, *Matilda*, pp. 7, 9.
39 See Daniel G. Williams, 'Realaeth a Hunaniaeth: O T. Rowland Hughes i Owen Martell', *Taliesin*, 125 (2005), pp. 12–27. Here, Williams contests Dai Smith's assertion that Welsh-language fiction cannot construct a convincing realism.
40 See Ivana Marinić and Željka Nemet, 'Two Languages, Number One Authors: The Influence of Bilingual Upbringing on the Literary Accomplishments of Roald Dahl and Dr. Seuss', *ELOPE: English Language Overseas Perspectives and Enquiries*, 5/1–2 (2008), p. 153.
41 See the editors' 'Postscript' in *The Nation in Children's Literature: Nations of Childhood*, ed. Christopher (Kit) Kelen and Björn Sundmark (New York: Routledge, 2013), p. 263.
42 Venuti, 'Introduction', p. 140.
43 Cronin, *Translation and Globalization*, p. 147.
44 Gouanvic, 'A Bourdieusian Theory of Translation', pp. 157–8
45 T. Llew Jones published a collection of ghost stories in 1975 under the title *Arswyd y Byd* (Llandysul: Gwasg Gomer). For further examples of traditional expressions in translations of Dahl, see Ffion Haf Pritchard, 'Cyfieithu Llenyddiaeth Plant i'r Gymraeg: Tair Astudiaeth Achos' (unpublished M.Phil. thesis, Cardiff University, 2014), pp. 47–8.
46 Dahl, *Matilda*, p. 142.
47 Dahl, *Matilda*, trans. Meek, p. 142; the insult 'Y twmffat [bach] twp' can be traced to the routine of the popular children's comedy duo, 'Syr Wynff a Plwmsan', who appeared regularly on S4C television in the 1980s.
48 Speller, *Bourdieu and Literature*, pp. 51–2.
49 Dahl, *The BFG*, p. 20; Dahl, *Yr CMM*, p. 20.
50 Dahl, *Matilda*, trans. Elin Meek, pp. 178–9.
51 Data from *http://statiaith.com/cymraeg/ysgolion/caisRhyddidGwybodaethLlywodraeth CymruED341.html*, accessed 2 January 2016.
52 See W. Gwyn Lewis, 'Addysg Ddwyieithog yn yr Unfed Ganrif ar Hugain: Adolygu'r Cyd-destun Rhyngwladol', *Gwerddon*, 7 (2011), pp. 66–88.
53 Roald Dahl, *Charlie a'r Ffatri Siocled*, trans. Elin Meek (Hengoed: Rily Publications, 2002), p. 96.
54 See Dahl, *Charlie a'r Ffatri Siocled*, pp. 171–4.
55 Bridget Fowler, *Pierre Bourdieu and Cultural Theory: Critical Investigations* (London: Sage Publications, 1997), p. 3.
56 Fowler, *Pierre Bourdieu and Cultural Theory*, p. 3.
57 Bourdieu, *The Rules of Art*, p. 20; Bourdieu, *The Field of Cultural Production*, p. 176.
58 Deborah C. Thacker, 'Fairy Tale and Anti-Fairy Tale: Roald Dahl and the Telling Power of Stories', in Alston and Butler (eds), *Roald Dahl*, p. 17.

59 Bourdieu, *The Rules of Art*, p. 347.
60 Fowler, *Pierre Bourdieu and Cultural Theory*, p. 161.
61 Said, *Reflections on Exile*, p. 186.

Works cited

Dahl, Roald, *Charlie a'r Ffatri Siocled*, trans. Elin Meek (Hengoed: Rily Publications, 2002).
—, *James a'r Eirinen Wlanog Enfawr*, trans. Elin Meek (Hengoed: Rily Publications, 2011).
—, *Matilda*, trans. Elin Meek (Hengoed: Rily Publications, 2008).
—, *Yr CMM*, trans. Elin Meek (Hengoed: Rily Publications, 2003).

Anderson, Kristine J., 'Children's Literature in English Translation', in *Encyclopaedia of Literary Translation into English: A–L*, ed. O. Classe (London and Chicago: Fitzroy Dearborn, 2000), pp. 276–8.
Boore, Roger, *Llyfrau Plant Mewn Ieithoedd Lleiafrifol* (Caerdydd: Gwasg y Dref Wen, 1978).
Bourdieu, Pierre, *In Other Words: Essays Towards a Reflexive Sociology* (Stanford CA: Stanford University Press, 1990).
—, *Outline of a Theory of Practice*, trans. Richard Nice (Cambridge: Cambridge University Press, 1977).
—, *The Field of Cultural Production*, ed. Randal Johnson (Cambridge: Polity Press, 1992).
—, *The Rules of Art: Genesis and Structure of the Literary Field*, trans. Susan Emanuel (Cambridge: Polity Press, 1996).
Butler, Catherine, 'Introduction', in *Roald Dahl* (New Casebooks), ed. Ann Alston and Catherine Butler (Basingstoke: Palgrave Macmillan, 2012), pp. 1–13.
Cronin, Michael, *Translation and Globalization* (London: Routledge, 2003).
Fowler, Bridget, *Pierre Bourdieu and Cultural Theory: Critical Investigations* (London: Sage Publications, 1997).
Ghesquiere, Rita, 'Why Does Children's Literature Need Translations?', in *Children's Literature in Translation: Challenges and Strategies*, ed. J. Van Coillie and W. P. Verschueren (Manchester: St Jerome, 2006), pp. 19–34.
Huws, Catrin V., and Hywel E. Roberts, 'Addasu, Cyfaddasu a Chyhoeddi yn y Gymraeg 1965–1995: Peth o Ffrwyth Ymchwilio'r Maes', *Y Llyfr yng Nghymru / Welsh Book Studies*, 3 (2000), pp. 69–87.
Inghilleri, Moira, 'The Sociology of Bourdieu and the Construction of the "Object" in Translation and Interpreting Studies', *The Translator*, 11/2 (2005), pp. 125–45.
Jones, Mairwen, *Publishing Children's Books in Welsh: Report to the Welsh Books Council* (2014).

Kelen, Christopher (Kit), and Björn Sundmark, 'Postscript', *The Nation in Children's Literature: Nations of Childhood*, ed. Kit Kelen and Bjorn Sundmark (New York: Routledge, 2013), pp. 263–72.

Lewis, W. Gwyn, 'Addysg Ddwyieithog yn yr Unfed Ganrif ar Hugain: Adolygu'r Cyd-destun Rhyngwladol', *Gwerddon*, 7 (2011), pp. 67–88.

Marinić, Ivana, and Željka Nemet, 'Two Languages, Number One Authors: The Influence of Bilingual Upbringing on the Literary Accomplishments of Roald Dahl and Dr. Seuss', *ELOPE: English Languages Overseas Perspectives and Enquiries*, 5/1–2 (2008), pp. 139–55.

Pritchard, Ffion Haf, 'Cyfieithu Llenyddiaeth Plant i'r Gymraeg: Tair Astudiaeth Achos' (unpublished M.Phil. thesis, Cardiff University, 2014).

Reynolds, Rhian S., *A Bibliography of Welsh Literature in English Translation* (Cardiff: University of Wales Press, 2005).

Rosser, Siwan, 'Thomas Jones, Dinbych, a'i *Anrheg i Blentyn*', *The Journal of the Calvinistic Methodist Historical Society*, 32 (2008), pp. 44–73.

Said, Edward, *Reflections on Exile and Other Essays* (Cambridge, MA: Harvard University Press, 2000).

Sigurðardóttir, Turid, 'Translation in Faroese Children's Literature', in *Northern Lights: Translation in the Nordic Countries*, ed. B. J. Epstein (Oxford: Peter Lang, 2009), pp. 181–90.

Sorvari, Hanna-Mari, 'Domestication and Foreignisation in the Finnish and Swedish Translations of *The BFG* by Roald Dahl' (unpublished MA thesis, University of Jyvaskyla, 2014).

Speller, John R. W., *Bourdieu and Literature* (Cambridge: Open Book Publishing, 2011).

Stallcup, Jackie E., 'Discomfort and Delight: The Role of Humour in Roald Dahl's Works for Children', in *Roald Dahl* (New Casebooks), ed. Ann Alston and Catherine Butler (Basingstoke: Palgrave Macmillan, 2012), pp. 31–50.

Thacker, Deborah C., 'Fairy Tale and Anti-Fairy Tale: Roald Dahl and the Telling Power of Stories', in *Roald Dahl* (New Casebooks), ed. Ann Alston and Catherine Butler (Basingstoke: Palgrave Macmillan, 2012), pp. 14–30.

van der Weg-Laverman, Jant, 'West Frisian Children's Literature', in *Handbuch des Friesischen/Handbook of Frisian Studies*, ed. H. H. Munske *et al.* (Tubingen: Niemeyer, 2001), pp. 223–32.

Venuti, Lawrence, 'Introduction', *The Translator*, 4/2 (1998), pp. 135–44.

—, *The Translator's Invisibility* (New York: Routledge, 1995).

Williams, Daniel G., 'Realaeth a Hunaniaeth: O T. Rowland Hughes i Owen Martell', *Taliesin*, 125 (2005), pp. 12–27.

Zubillaga, Naroa, 'A Corpus-based Descriptive Study of German Children's Literature translated into Basque: Preliminary Results', in *Translating Fictional Dialogue for Children and Young People*, ed. M. B. Fischer and M. W. Naro (Berlin: Frank & Timme, 2012), pp. 81–98.

9

Dahl's Cardiff Spaces

Peter Finch

1. The Bay (he would have had no idea where this was)

Going down the grand boulevard is a mile-long pull. Ahead I can see the refracted light of the new Cardiff – the helmet metal of the Millennium Centre, William Pye's shining silver tower cascading with water, the high-risen apartments edging the Oval Basin, the cranes building more. They haven't finished reinventing this place even after thirty years. The Bay is still a rush of sparkling change.

The road I'm on is a French-style, tree-lined dual carriageway that, in true Welsh fashion, doesn't actually go anywhere at all. When this line in the silt was called Collingdon Road it was edged with flour mills, grain stores and warehouses strung out along the Bute West Dock. Then it had a purpose. Its air was thick with coal and industrial dirt. Trade and more trade rolled along its uneven, potholed top. Now Collingdon has been widened, resurfaced, and redesignated as the first section of the A470, the only thing we have in Wales that links the north with the south. It runs from the Flourish at the top of the Oval Basin to roar up from the Bay in a perfectly straight line. Your drive, you zoom, and then you stop. You hit the embankment of the main Swansea to London rail link. Traffic lights, turns, tunnels, underpasses. Grand vision turned folly. Who thought this up?

When it was first completed in 2000 the boulevard was called Bute Avenue. There's an engraved stone at the southern extremity to this effect. It is situated just along from the road's actual nameplate. This brands the highway Lloyd George Avenue, named thus by the city fathers in celebration of the great Liberal politician. Lloyd George, the man who introduced social welfare, won the First World War, reordered Europe and created an independent Ireland but saw no point in doing the same for Wales.

This is all so alien from the world Roald Dahl once inhabited. He would have been here in 1916 getting himself christened. He would then have been brought as a toddler to sing Norwegian hymns at the church. And later he'd come to crawl on the wooden floors of his father Harald's office, to take in the sights of steam ships and sailing brigs, clanking steam trains, men in bowlers making money, dockers with hard hands getting by, coal dust whirling everywhere, entering every pore.

We know this is Dahl's place because the Bute West Dock Oval Basin has been renamed in his honour. This ship-holding salt water impoundment just to the south of Bute's first dock has been hard-core refilled, pasteurised with amphitheatre stone seating, and embellished with stone column lighting. It now faintly recalls Barcelona. The Oval Basin opened in 2000 as a great new space for the city to call its own. It was renamed Roald Dahl Plass in 2002. It's now home to a rolling smorgasbord of car shows, craft markets, food fayres, drinks festivals, people dressed in French costume playing accordions, Eisteddfod shenanigans, open-air opera, and Cardiff's own all-weather artificial sand beach, fun fair and paddling pool (annually every August).

In the pub I ask how much they know of this great native son of the Welsh capital. Willie Wonka, they say. Charlie. Beyond that they know little. It's as if Cardiff is a Dahl-resistant city, a place that manages pretty well without mentioning him at all. I've done so much of this stuff, hunting the vanished, looking for things that are no longer there, checking for the past that lies just below the present, searching for traces. When I've been lost I've always sought support in the company of someone who knew exactly where I was. But on this trip I'm on my own.

The Plass today is empty. A Japanese tourist or two at the base of the silver tower looking for Torchwood's fictional HQ, no sign of the author's memory or trace of his spirit in the air. In the early nineties, before the building of Jonathan Adams's Wales Millennium Centre, there was an audacious plan to make Cardiff a Dahl capital. Those with their hands on the city's future at this time had just rejected Zaha Hadid's proposals for a decade-defining Cardiff Bay Opera House. This was a failure of nerve and vision of the kind that marks so much of Welsh life. Roald Dahl had died at the end of 1990. Dahl and Dahl, the trust which managed the Roald Dahl estate and its not inconsiderable wealth, were looking for a permanent home. There was a proposal to build one in Cardiff Bay, a spinnaker tower of a children's centre to be erected at the end of a dock pier right in the midst of the Severn's estuary sea.

Literature was on the rise. Why not mark the capital as the centre for children's stories, a place to celebrate the form's greatest practitioner? The Dahls were interested. But as with all audacious plans, it takes nerve and cunning to deliver. Someone somewhere fumbled. Instead, Dahl and Dahl acquired a group of buildings in Great Missenden, Buckinghamshire, where Roald had moved in 1954 and where most of his classic books were written. His writing hut had been preserved. So had his writing chair. His vast archive of manuscripts, drawings, story ideas, books and other documents was ready to go on display. The Trust opened their Roald Dahl Museum and Story Centre in 2005. They could have been out there in Cardiff's prevailing salt westerlies, Dahl back in his now sparkling birthplace. Instead, with the Big Friendly Giant looking over the wall and the crocodile disguised as a bench, they were safe in the quiet centre of England.

Cardiff rolls on, Dahl an absence. He isn't in our street blood the way Dannie Abse and Frank Hennessey are. They didn't celebrate him to mark devolution and the opening of the Welsh Assembly. For that they had Tom Jones, Bonnie Tyler and Shirley Bassey in her *Draig Goch* dress. Beyond the Dahl Plass itself there's little named after him. By way of comparison, go to Laugharne and check how many things have incorporated Dylan Thomas into their nomenclature. There are no Dahl Burger Bars or Dahl Cafés and Diners here in Cardiff. No Dahl bookshops, no Roald Dahl literature awards or Dahl story festivals sprawling across the Oval Basin.

Cardiff isn't explicitly there in his work, either. Roald Dahl was Norwegian, son of Norwegian parents. He was born here in Welsh Great Britain by sheer chance. If Dahl was anything then he was English. He adopted English ways, at least he did when he wasn't following his 'gypsy' predilections for gambling and poaching. A cultural schizophrenic, half-toff, half-backwoodsman, Cardiff vague on his tongue.

I do a round of the Plass. I check the name plaque, a bilingual slate oval – English, Welsh, no Norwegian. Russell Goodway, Council Leader and friendly giant, was here in 2002 in the company of both

Liccy, Roald's second wife, and the Norwegian Ambassador. Together they'd marked Cardiff as a Dahl place. A highly commendable act, but there's still so far to go.

Cardiff Bay may not be exactly a Dahlian epicentre but there are a few traces. There's a Norwegian church. A white-painted corrugated iron shack had been erected in 1868. This was on land donated by Lord Bute on the edge of his West Dock, just south of the engine works and opposite warehouses belonging to the South Wales and Liverpool Steam Packet company. The building was half Christian chapel and half seamen's mission. A place of refuge, God, soup, Norwegian newspapers and Norwegian talk. Norwegians had been sailing into Cardiff since the beginning of the industrial revolution. They delivered shipments of wood from which pit props (known as 'Norways') were made, and they took back iron and coal. When the docks declined, so, too, did the church. Fewer Norwegian congregants, diminishing numbers of refuge-seeking sailors. By 1974 it had been deconsecrated and had fallen into disrepair.

When regeneration began in the Bay during the eighties, the abandoned Norwegian structure found itself in the wrong place. That sliver of dock edge was marked as ground for the incoming Wales Millennium Centre. I walked over this levelled-but-not-yet-built-on earthen patch once with a trumpet player from the Opera's orchestra. He was going to deliver the first performance in this new cultural arena even if all that existed at the time was a set of hoardings surrounding a bleak slice of cleared and infilled ground.

I forget what he played. Not *Cherry Pink* or anything very military, but it sounded welcoming. It was to be the trumpet-call of a socialist future when the people would own this creative space, this cultural furnace. Except that never quite happened. Bills have to be paid, debts defused and obligations discharged. The new centre responded accordingly.

The church was rebuilt a few hundred metres south. This is now Harbour Drive but back then was mainly rail sidings holding coal in wagons ready for loading in the Roath Basin. The church got itself a new roof, new wooden walls painted bright white, a new spire and a new floor. Same church, said the preservation trust running the show. The one where Roald Dahl was christened.

Despite the bodily relocation and structural tinkering, the Dahl spirit still hangs in the air. Inside the church is the Roald Dahl Gallery. This mounts exhibitions of paintings and framed photographs, as well as showing the Dahl family christening bowl, used to name Roald and his siblings. On Roald Dahl Day, the anniversary of his birth, the church holds Dahl readings and competitions. Liccy has been here. So have children dressed as chocolate factory characters, Matilda, the BFG, and the Grand High Witch of All the World. Willy Wonka himself once perambulated the church handing out chocolate bars. But then September was gone and the bleak rains of October came rolling back. The church returned to its role as café, rentable meeting space and venue for folk concerts and poetry performances. Twm Morys read here, pulpit-standing like a wild north Wales preacher. So did Benjamin Zephaniah, Dannie Abse, Grace Nichols and other literary luminaries. So did I, launching a volume in the *Real Cardiff* series, standing there talking about the city, looking out at the soft-shoed tourists grazing the Bay's edge, wondering just where the reality had actually gone. Dahl's name blurs.

Ronnie Dickens, Juggler
Ron Dawkins, Backwoodsman
Ronald Davies, Pork Butcher
Ronald Dawes, Confectioner
Ronald Drift, Handyman
Ronald Dill, Steam Brakeman
Reginald Dosanquest, Reporter
Reggie Darling, Coal Cutter
Rennie Derringer, Chemist
Rollie Dark, Magician
Roland Desketh, Government Agent
Roland Delwydd, Farmer
Roland Dafis, Church Decorator
Ronal Despor, Rodent Remover
Roland Dal, Manufacturer of Ship Stays
Roland Dil, Iron Moulder
Roland Doll, Air Pilot
Roland Dell, Pencil Maker
Roland Barthes, Philosopher
Song of Roland, Musselman
Reggie Dahl, Gunrunner
Roland Dahl, Awdur
Roald Dahl, BFG

Cardiff's Norwegian connection perseveres. For decades the Christmas Tree erected in the gloom of the early twentieth century outside City Hall was a gift from the people of Norway. There'd be a ceremony, the mayor would speak, there'd be applause, and then some local celebrity, a famous fishmonger or footballer, Lennie the Lion or Dorothy Squires, would press the switch and the tree would light up. We might sing something, briefly. After that we'd all go home. By the late twentieth century that tradition had morphed. Cardiff is now twinned with the Norwegian town of Hordaland. The council there sent us a tree that was permanently planted outside the Bay's Norwegian church. It gets decorated each Christmas, formally lit, and a band plays. After that we all go inside for Norwegian drinks or up to Roald Dahl Plass to engage with Cardiff's craftspeople selling wooden bird houses, knitted hats and bread boards with your name burned onto them. I guess we should send the people of Hordaland something back. I don't think we do.

Over at the Eli Jenkins pub I'm trying to track Harald, Roald's father. The Eli Jenkins is on Bute Crescent. It stares out across the Plass at the metres-high lettering of the Gwyneth Lewis poem that fronts the Wales Millennium Centre. *In These Stones Horizons Sing – Creu Gwir fel Gwydr o Ffwrnais Awen*. During construction one dismal Christmas a decade or so ago, some wag went home for his fortnight break leaving only four letters illuminated. *F oFf* they read, pouring their light expletively right up James Street. Below this sheet metal verse is the Portmeirion book and gift shop. It's the nearest store to where the Norwegian church originally stood. Do they have Dahl titles in stock? They don't.

The Eli Jenkins may look old, as if it had once flogged ale to parched dock hauliers and coke tippers. It opened in the mid-1990s, just when that line of great original docklands taverns – The White Hart, The Ship and Pilot, The Big Windsor, The Bute Dock – were starting to close. It majors on cheap pub food. The bar is full of turned wood, pine stools, dado rails. It occupies the site where Roald's father Harald, as one half of Aadnesen and Dahl, had his business office. He was a colliery and ship agent, drawn to Cardiff by the south Wales coal boom at the turn of the twentieth century. He supplied arriving ships with all the consumables they needed. As his business developed he expanded it to include coal export. You want to make money? Come here.

Harald had done that in 1897, the year of Queen Victoria's Diamond Jubilee and the apogee of Empire. He settled first at 3 Charles Place, Barry, facing David Davies's docks. There he learned his trade. In 1901 he set up a shipbroking and coal-exporting business with fellow Norwegian exile Ludvig Aadnesen. They had a small office in the rabbit warren of Pier Head Chambers at the bottom of Bute Street. Their business boomed. They expanded to Newport, Swansea and Port Talbot. By 1915 they'd shifted their HQ to larger premises on Bute Crescent. No. 6. Right where Eli Jenkins now serves beer. You can see the pair of them out there, walking down the Crescent, high, stiff collars, business-suited among a local population of dock workers in rough clothes and mufflers. They blow on their hands. It's cold. They turn up the entrance steps and enter the Bar. Harald goes to his desk, Ludvig to a side room where the files are kept. It's a toilet now. A guy in a tracksuit exits, goes back to his mid-morning beer.

Today, a Tesco Express occupies the site of Pier Head Chambers. The chain sells cheese and tuna sandwiches to office workers. It also does a good line in top-up supplies to the district's eclectic mix of Bute Town residents and Johnny-come-lately Bay apartment renters. The area is one of transience, at least as far as flat life goes. One-person edifices of glass and chrome abound. Undercroft parking no problem. Reasonable service charges. Views of the water. Of the industry and dirt that created this place there's little trace. The road is pedestrianised, euphemised, scribbled on with strolling visitors. Art reproductions, ribboned gifts, celebratory Welsh cakes. Nothing a resident would really ever want to own.

Looking for Dahl down here is hopeless. The psychogeography is all wrong. He's present but only in the way that Peppa Pig and Ronald McDonald are, pressure-sprayed onto the district's surface by vested interests. This is the Bay, after all, centrepiece of regenerated Cardiff. Cardiff, Europe's youngest capital. Cardiff, a family friendly, hands-on place. Cardiff, green and endlessly cultural. Cardiff, streetwise and hip hop proud. Cardiff, the fastest-growing of cities, centre of dragons, skateboarders, rugby balls and smiling middle-class visitors. You drink and dine, marvel at the cultural wonders and the impounded waters. I write it up for my books. It's what people want to read. But Roald's Cardiff, if there ever was one, was never really here.

Peter Finch

Dahl By Numbers

If it's not:
19222 74527
19254 74600
19163 74546

then it has to be:
19464 72584
13434 80467
12725 80933
15408 78111

(Check yourself:
http://www.gridreferencefinder.com)

The Dahl ghosts are north, well out of the city, in places where the past is still occasionally visible. They run like a ley from the north edge of Radyr following the river down into the ecclesiastical city of Llandaff. Dahl tracks. Places where he'd spent enough time to have left just a fleck of himself in the fabric of the air. Where the trees he'd seen might still grow. Where the woodland paths he'd walked might not all have been paved.

When you had money in the early and still grubbily industrial twentieth century you tried not to live in the heart of cities. Cities were filled with bad air. Their road surfaces were a mash of horse dung and mud. They were thick with workers' housing, and even thicker with workers themselves. Men in caps, women in headscarves, housed in the tight streets of Adamsdown, Newtown, Splott, Grangetown, Butetown's Tiger Bay and the residential Docks. They were noisy places, abundant with hooters and rushing steam, ships arriving, trains clanking. Trees faltered. Green spaces were layered with dust. If you had the cash then you built yourself a great house out there in the hills – in Llanishen, on the slopes of Penylan Hill, in flourishing Cyncoed, in the green pastures of Whitchurch and in the woods of Radyr. These were places that had not yet been incorporated into the thriving metropolis. They were close enough to Cardiff's working centre to allow for easy transportation, yet they remained places apart.

Harald had the cash. Despite an earlier attempt to lead the bohemian life in Paris in the company of his brother Oscar, Harald had made good. His shipbroking business was doing well. Well enough for him to escape the grime of Barry for a new mansion, built to his own designs, on the edge of Llandaff.

The Dahl ley is a crooked leg. It's a line south but it does nothing in the right order. Death comes before life. You see the memorial and then you see the birth. It streams and sparkles then it bends left and then right, picking at history. But it's a ley alright. A line of Dahl force running into the city, north to south. The Roald Dahl trail. On paper, tourism operators would love the idea. In practice, it's something else.

2. Walking It

On foot is the only way to see anything. So perversely, at Cardiff Central, I start on the train. I catch the City Line which began at Coryton and now, after looping in a great U through the eastern suburbs, is about to take me north. This line could so easily have been a circle. It almost was. That was at a point somewhere between the unsparing slum clearances of the sixties and the start of redevelopment signalled by Cardiff Council building itself a new pagoda-like headquarters right in the middle of the otherwise deserted and devastated post-industrial Bay. A forward thinker suggested the lines be linked. There were extant but abandoned trackbeds ready to be reused. Only a small amount of new build would be necessary. But the spirit of that age was the motorway, on stilts, running right into the hearts of cities. Proposals for new rail lines stood no chance. The metro was never built.

The City Link is the nearest to a metro that we now have. It is the welding together of two once separate rail lines operated by different companies. I'm in the two-car diesel and I'm standing. Every single seat is occupied by pupils from Bishop of Llandaff High School. Kids, bags, blazers, headphones, chewing. The windows stream as the train steams. Around us is railway land, an industrial cityscape full of rail sheds, engine bays, carriage washeries, repair shops and assembled new track in stacks like a giant train set. Passenger usage at Cardiff Central has risen and risen. It's hitting twelve million annually now. A decade back it was less than half that. Expansion is in the wind. There's already a surreal-sounding Platform 0 with direct access to the Millennium Stadium. Work is also almost done on the new Platform

8. If Network Rail's development proposals under a set of initiatives called Control Period Six succeed (which make it all start to sound like a science fiction film) a new Platform 8 will be only the start. Enfolding shopping malls, underways, electric tram complexes and a massive new urban light electric rail system for the south-east will spring into being. Well, hardly spring. It'll take five years to raise the money and then a further five to use it. So don't hold your breath.

This south-west of the city on view from the tracks is the capital with its guard down. Backs of mosques, tottering streets, unkempt gardens, the yards of the brewery, open land where the paper mills once stood, warehouses stacked with building materials, and even more open and right now empty rail beds. It reminds me of London, how the land looks as you reach Paddington or Waterloo.

But it doesn't last. After the carriages have disgorged a hundred uni-formed school kids at Fairwater, the cuttings emerge, wooded banks and scrub masking the housing above. It's leafy suburbia giving an impression of empty countryside. A green west Cardiff, a place that doesn't change.

It's freezing. The train has reached Radyr where it will rest a while before returning the way it came. I'm off, up the footbridge steps, plastered thickly with Network Rail road salt. No one but no one will slip and sue here. In a previous, smaller, steam-filled incarnation, the Radyr train would have served Harald Dahl who did a daily commute into what was then called Bute Road Station. His ghost is there on the platform now, eye glasses, one arm, three-piece suit, white starched collar. He looks like a disapproving headmaster. His Taff Vale railway season ticket was found inside his expensive leather wallet when he died in 1920. That was on 11 April. The ticket was valid until the 23rd.

In 1917, dissatisfied with Villa Marie – the house he'd built for his first wife, the Parisienne beauty, Marie Beaurin-Gressier (who had died car-rying their third child), Harald bought Tŷ Mynydd (Mountain House), set on rising ground a mile north of the rail station. This was life on a grander scale. One hundred and fifty acres of land, outbuildings, cot-tages, a piggery, lawns, formal flower borders, terraces, its own electricity generator and an enormous Victorian house. An estate. The Dahls had now become part of the English-accented county set. Roald, from the recordings I've heard, sounded more home counties than west-of-the-Severn. The Cardiff buzz-saw tonalities come into it not at all. I've no idea what Harald might have sounded like. Norwegian, I expect.

The Radyr house was huge. In photographs it looks like part of Hogwarts. It had multiple chimney stacks, mock Tudor gables, a tiled roof larger than most churches' and greenhouses to the side to rival those of Dyffryn House, to the west of Cardiff. This is the place Roald remembers with nostalgia, recalling the fields full of shire horses and dairy cows. There are photographs of him as a four-year-old out on the lawns and terraces, in the fields among the sheaves of corn, sitting on the wall of the piggery and of the house itself, which is resplendently decorated with both the Union Jack and the Norwegian flag. No Welsh dragon in sight.

Tŷ Mynydd had been built in 1883 by George Fisher, general superintendent of the Taff Vale Railway. When he died in 1891 the property passed to his son, H. Oakden Fisher, chair of both the TVR and the Cardiff Gaslight and Coke Company Ltd, although his real interest lay with the military. He was Lieutenant Colonel of the Glamorgan Volunteer Artillery. Harald bought the estate in 1918. When he died in 1920, his second wife, Sofie Magdalene, moved to smaller premises back in Llandaff. Tŷ Mynydd then became the property of the architect Sir Beddoe Rees MP, and for a brief time in the 1930s was turned into St Maur's College, a small private boarding school for girls.

In 1967 the house and most if its outbuildings were demolished. This was the first full-blooded rush at clearance following the war. Cardiff was expanding. Property developers had no interest in the preservation of inefficient, draughty piles such as Tŷ Mynydd. On its lands a whole housing estate could be built. It had to come down.

I take the road up out of the station's gully. Already the old shunting yards and waste ground lining the river have been populated with high-density brick town housing. There's little public space. Most structures are distinct from each other, laid at angles as if thrown there like dice. Room for breath is restricted and corners are rounded. Access is on turning roads named after De Clare, Norman lord of the city, Aradur Hen, an ancient local croft that gave us the name Radyr, and Goetre Fawr, the farm that once worked these lands. Behind the aptly named Junction Terrace is a field replete with three grazing llamas, tall-necked beasts which, despite the ll of their name, are about as common in Wales as kangaroos. Food To Go which has signs offering coffee and warmth is closed. I head up along rising Heol Isaf in the direction of the Village of Fire.

In 1841 the ten cottages of Pentre Poeth (Warm Village) were all that existed of what is now Morganstown, upper Radyr – that part of

Cardiff north of the M4's *périphérique* grip. This is where the workforce of the developing fire-filled ironworks at Pentyrch lived, an element of Cardiff's lost industrial heritage. Heol Isaf was and still is the main road to Tŷ Mynydd. It's no distance to cover. In my ears I've got Emmylou playing through the buds. 1970s country, when what she sang was the edge. Alabama downhome. Dahl wouldn't have stood for this. He preferred Beethoven.

The Tŷ Mynydd estate has been built on; the fields are gone. The line of the original entrance path running up from Tŷ Mynydd Lodge has been preserved in the rising bends of Maes Yr Awel. The detached late sixties houses along it turn eventually to a U-shaped cluster of apartment blocks. Cwrt Tŷ Mynydd is the appropriately named first; after that the developer gave up and resorted to names with a strong English resonance – Norfolk Court, York Court, Windsor, Argyll. It's a marketing thing. Here, near the eastern edge of Wales, where the language thins, the Anglo norm dominates.

Beyond the apartment courts, circled like a residential wagon train, there's a copse, ancient pine trees, all that remains of what once was here. For the Dahls of the nineteen-teens this would all now be virtually unrecognisable. A local walking his young daughter to the primary school at the former estate's southern end tells me, yes, he knows about Dahl and the great house. He points me back towards the still extant Tŷ Mynydd Lodge which faces Heol Isaf. And there it is, the gate house preserved. There are 4x4s parked out front and a family inside. Over the years since Roald would have known it the building has been much extended. But there's enough original left for the Dahlian spirit to soar. I can see him outside, short pants, laced leather shoes, hat, overcoat with enormous buttons. Mama holding his hand.

Back at Radyr station Food To Go is still closed. Clearly, they don't do mornings here.

3. The Poetry of It All

I decide to hike it back along the bone of this Dahl route I've found. With the llamas once more on Junction Terrace I find the entrance to Radyr Woods which I last visited a decade ago when I was researching outlying parts of the city. What I was interested in then – the Radyr Burnt Mound, a scheduled ancient monument known locally as the

Junction Terrace Cooking Mound – remained elusive. I couldn't find it anywhere, although I did not let this failure prevent me from writing up the whole experience. That's part of a psychogeographer's life, hunting for the lost, the invisible, the once was, the unfound. Staring at void space, the absences above playing fields, the gaps between trees, the undulating lie of vacant land. Not there today but once was. Shimmering in empty air.

Today I find the Radyr Mound by simply walking up to it. It is a grass-covered two-metre-high dump of once heated rocks and animal bones. This was our ancestors' version of Burger King. It is described on the woodland interpretation board as an Iron Age Hearth. I photograph it with my phone but it comes out looking like nothing more than a pile of grass and earth.

The paths are empty and even in the leafless winter foggy dark. They run across a duckboarded wetland of pond and drainage ditch before rising steeply up Beechwood Bank. There they follow the ridge first below Radyr Comprehensive School and then below the splendours of the Danescourt Estate. These woods and their paths are old. Roald could well have walked through them. Could this be the Forest of Sin where the Whangdoodles, Hornswogglers, Snozzwanglers and Vermicious Knids hang out? If it is, then they are uncharacteristically quiet today.

Woodland doesn't normally lend itself to the kind of poetry I engage in but with Dahl's narrative lines clouding my creativity today I decide to glory in the contingent prompts of the postmodern. As Bob Cobbing taught me, anything can be poetry, it's merely a matter of application. Over the years I'd watched him perform the folds in an anorak, the blurred labels of decomposing tea packets, smeared print pulled from a jammed photocopier, misaligned wallpaper and junk mail found beneath a hedge. In Cobbing's poetry universe, material is everywhere. I attempt to read the letter shapes discerned in the path below my feet. I use them to launch phonemes from which I can build poetic structures. This all might sound esoteric but it does have a solid basis. Paula Claire showed me how in the nineteen-nineties when she sliced leeks into fragments across the floor of the Oriel Gallery and then performed them in a sort of verbi-vocal tea-leaf-reading exercise. Concrete poetry as future diviner, leaves that speak, the sounds of the other world.

The letters come up like a chant by Jackson Mac Low. *Kness the real. Tell whole hing lankness an't. Contradictions cover. Re pen remember were. Yu ions range.* I'd driven Mac Low near here once, in the early seventies. Llantrisant Road, not too distant. But we hadn't stopped. We'd gone for an interview at the BBC. 'Poet visits Cardiff' was their line. The interview had made it sound as if they never did. After this, Mac Low had fancied seeing a bit of the Welsh countryside before returning to the grubby room above a pub in Cardiff Central's Frederick Street where we were running the No Walls readings. Poetry mostly soothes, but with its angular stops, elisions and restarts, never Jackson's.

This reading the landscape as text has happened before. Last time was with the late blind poet David Reid who'd tried to turn sections of a path up over Pen y Fan in the Beacons into a braille text. It had sounded like Henri Chopin filtered through Wynford Vaughan Thomas, a sort of county Welsh pronunciation overlaid with the Grundig-powered shimmers and swirling stutter typical of the Frenchman. Mac Low employed systematic chance operations as the core of his working method. Like John Cage, he was a twentieth-century giant in this form of poetic and musical practice. Where others would fail from the sheer boredom of the process, its testing duration, its multiplicity of arbitrary conjunctions, Mac Low ploughed on. His output was prodigious. The results were often grey and foggy, but just as often sublime.

By contrast, Roald Dahl waited for the lightbulb moment. His process relied entirely on using his life experience as a jumping-off point and then allowing plot lines to flow from that. When he had an idea he wrote it down before it vanished and then, if he decided to run with it, took at least a year to push it into shape. Stop writing only when it's going well, always leave somewhere to move on to, never return to face a blank page, that's the worst thing in the world. Keep going. Write every day. With Dixon Ticonderoga pencils, a tray on your lap and corrugated cardboard over your knees.

As the path rides up and on, Danescourt begins to intrude from the far side of the restraining fence. There are graffiti much of the way and then a crop of lost-cat notices. Bimbo, white and black wearing a collar, nervous, went missing from Blethin Close. Phone number. No indicator of when. Could the cat still be stuck up a woodland tree? I look but there's nothing.

The alien-sounding portmanteau name Danescourt derives from the two great houses that once stood in the fields on which the present 1970s Wimpy housing estate was built. The powerful Radyr Court and the lesser Danesbrook House. Memory of the Court continues in the Radyr Court pub, a Victorian structure built on top of the remains of an earlier great house of the same name that was destroyed by fire at the start of the nineteenth century. Its foundations are still there, below. Dungeons, runs the local legend, but I doubt that. Of Danesbrook House no one is quite sure. Lost Radyr Isha and Radyr Ucha, both manorial seats, are celebrated in the local histories. The Danes, who locals believe never actually came here, are not.

Sils ap Siôn, amateur bard, feckless drunkard, a fool carousing from fair to fair, once lived in this place. In the sixteenth century he spent time at Radyr Ucha, now subsumed by the houses of Heol Aradur. His fame was for beating the professional bards at their own game and doing so while pissed. Iolo Morganwg celebrated him. He was a sol-dier, merchant, wanderer, farmer, leader of a wild life. It's good to see that here, that tradition rolls on.

Making it up from the wood through the winding post-Radburn Danescourt is like entering a maze. The housing stock is uniform brick, still new enough to lack pollution stains and multiple-owner-applied alterations and amendments. No assorted front doors and mixed replacement windows, colourful extensions and sagging gates yet. I check a wheelie bin to work out just where I am. I climb through De Braose onto Timothy Rees Close and then out onto Danescourt Way. William de Braose, one time lord of these lands. Timothy Rees untraced, but patron of a cul-de-sac in what is, according to the 2011 census, the least deprived area of Wales. Parked with Clios and Fiestas. Statistics tell you what you want to hear.

4. Church

The geographic centre of the Danescourt reaches of Radyr remains the medieval parish church of John the Baptist. It has a thirteenth-century chancel arch and aged corbels that once held a rood screen. It stands in what was once the heart of a Norman buffer zone hold-ing back the Welsh to the north, much as the M4 now does, keeping Morganstown distant and distinct from the real Radyr. I'm here because this is where Harald is, dead of a broken heart. In February 1920 his eldest daughter, Astri, died suddenly of a burst appendix. Infection, peritonitis. Harald never got over it. He, too, died in 1920. They are here together in the graveyard of St John's.

Up against the burial ground's western wall, mock Tudor houses beyond, watching the pub and its business due east, is a Celtic stone cross, unexpected and dominant. It was erected by Sofie Magdalene – an act that offered, perhaps, a public demonstration of her commitment to Wales, land of Roald's birth and Harald's death. Its base is dressed with creeper and bramble. I pull the leaves back to reveal the inscription. *Harald Dahl who died at Ty Mynydd. 1920. Aged 56. And his daughter Astri aged 7.* Round the side the carved letters continue: *and His Wife Sofie Magdalene who died 1967. Aged 82 years.* Her ashes were scattered here. With her unbending Norwegian solidity she outlasted her undemonstrative husband by at least another life.

My Dahl trail turns back to pour down the lane leading to ancient Radyr Court Road. This highway predates the Danescourt infill and runs alongside the Taff most of the way south to Llandaff. I pass new build after new build cowering behind their house insurance flood barriers and then, suddenly, there's Riversdale House. I recognise this place. It is now emboldened with a new roof and multiple extensions and is hemmed in by other properties. When I first came here it was the only house on this road for miles. It was a farmhouse that had lost its lands, an aged wreck, where Witold Klimaszewski, Count of Poland (so he claimed), lived with his dogs, his drink and his utterly frantic ideas. Klim was a poet, a filmmaker, a performer, a creative man of philosophy and power. He wanted to run the world and make it again in the Polish image. Except he never did much beyond talk, dropping his hard Polish accent for his easier Cardiff one, inviting us to drink ourselves into the ground in his smoke-ridden back room. He'd have Janis Joplin on the player and then occasionally The Doors. Conrad he talked about. And Hemingway. Hard men, like him. But there was no evidence from either our conversations or the shelves in his room that he ever actually read anything at all. Like that loud late-sixties world, he's gone – a ghost now, shouting in the road.

Harald is in the back room with Klimaszewski, both pulling on cigars. Klim has just expounded his theory about creativity. It comes from ideas bumping together like clouds, he says. Harald is nodding. Jimi Hendrix is on the player. The pair both tap their feet as they down their wine. Harald is entranced with the bohemia he has found. Here, just down from his big house. Such serendipity. He never needed Paris. It was all waiting for him here.

5. The Ley Heats Up

The Dahl trail fairly shoots now, running with the river. It plunges with descending zip along the back of the soon-to-be-abandoned BBC studios on Llanishen Road. The BBC will move from the ease of Llandaff to the new and glittering but tightly marshalled premises to be built outside the main rail station in the city's Central Square. When you dismount from the new electric rocket train from the moneyed east, what will greet you? The British Broadcasting Corporation.

The path tracks the river, the now clean Taff, which would have been emulsified with coal dust from the up-valley pit washeries in Roald's day. I skirt the rowing club and descend towards the weir. It's here that the Taffside track becomes Ffordd y Meirw, the road of the dead. Coffins were carried along this route from outlying Whitchurch to the cathedral burial grounds. There are goal posts visible through the trees, set up on the disputed meadow by Cardiff Metropolitan University who insist this land belongs to them. Locals disagree. This is an ancient free green space, common land used for centuries by Llandaffians walking their dogs, maypole dancing and celebrating both the arrival and the passing of Christ with religious and alcoholic zeal. There are Public Notices attached to the gateposts offering public discussion of the field's future, but I fear the whole thing is now lost.

I hit the southern edge of the cathedral and negotiate the fast and strenuous rise up the Dean's Steps to emerge at the top end of Llandaff Green where the original Cathedral School buildings once stood. The new ones lie south of the cathedral, embracing the wrecked Bishop's Palace with their educational arms. Roald attended between 1923 and 1925. Donald Sturrock says the school on the Green was 'an elegant three-storey Georgian building . . . an educational institution with a pedigree that dates back to the ninth century', which might stretch its lineage slightly, but whatever, it's now gone. It was demolished in 1958 to be replaced by unobtrusive private residential accommodation. This has splendid views of both the Llandaff Preaching Cross where Archbishop Baldwin and Giraldus Cambrensis both recruited for the Third Crusade, and the hatted statue of moderniser and benefactor, James Rice Buckley, Archdeacon of Llandaff, 1913–1924.

I stand, staring into empty air again, looking for motes of power which might recall Dahl. There are more here than where I've been so far, for sure. On Llandaff High Street stands the Great Wall Chinese

Take Away. I have memories of queuing here for chips after some dull poetry reading held in a nearby pub. Rain outside, windows streaming. Today, inside, they offer Egg Foo Yung where once, according to the Llandaff Society's blue plaque, they sold sweets. This was the place where Dahl carried out the daring mouse plot as celebrated in the bent-truth *Boy*. Each year on Roald Dahl Day the Society now fills the window with pictures of sweets from the twenties: Fruit Gums, Peppermints, boiled sweets in screws of paper, Rowntree's Motoring Chocolates, Aero Bars, Dairy Box Selections.

The ley is burning. Around the corner on Cardiff Road is No. 47, the onetime home of Ludvig Aadnesen, Harald Dahl's business partner. His building is long gone, replaced by a sixties stone-veneered concrete monstrosity housing Barclays Bank, the Cathedral School shop and Darlow's Estate Agents. No one there has heard of Aadnesen, but Roald, yes.

Outside, the adult Roald is checking properties available locally. He's taller than most remember him, almost regal. These days he has a longing for the familiar and there are plenty of things about this place that he enjoyed enough to want to come back. Fields. Empty streets. The sound of Mama's voice, calling. He spots somewhere that sparks a memory. Big house, sloping eves. The price is enormous, a million and a quarter. He'd need a mortgage to buy it but he could raise one. Go for it? Why not.

Crossing the main road I turn from the true path south to walk along Fairwater Road. This heads away from Llandaff towards Cardiff West. Nearby was the birthplace of Felicity Ann d'Abreu Crosland – Liccy, Roald's second wife. The Cardiff Dahl connection made just that bit stronger. But the main attraction out here is Villa Marie, the birthplace. This is a spot that should burn a hole in the Dahl continuum. If this was America, then by now we'd have paid money to get in, marvelled at the Dahl exhibits, engaged with the multi-media display, watched the films, and would be eating Dahl burgers in the extensive gift shop. As it is, Villa Marie has been renamed Tŷ Gwyn (White House) and is up for sale for a price approaching a million and a half. Viewing strictly by appointment. Don't knock, ring up. Its eaves slope groundward in arts and crafts style, simultaneously grand and demure. Of Roald there's nothing. No memorial, no mark, no resonance. The motes, if there were any, have been washed away by decades of rain.

6. Cumberland Gap

But Dahl is not over. There is one more place. With fear of failure
driving me, half a dozen false starts made by walking up inappro-
priate side roads and asking passers-by, I find it a few days later.
Cumberland Lodge. No connection whatsoever with the Lonnie
Donegan song of similar name. It sits on Cardiff Road, in sight of
the Cathedral School with front bedroom windows that gaze out at
the expanse of Llandaff Fields. It was here in 1920 that the newly
widowed Sofie Dahl moved with her six-strong family, unable to
cope with the running of the Tŷ Mynydd estate. It may have been
smaller than the Radyr great house, but by contemporary Cardiff
standards, Cumberland Lodge was still vast. Long corridors, great
drawing rooms, a soaring hall lit by a magnificent stained glass window, multiple bedrooms and a tennis court. Roald lived here until
1927 when his mother sold up to move to Oakwood in Bexley, Kent.
Lived here is perhaps putting it too strongly. Spent time would be
better. This period coincides with the start of the boy Roald's formal
education. This included a period at Elm Tree House kindergar-
ten, two years at the Cathedral School, and then banishment as a
boarder to distant St Peter's School, across the grey-brown channel
in Weston-super-Mare.

It was from there that Roald gazed back, imagining he could see his
mother's house twenty or more miles distant through the sea mist. He
could make out the roof tops. He could see the slates. I've spent time in
Weston-super-Mare, walked the promenade there, looked homewards
from the end of the pier. I've stood in well-to-do England trying to
touch poor man's Wales. I've written it up in my study and travelogue
of the whole Severn Sea, *Edging the Estuary*. Could I see the houses and
the people? Not a chance. Roald hated the whole St Peter's experience
and being away from home. He faked illnesses in order to get back.

Cumberland Lodge was one of a group of similarly large Victorian
mansions built on land that once formed part of the farms south of
the Bishop's Palace. Ecclesiastical country, Llandaff not Cardiff, and
late in gaining the civic benefits that incorporation into the future
capital would bring. These included mains drainage, paved roads and
street lighting.

All the houses in this group – Hazelwood House, Bryn Taf, Oaklands
and Cumberland Lodge itself – have by now been purchased by

Howell's School. This was initially as accommodation for girl board-
ers, but now that Howell's have abandoned boarding completely, the
buildings have become teaching space. Cumberland Lodge has been
extended considerably to serve as both Howell's Nursery School and
its Music Department.

From the outside, there's nothing to tell you this building was once
Dahl space. It stands dark and half hidden by perimeter walls. And
since it's a nursery school you can't arrive from the street and just poke
about. But if I'm tracking the Dahl scent, no matter how faint, then I
should explore. I arrange a visit.

From within the school grounds Cumberland Lodge looks far
more like an actual house than it does from without. Three sto-
reys of red brick intact, decorative bargeboards and gables, and,
despite the extensions, largely unspoiled. It is also resolutely Dahl.
It is surrounded by the nursery playground, animal fences, play
huts, climbing frames, slides, model giraffes, and child-friendly fenc-
ing. There's a blue plaque put up by the school which celebrates the
fact that Roald lived here. There's also an outdoor display panel
showing his letters sent back home to his mother, signed 'BOY' in
a scrawly hand. 'Please could you send me some conkers as quick as
you can?'

Inside, I narrowly avoid getting sucked into the Nursery School's
St David's Day eisteddfod, an exercise that would have been alien
to Roald Dahl. Dozens of three- and four-year-olds dressed in Lady
Llanover-created Welsh costume, miniature stovepipe hats, tartan
skirts, shawls, most of them with daffs fixed about their tiny persons,
are gathered in what would have been the Dahls' drawing room. They
sing and recite and dance.

Despite this diversion there is more of Roald here than anywhere
else I have so far found. The walls carry Dahl quotations. 'If you
have good thoughts they will shine out of your face and you will
always look lovely.' 'And above all, watch with glittering eyes the
whole world around you because the greatest secrets are always hidden in the most unlikely places.' There are exhibition panels showing
Quentin Blake's Dahl illustrations and further Dahl boyhood letters,
a school report, and a photo of Roald and Mama in the grounds of
Cumberland Lodge.

This house is a place of children. It was, too, in Roald's time. He'd
be glad to know it remains so today.

Metro Dahl

Tŷ Mynydd (Copse)
Lodge
Food To Go (open high days & holidays)
Radyr Jct
St John's Cross, Danescourt
Cathedral School
Cardiff Road
Great Wall
Villa Marie
Cumberland Lodge
Elm Tree
Ninian Park
Plass
Portmeirion
Norwegian Church
Norwegian Church
Pier Head Chambers (lost)
Eli Jenkins
Story Centre (opens 2060)

7. Dahl's Books On Finch's Shelves

Back home I untangle my notes into Word, the writer's daily task. Dahl
the real, Dahl the imagined. On my shelves are all his books, in their
day read to children, read by adults, and assiduously collected as a
vital component of Welsh literary art. If you are born in Wales or have
come to live here, then, according to my lights, that makes you Welsh.
I've done twenty-three years as a bookseller in the Welsh capital, at
Oriel, 1974–1997. I learned early that to keep turnover up you had
to make Wales as big as you could. Dahl was stocked alongside fellow
Anglo-Welsh authors Jack Jones, Glyn Jones, Emyr Humphreys and
Gwyn Thomas. His book sales massively outshone theirs. I turn for my
collection of his titles but they are gone. Abandoned in a downsizing
exercise a few years back. I recall trying to fit a lifetime's collection,
ten thousand books, onto shelves with space for only half that number.
Things had to go. Dahl, I must have decided, was not Welsh enough.

I one-click at Amazon and the texts I need start digitally arriving. It's hard to believe that Roald created all this wonder with pencils on pads of yellow ruled paper, sent from the States. No keying. No spellchecking. No cloud storage. His arm doing the work.

My Dahl walk has been a journey of chasing echoes and summoning ghosts. I've been to all his Cardiff spaces both extant and lost, stared at bricks, gazed at empty air. It would be easy to say that if there was a Welsh Dahl then I didn't really find him. But that wouldn't quite be true. Dahl is here but hidden. As it says on that Howell's School Cumberland Lodge wall: 'the greatest secrets are always hidden in the most unlikely places.'

Index

Index

Index